HIMALAYA

A Conway Book
© Conway Publishing 2013

First published in Great Britain in 2013 by
Conway
A Division of Anova Books Ltd
10 Southcombe Street
London W14 0RA
www.anovabooks.com
www.conwaypublishing.com
Twitter: @conwaybooks

Distributed in the US and Canada by Sterling Publishing Co. Ltd
387 Park Avenue South, New York, NY 100016-8810

British Library Cataloguing in Publication Data:
A catalogue record for this book is available from the British Library.

ISBN 9781844862214
Printed by Craft Print International Ltd, Singapore

To receive regular email updates on forthcoming Conway titles, email conway@anovabooks.
com with Conway Update in the subject field.

HIMALAYA

THE EXPLORATION & CONQUEST OF THE GREATEST MOUNTAINS ON EARTH

EDITED BY PHILIP PARKER

FOREWORD BY PETER HILLARY

CONWAY

Himalaya Contributors

PHILIP PARKER (General Editor) is a historian specializing in the classical and medieval worlds. He was General Editor of *The Great Trade Routes: A History of Cargoes and Commerce Over Land and Sea* (2012) and a contributor to *Mountaineers: Great Tales of Bravery and Conquest* (2011). Among his other works are *The Empire Stops Here: A Journey around the Frontiers of the Roman Empire* (2009) the *Eyewitness Companion Guide to World History* (2010) and *The Northmen's Fury: A History of the Viking World* (2014).

PETER HILLARY is the son of Sir Edmund Hillary and he has been on over 40 mountaineering expeditions around the world, including five on Mount Everest. He works with his father's Himalayan foundations to provide health, environment and education services for the people in the Himalaya – all programmes are at their request and with their cooperation. Peter is a writer, speaker and adventure travel operator.

MADELEINE LEWIS (Chapter 1) is a creative multimedia specialist focusing on the environment and sustainability. She has worked as a BBC online and radio producer, and a freelance writer, including co-writing, with Richard Sale, *The Times Explorers: A History in Photographs* (2004).

GEORGIOS T. HALKIAS (Chapter 2) holds a DPhil in Tibetan and Himalayan Studies from the University of Oxford. He has extensive fieldwork experience in India and Nepal. His specialized interests are Himalayan history and culture, Tibetan Buddhism and the transmission of Buddhism to Tibet. He has written several works on the cultural and religious history of the northwestern Himalaya. He has been a Fellow at the Oxford Centre of Buddhist Studies since 2009.

STEWART WEAVER (Chapters 3 and 4) is a Professor of History at the University of Rochester in Rochester, New York. He is the co-author (with Maurice Isserman) of *Fallen Giants: A History of Himalayan Mountaineering from the Age of Empire to the Age of Extremes* (2008).

AMANDA FABER (Chapter 5) is an independent film, television and theatre producer and director. Introduced to climbing by Commander Jim Simpson and Mike and Sally Westmacott, she worked as a trek leader for a number of years and has climbed, mountaineered and trekked in Europe, the USA, Africa, New Zealand, Australia, the Himalayas and Central Asia. She is a fellow of the RGS (with IBG), an aspirant member of the Alpine Club and a member of the Royal Asiatic Society.

During a mountaineering career spanning more than 40 years, **STEPHEN VENABLES** (Chapter 6) has made many first ascents in South America, Antarctica and the Himalaya, where he became the first Briton to climb Everest without supplementary oxygen. Of his 11 books on mountain travel and mountaineering history, two have won prizes at the Banff International Mountain Festival and his first, *Painted Mountains* (1986), won the Boardman Tasker Prize. He also wrote the screenplay for the IMAX film 'The Alps' and has taken part in several radio and television documentaries. He has lectured throughout the world and leads regular sailing-climbing expeditions to the mountains of the Southern Ocean.

MICK CONEFREY (Chapter 7) is a documentary maker and writer specializing in exploration and mountaineering. He is the director of 'The Race For Everest', made for the BBC to commemorate the 50th anniversary of the first ascent, and author of the widely acclaimed book, *Everest 1953* (2012).

PETER GILLMAN (Chapter 8) is one of Britain's leading mountaineering writers. His biography of George Mallory, *The Wildest Dream*, co-authored with Leni Gillman, won the Boardman Tasker Prize for mountain writing in 2000. He has won a record six awards from the British Outdoor Writers & Photographers Guild.

DOUG SCOTT (Chapter 9) has made 45 expeditions to the high mountains of Asia and has summited 40 peaks, half of which were first ascents, and all were climbed by new routes or for the first time in Alpine style. Doug and Dougal Haston became the first Britons to summit Everest in 1975 when they made the first ascent of the Southwest Face. He is a past president of the Alpine Club. He was made a CBE in 1994, and in 1999 he received the Royal Geographical Society's Patron's Medal for his contribution to mountaineering and the knowledge of mountain regions. Following on from Walter Bonatti and Reinhold Messner, Doug was awarded the Piolet d'Or in 2011.

Contents

Foreword

Peter Hillary

Father and son Peter Hillary with his father Edmund in 1990, shortly after he made his own first ascent of Mount Everest

The Himalaya is the greatest mountain range on Earth and its story is equally grand in all the realms: geology, biology, meteorology, human culture, migration and high adventure.

The story starts with the incredible formation of the mountains caused by the plate tectonic collision around forty-five million years ago and the extraordinary consequences of when continents collide. A youthful range of mountains rose that changed the weather and the nature of the monsoons, concentrating the force of the rains to the south of the Himalaya and sentencing the high plateaux of Central Asia to aridity in the rain-shadow of this great divide.

A rich abundance of forests, shrubs and animals thrived upon the flanks of the mountains and they dominated the convoluted landscape of the growing Himalaya for tens of millions of years. This was an astounding richness of vegetation and of wildlife that filled a narrow band from south to north of just 100 kilometres (60 miles), ranging from tropical to Alpine: from elephants and the mighty gaur on the plains, to langur monkeys in the jungle-clad foothills, and the secretive snow leopard, the lammergeyer and the Alpine chough along the crest of the Himalaya. The Himalaya was all theirs until out of Africa came a bipedal being that spread along the coasts of southern Asia and much later colonized the great plains of the Indus Valley and the Ganges.

For millennia stacked upon millennia the land that we would eventually call India received waves of immigrants. Different ethnic groups and traditions were absorbed, creating India's rich multicultural mix of peoples. And as people tilled their fields down by the life-giving river personified as the mother goddess Ganga, they would look to the north and see the glistening white of the 'Abode of Snow', the Himalaya. This was where the rivers originated, where the monsoon clouds rose in billowing columns and thunder boomed; for them it was the abode of the gods. As Indo-Aryan people colonized the foothills from the south and Tibeto-Mongolian people colonized the Himalayas from the north, a tapestry of ethnicities and traditions spread across the valleys of the greatest mountain range on Earth.

People have always been fascinated by the Himalaya. Hindu ascetics travelled up the rivers into the high Himal in search of inspiration and enlightenment. Temples were built deep among the mountains and pilgrims would come and go. Buddhist and Muslim theologies followed a thousand years apart, and all the while the mountain farmers cut their tracks, dug terraced fields and built stone houses in improbable locations upon the flanks of the rising Himalaya. For them this was home; the landscape spoke to them, and they in turn felt a part of the Himalaya.

More recently great empires came to the edge of the mighty Himalaya. Ashoka brought Buddhism to his Indian empire in 500BC, the Mughals brought Islam and architecture, and the British brought railways and commerce. The Himalaya was a political boundary between these empires and the ones in the north: the Tibetan empire, the marauding Mongols and the procession of dynasties in China. And then as the 'Great Game', as Kipling called it, developed between Russian and British ambitions in Central Asia, there was a small group of eccentric British bluebloods who took up a pursuit called 'mountaineering'.

This new pastime evolved in the European Alps, but as the Great Game expressed itself across the wide Himalaya as a thirst for geographical knowledge and influence among its peoples, the opportunity to climb where no one had gone before began in earnest throughout the Himalaya.

The great French mountaineer Lionel Terray described Alpine climbers as 'Conquistadors of the useless' but he knew better than most that mountain climbing was a quest for the human spirit. Anyone who has reached the summit of a mountain knows that long after the blisters and the wretched fears of vulnerability have subsided the pleasure of having gone 'beyond' is with you always.

When my father and Tenzing on the British Mount Everest expedition were making their attempt on the summit of Mount Everest on the morning of 29 May 1953 they had their doubts about the conditions. Just below the South Summit the snow was dangerous and prone to avalanche, and my father reflected that if he were back in the Southern Alps he would most likely have chosen prudence and turned around, but something snapped inside of him and he told himself, 'Ed, my boy. This is Everest!' As a child he told me that sometimes you have to go 'the extra distance' to achieve your goal – and up there on Everest was one of those times.

The truth is we are all liberated by the successes of others because their successes show that it can be done. And that is what the first ascent of Mount Everest or any of the Himalayan giants came to symbolize. For me that makes any great endeavour to be one about stretching human potential – and that has been the history of the Himalaya, and will no doubt continue to be into the future. Today the great mountaineers push this envelope every day and the Himalaya is their ultimate playground – the abode of mountaineers – but the world's greatest mountain range has for far longer been a place for human self-realization and philosophical development.

Nowhere is the search for wisdom or the spirit of exploration better manifested than in the Himalaya.

Peter Hillary

www.peterhillary.com
www.edhillary.com
www.himalayantrust.org

Introduction

It is now more than 60 years since the first summiting of Everest, the world's highest mountain. Undeniably one of the defining achievements in mountaineering history, it also signalled a key moment in mankind's interaction with Earth's greatest mountain range. Celebrated though it is, that climb by Edmund Hillary and Tenzing Norgay is just one point in our long relationship with the Himalaya, the 'Abode of Snow'.

Himalaya recounts the whole of that rich history, from the first ancient accounts in the Hindu scriptures, through the establishment of complex cultures and kingdoms in the region, to the beginnings of European exploration in the seventeenth century, the great surveys of the region (principally under British direction from 1800) and then the birth of Himalayan mountaineering in the late nineteenth century. The book relates the astonishing decades from the 1920s when the peaks were first climbed in earnest, and then conquered one by one, and carries the story of the mountains into our own era, when new routes and new techniques have heralded achievements that would have been unthinkable 60 years ago.

The Himalaya, whose crowning peak Everest is, contains all of the world's 14 summits in excess of 8,000 metres (26,246 feet), strung across Central Asia like a lofty but lopsided smile. The mountains were already old when our own species was young, their vast 2,400-kilometre-long (1,500-mile) bulk formed some forty-five million years ago by the collision of the Eurasian and Indian tectonic plates. The discovery of the Himalaya was a long process, as full of misunderstandings as of sudden revelations. The first mention of the range in European sources, in the writings of Herodotus, the fifth-century BC Greek historian, refers to the 'gold-digging ants' to be found there, a species even more elusive than the yeti, a huge (and shy) hairy anthropoid whose traces various twentieth-century expeditions to the Himalaya are said to have come across.

From the earliest times, the Himalaya have sat upon a series of fault lines, as much psychological as the physical one that gave birth to the range; they have held a fascination for all who encountered them, an allure both fascinating and terrifying, that at various stages in human history has manifested itself either as religious awe or an exhilarating determination to tread on their uppermost reaches. And they sit on a political fault line, too, where the historical leviathans of China and the Indian subcontinent rubbed against the complex and shifting cultures of Central Asia and the mountains themselves – a process that the solidification of frontiers in the twentieth century has not halted entirely.

The first Europeans to venture into the Himalaya, Jesuit missionaries in the

Eastern Himalaya
A NASA Terra satellite false-colour composite image of the eastern-most Himalaya creates a dramatic perspective on the range. The mountainous slopes and snow-capped ridges are highlighted in red and white respectively, while the rivers, which snake through the valleys between the peaks, are picked out in blue.

Siniolchu A view of the crest of Siniolchu taken by the great Italian mountain photographer Vittorio Sella during Douglas Freshfield's 1899 expedition to the area around Kangchenjunga. In viewing the 6,888-metre (22,598-foot) peak across the Zemu Glacier, Freshfield remarked that the beauty of its ice and snow-encrusted precipices stood out among the surrounding peaks in the manner of 'Giotto's Tower to the rest of the Italian Domes and Campanili'.

seventeenth century, did so for practical reasons, first to garner converts and then, when the crop seemed unlikely to be a rich one, to act as diplomatic conduits to the ruler of the region and, especially, to reach the most mesmerizing destination of all: the court of the Dalai Lamas of Tibet. The desire of the nineteenth-century British imperial administrators of the Great Trigonometrical Survey to measure, define and capture the mountains, to set them down in clearly defined contour lines on a map, makes them seem like heirs to this pragmatism, but theirs was soon succeeded by a spirit that combined both a sense of adventure and one of pilgrimage, as the first mountaineers came to test themselves against the peaks.

The century and a quarter that separates Martin Conway's pioneering 1892 expedition to the Karakoram from today's organized tourist expeditions to the summit of Everest have seen so many achievements, so many expeditions, conquered peaks, acts of bravery and, sadly, deaths on the unforgiving slopes, that it is impossible to pick out any without doing an injustice to the rest. Suffice it to say that the topmost reaches of the Himalaya, the 8,000-metre (26,246-foot) peaks, resisted all attempts to conquer them until Maurice Herzog and his climbing partner Louis Lachenal summited Annapurna on 2 June 1950. From then on the pace quickened, until in

1986 Reinhold Messner, from Italy's South Tyrol, became the first person to have reached all the 8,000-metre summits (including the first ascent of Everest without oxygen), beginning a select club that to date has only around 30 members.

In this book the achievements of Conway, Herzog and Messner are catalogued, as well as those of scores of others, from Fanny Bullock Workman, a precocious pioneer of women's mountaineering in the early twentieth century, to George Mallory and Sandy Irvine, who disappeared high on Everest in 1921, the mystery of whether they reached the summit never yet fully resolved, and the Tibetan-Chinese team that summited Shisha Pangma, the last of the 8,000-metre peaks to be scaled, in 1964.

Yet even when the principal peaks had been climbed, the story of the exploration of the Himalaya was not done, and the final chapter of this book recounts the further pushing of the boundaries of Himalayan mountaineering, with the pioneering of new routes, the conquest of summits solo or without the use of oxygen, the introduction of Alpine climbing techniques and the achievement of ever more technically difficult summits. New challenges have emerged, too, as the advent of large-scale tourism in the region has raised problems both environmental, as the melting of glaciers due to global climate change modifies the landscape and an increased use of the mountains brings with it a higher level of pollution, and ethical, as the growing number of tour companies wishing to reach the summit of mountains such as Everest brings dangers of its own (while at the same time, as with tourism everywhere, local communities in the Himalaya may not derive the benefit they should from this influx).

Managing these difficulties will make the coming years among the most testing in mankind's long history in the Himalaya. New entries, too, will be added to the chronicles of the explorers, pioneers, pilgrims and adventurers who have travelled its valleys and scaled its peaks. And, as time goes on, even the long-established contours of the mountains will change as the Indian tectonic plate is rising steadily, a process that outweighs the countervailing trend of erosion.

The matter of heights in the Himalaya is, indeed, a vexed one, with minor variations appearing in the literature over the years as more accurate surveys become available. To take just one example, the height of Everest itself, long agreed to be 8,848 metres (29,029 feet), may soon be subject to a slight raise, as a National Geographic Survey in 2012 measured it 2 metres (6.5 feet) higher (though this change was not immediately accepted by the government of Nepal).

I would like to thank all the contributors to this volume, who worked to an unforgiving schedule and responded to all the demands of the General Editor with surprising good humour. Together they have produced a compelling, accessible and comprehensive survey of the Himalaya in all its aspects. Thanks are also due to the editorial and design team who have turned that raw material into a polished and lavishly illustrated book: John Lee, the publisher at Conway, whose vision and patience have been fundamental to the project; Christopher Westhorp, for whose exceptionally skilful editing I am sure all the contributors are grateful; Jen Veall for her resourceful picture research, which has unearthed a trove of fantastic imagery; Martin Brown for his wonderfully crafted cartography, which illustrates the routes taken on the principal mountaineering expeditions; and Friederike Huber and Georgina Hewitt for the design that so beautifully creates the panorama within which the story of the Himalaya can be told.

Philip Parker
London, May 2013

1

Anatomy of the Himalaya: The formation and topography of the range

MADELEINE LEWIS

For thousands of years the Himalaya has captured the imaginations of explorers, writers, and those who have lived among this spectacular, remote and often dangerous landscape. This is a land that demands superlatives – it is the highest mountain range in the world, one of the youngest mountain ranges in the world, home to all of the world's independent mountains exceeding 8,000 metres (26,246 feet) above sea level, the 'eight thousanders', and some of the greatest rivers systems on Earth.

The Himalaya is 2,400 kilometres (1,500 miles) long and spans Bhutan, India, Nepal, China and Pakistan, bounded at either end by the Indus and Brahmaputra rivers. It reaches from Pakistan's Nanga Parbat in the west to Tibet's Namcha Barwa in the east, and – as in this book – it is normally taken to include the Karakoram range in the northeast. Himalaya, properly used always in the singular, means 'Abode of Snow' in Sanskrit. By sheer virtue of its size, the range acts as a barrier between the warm, wet monsoon weather to the south and the dry, cold winds from the north. And just as it is instrumental in the climate of the regions around it, it is instrumental to their water supplies too.

The Indus, Ganges and Brahmaputra rivers provide not only transport and irrigation for the millions of people living in their river basins in Pakistan, India, Bangladesh and Myanmar, but also carry the sediments that make this region so fertile for agriculture. Largely originating north of the mountains in Tibet, these waterways cross through the Himalaya and are fed by glaciers before twisting, turning and converging to become the great rivers that reach the sea. The Indus system ultimately flows into the Arabian Sea, and the Ganges and Brahmaputra meet in Bangladesh before draining into the Bay of Bengal.

The rivers are thought to be older than the mountains themselves, managing to cut through such an ordinarily impermeable barrier by forging their way at the same time as the mountains thrust upwards. This is the cause of such deep gorges as the Yarlung Tsangpo Canyon in the Eastern Himalaya. China is currently eyeing the canyon as a source of hydro energy, illustrating just one of the increased pressures being brought to bear on the region.

And water isn't the only problem facing the peoples of this part of the world. On top of the political disputes affecting the border areas, other environmental and social issues are starting to bite. Deforestation is one – a 2006 University of Delhi study suggested that 15 percent of the forest cover in the Indian Himalaya region was lost between 1970 and 2000. Other issues include climate change, pollution, food security and biodiversity loss.

Himalaya from the air This aerial photo shows the full length of the Himalaya, a great arc stretching some 2,400 kilometres (1,500 miles) from Gilgit in the west to the Brahmaputra River in the east, and then a further 160 kilometres (100 miles) northwards into the highlands of Tibet.

The Ganges river dolphin, one of only four freshwater dolphin species, is endangered. Found from the Himalayan foothills to the Bay of Bengal, it is decreasing in number because of pollution, overfishing, and changes in habitat and decreased food levels due to the construction of dams and other irrigation projects.

Geological formation

The topography and geography of the Himalaya and lands surrounding it are largely the result of one single geological event – the collision between the Eurasian and the Indian tectonic plates around forty-five million years ago.

Eurasia is sometimes described as a 'composite continent', with which various landmasses have collided and joined over the past 800 million years. Most of these 'sutures' are older than 200 million years. The Indian Plate is Eurasia's most recent addition, joining the continent along a front of around 2,400 kilometres (1,500 miles).

The Indian Plate broke off from the supercontinent Gondwana around 120 million years ago, and by around sixty million years ago, it was travelling some 5,000 kilometres (3,100 miles) towards Eurasia at a rate of 15–20 centimetres (6–8 inches) per year. That's pretty fast when you compare it to the rate at which Europe and North America are moving apart – a comparatively sedate 2–4 centimetres (under 1–2 inches) each year.

Yet, while the collision with Eurasia around forty million years ago slowed down this movement, it did not stop it, and the Indian Plate has continued its relentless march for around a further 2,000–2,500 kilometres (1,240–1,550 miles). Several mechanisms have been identified to explain what has happened to the displaced crust (or displaced lithosphere) after the two plates collided.

One mechanism describes the Indian Plate subducting below Tibet; the second suggests that India acts as a 'wedge', effectively splitting Eurasia and pushing Indochina out to the west; the third is orogeny – the thrusting and layering of the continental crust upwards to create mountains. All three have likely been at play, but it is the latter that gave rise to this most spectacular of mountain ranges.

The collision between India and Eurasia is not for the history books; it continues to this day, with the Indian Plate pushing into Eurasia at a rate of around 5 centimetres

Glacial melt Water forms under the Khumbu Glacier in Nepal, a sign of the warming which has caused many glaciers in the Himalaya to retreat. A number of new glacial lakes have formed in the mountains and the raised flow of water into major rivers such as the Brahmaputra and Ganges is likely to lead to an increased risk of flooding in the region.

Mountain source An 1890s' photograph of the Gaumukh ('Cow's Mouth') cave, formed at the terminus of the Gangotri Glacier. It is the source of the Ganges River. Each year many thousands of devotees trek here during the Kavad Yatra festival in July–August to collect water from the sacred Ganga and offer it at temples back home.

(2 inches) a year, which is the cause of seismic activity in the wider region. This rate of uplift in some places is thought to outpace erosion, meaning that – like a teenager – parts of the Himalaya are probably still growing.

The three major zones of the Himalaya

Three parallel mountain zones make up what we know as the Himalaya: the low Sivalik Hills, or foothills, of the Himalaya; the Lesser, or Middle, Himalaya; and the Greater Himalaya, home to the mighty Everest. From north to south, these three ranges measure from 240 to 320 kilometres (150 to 200 miles) across, and from west to east they curve gently south and east in a sort of lopsided smile.

Hill Station Kangchenjunga, the most easterly of the world's 8,000-metre (26,246-foot) peaks, can be made out from Darjeeling in West Bengal, India. Land was first acquired here in 1835 by the British, who established a hill station, attracted by its healthy climate, at just over 2,000 metres (6,562 feet). Tea production began in the 1850s and the region now produces a highly sought-after blend.

The Sivalik range, also called the Sivalik Hills or, in Nepal, the Churia Hills, is the youngest and lowest mountain range in the Himalaya – the 'sub-Himalaya'. In Hindu mythology, Shiva has his home in the Himalaya – in fact, Sivalik (or, in an alternate spelling, Shivalik) means 'belonging to Shiva'.

Running south of, and parallel to, the Greater Himalaya, the range has an average elevation of 1,066–1,220 metres (3,500–4,000 feet), and is narrow in places, ranging from 10 to 48 kilometres (6 to 30 miles) wide. One of the principal passes is the Mohan Pass, on the road linking Saharanpur, Dehradun and Mussoorie hill station. The range was once densely forested and home to much wildlife, including tigers, bears and elephants. Fossils of giraffes and tortoises have also been found. But deforestation and development mean that wildlife is now largely confined to sanctuaries.

Between the Sivalik Hills and the Greater Himalaya lies the Lesser, or Middle, Himalaya, separated in many places from the Sivalik by broad plains called Dun. Older and geologically more complex, the Lesser Himalaya is on average 96 kilometres

POLITICAL FAULT LINES

There is more than seismic activity rumbling in the Himalaya today. Politically, this is a highly sensitive region, and tense relations along the border continue between India and Pakistan over Jammu and Kashmir and between India and China over Aksai Chin (also in the Kashmir region) and Arunachal Pradesh. These stretches of remote and mountainous border territory are considered some of the world's most dangerous places because of these occasionally violent disputes.

In Kashmir, the Line of Control was agreed in 1972 under the Simla Agreement, but because it is not legally recognized as an international boundary it has remained an uneasy and ongoing source of tension. As well as the claims of the two states over the area, there is also a strong independence movement in the Kashmir Valley. Depending on whom you believe, it is estimated that the conflict has resulted in 40,000–100,000 deaths.

China also claims part of Kashmir in Aksai Chin, a high-altitude desert bordering on Jammu and Kashmir and Xinjiang in China. Between the two lies the (confusingly similar) Line of Actual Control, which more or less represents the unofficial but effective border.

Similarly, right at the other end of the Himalaya, China and India dispute Arunachal Pradesh – the easternmost state of India, which is described by China as South Tibet. India recognizes the McMahon Line as the border – a frontier agreed between British and Tibetan representatives in 1914 – while China claims as its own a large part of the state south of the line.

As the world's economic centre of gravity moves eastwards to Asia such border disputes, between nuclear-armed neighbours who are amassing some of the biggest armies on the planet and building the infrastructure to support them, are a cause for concern. The Himalaya is one of the fault lines on which these regional powers are flexing their muscles.

The Kashmir conflict and tensions with China have resulted in the Indian military improving access to the region. Key passes include the Rohtang Pass, on the Manali–Leh Highway, and the Zoji Pass (or Zoji La), on the highway between Srinagar and Leh.

Both passes are only open for a portion of the year and, as confirmation of the unpredictability of its weather, Rohtang literally means 'pile of corpses'. Because of this inclemency, India is currently building what will be one of its longest tunnels (9 kilometres/5.5 miles) to enable year-round access and provide the military with the ability to make a more rapid deployment.

(60 miles) wide. Although not as high as the Greater Himalaya, it stands proud on the world stage, and is home to peaks of over 4,877 metres (16,000 feet), which is higher than Mont Blanc.

The Lesser Himalaya is protected by the mightier Greater Himalaya, resulting in a temperate climate that is home to deodar forests, tea plantations and other agricultural activity. And it's where the famous British summer hill stations stand, such as Darjeeling and Shimla, built as summer havens away from the searing heat of the cities at lower altitude.

The final zone is the Greater Himalaya, where its myths were born. This region is the top of the world: sparsely populated, with limited flora and fauna, it is home to the highest peaks on Earth. The crest of the Greater Himalaya rarely drops below 5,486 metres (18,000 feet) except where rivers or passes cut through it.

Due to its complexity and size, the Greater Himalaya was classified at the beginning of the twentieth century into six parts or zones by Sir Sidney Burrard of the Survey of India. Later adapted by Kenneth Mason, a soldier, geographer and author of an influential history of the Himalaya, *Abode of Snow* (1955), this system of classification remains in use today to make sense of this vast and intricate landscape. From west to east the six regions are: the Punjab Himalaya, the Karakoram, the Kumaon Himalaya, Nepal Himalaya, Sikkim Himalaya and Eastern Himalaya.

Punjab Himalaya

This area is the source of four of the rivers from which the Punjab gets its name (Punjab literally means the land of 'five rivers'): the Jhelum, the Chenab, the Ravi and the Beas. (The fifth, the Sutlej, has its source just above the Himalaya – on the Tibetan Plateau.) As tributaries of the Indus, they transport minerals and silt down to create the fertile plains below. This zone includes, or abuts, the two disputed provinces of Jammu and Kashmir (administered by India but contested by Pakistan) and Aksai Chin (administered by China but contested by India).

The crown of the Punjab Himalaya is Nanga Parbat, the ninth-highest mountain in the world, and one of the 'eight thousanders'. It is a spectacular peak, rising sheer up from the Indus Valley below. But with its dramatic beauty comes danger – it is a notoriously difficult climb and thus has born witness to more than its fair share of climbing tragedies.

Karakoram

Spanning Pakistan, India and China, the Karakoram region is north of and roughly parallel to the Punjab Himalaya. The range gets its name from Turkic words meaning 'black' and 'gravel' or 'rock', and was so named by traders due to the millions of tons of largely black slate that lie throughout its valleys. Although the Karakoram sits slightly north of the Himalaya range as a whole, it is normally taken to be part of the Greater Himalaya due to much shared history and it having been created through the same tectonic collision between Eurasia and the Indian Plate.

Even for the Himalaya the Karakoram demands superlatives, and within its boundaries lie the highest concentration of peaks over 8,000 metres (26,246 feet) in

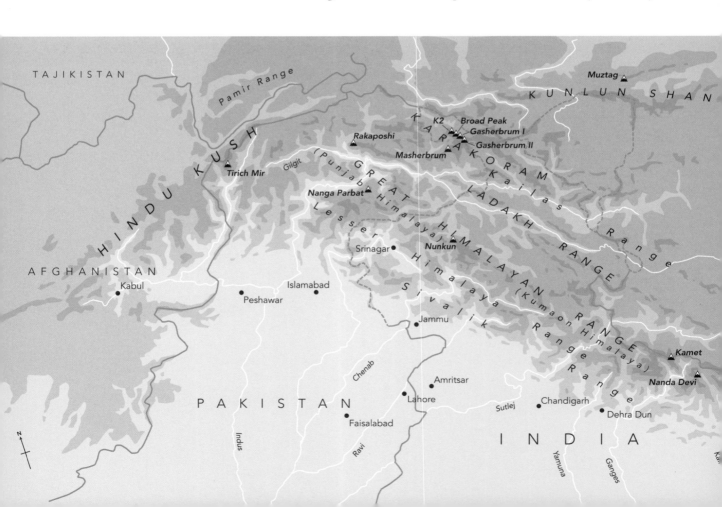

the world. Taken alone, it is the highest mountain range on Earth, with an average elevation of 6,100 metres (20,000 feet) along its 480-kilometre (300-mile) length.

The Karakoram is home to K2, the second-highest peak in the world, just a few hundred metres shy of Everest, and known as the 'savage mountain' due to the high fatality rate of those attempting to scale its peak. It was so named by the Great Trigonometrical Survey in the nineteenth century (1802 onwards) because the surveyors couldn't find evidence of a local name, probably because of its remoteness and inaccessibility.

That all changed in 1979 with the development of the Karakoram Highway. It connects China and Pakistan through the range's Khunjerab Pass, where it becomes the highest paved international road in the world, at 4,693 metres (15,397 feet). The highway has opened up this remote mountain range not only to China–Pakistan trade, but also to a growing market in adventure tourism.

The Karakoram is also the most glaciated place outside the Earth's polar regions. The Siachen Glacier – a major source of the Indus – is, at 70 kilometres (43 miles) long, the second longest glacier outside the poles, and has become an icy battleground in the Kashmir dispute between India and Pakistan. The glacier was not clearly defined as part of the Line of Control (see box, page 17), possibly because the area was thought to be too inhospitable to be relevant. And so both countries now station troops up in this barren landscape – how many lives have been lost is unclear, possibly thousands, with more killed by the extreme conditions than by combat.

The Kashmir conflict and tensions with China have resulted in the Indian military improving access to the region. Key passes include the Rohtang Pass, on the Manali–Leh Highway, and the Zoji Pass (or Zoji La), on the highway between Srinagar and Leh. Both passes are only able to remain open for about half the year due to

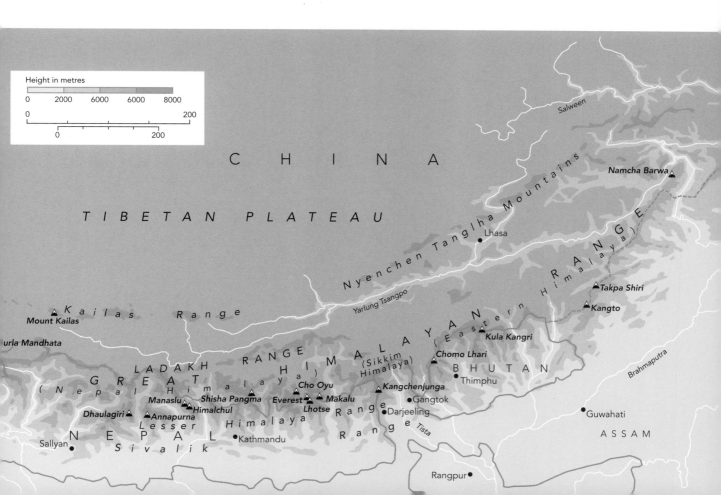

snowfall and the fierce and capricious weather. Because of this, India is constructing what will be one of its longest tunnels (9 kilometres/5.5 miles) to provide access all the year round and give the Indian military the ability to mount a rapid response should it be needed.

Kumaon Himalaya

This area lies to the southeast of the Punjab Himalaya in the Indian state of Uttarakhand, which borders on Tibet and Nepal. This region is the source of the infant tributaries of the Ganges and Jumna rivers – and contains Nanda Devi, considered the throne of Parvati, Shiva's consort. Kumaon has some of the most visited sites and shrines in India. At 7,816 metres (25,643 feet) Nanda Devi is also India's highest peak, if Kangchenjunga at 8,586 metres (28,169 feet), which is 'shared' on the border with Nepal, is discounted. Nanda Devi is actually a two-peaked massif that is encircled by a spectacular rampart of others between 6,000 and 7,500 metres (19,685–24,606 feet) in height, including Dunagiri (7,066 metres/23,182 feet) and Trisul I (7,120 metres/23,359 feet).

Nanda Devi is also one of the steepest peaks in the world, which has made its exploration difficult. Inside the circle of mountains lies the Nanda Devi Sanctuary, a glacial basin that is part of the Nanda Devi National Park, a UNESCO World Heritage site. Getting into this sanctuary in order to climb Nanda Devi requires traversing the Rishi Ganga Gorge, a steep canyon draining the sanctuary to the west.

Nepal Himalaya

The fourth zone is named after the landlocked state that is home to the crown jewels of the Himalaya – eight of the 14 'eight thousanders'. The Nepal Himalaya is often separated further into sections corresponding to three major river systems. From west to east, these are the Karnali, the Gandaki and the Kosi. The Karnali section includes the seventh-highest peak on Earth, Dhaulagiri I (8,167 metres/26,795 feet), and the eighth highest, Manaslu (8,156 metres/26,759 feet). They are separated from the Annapurna massif by the Kali Gandaki Gorge, which according to some measurements is the deepest gorge in the world, and a centuries-old trade route between Tibet and India.

Further to the east, the Kosi River and its tributaries drain one of the most incredible parts of the Himalaya, because it is home to four of the six highest mountains in the world – Cho Oyu, Everest, Lhotse and Makalu. Everest continues to draw people to its summit despite its increased commercialization in the last couple of decades, with bottlenecks and queues frequently being seen on the upper reaches of the mountain. In 1996, 15 people died attempting the summit, eight in just two days of May, and other instances of climbers being left to die has prompted a fierce debate about climbing ethics.

Just west from here is a key route connecting Lhasa and Kathmandu – the China–Nepal Highway, also known, on the Chinese side, as the Friendship Road and, on the Nepalese side, as the Araniko Highway. The highway passes through the Yarlung Tsangpo Valley where it provides incredible views of Everest and the surrounding peaks. On the Nepal side, the road is one of the most dangerous in the country due to the steepness of the slopes surrounding it and the high risk of landslides.

Sikkim Himalaya

Kangchenjunga – the third-highest mountain in the world – sits on the border between Nepal and the Sikkim Himalaya section. The name of this mountain with five peaks translates as the 'five treasures of the snow', which according to legend are gold, silver, gems, grain and holy books. Out of respect for its spiritual significance, by tradition all climbs stop just short of the summit. Kangchenjunga is surrounded by a number of other notable peaks, including Jannu (7,710 metres/25,295 feet) and Siniolchu (6,888 metres/22,598 feet).

On the other side of Sikkim, in the Chumbi Valley near the border between Sikkim (India) and Bhutan, an old and important offshoot of the Silk Road was reopened for trade in 2006 – almost half a century after its closure in the Sino–India War of 1962. Connecting Sikkim's capital Gangtok with Lhasa, the route crosses the border at Nathu La. This whole area is strategically important and subject to ongoing negotiations involving China, Bhutan and India.

Eastern Himalaya

The Himalaya continues into the last of Burrard's regions, which is Eastern Himalaya, spread across Bhutan, Tibet and, in India, Assam and the disputed region of Arunachal Pradesh. As it contains no 'eight thousanders', it has attracted less attention than the more westerly sections of the Himalaya. Namcha Barwa is its most well-known peak, which sits inside the great bend of the Yarlung Tsangpo and its grand canyon, one of the deepest in the world. The river becomes the Brahmaputra and it marks the eastern anchor – and end – of the Himalaya.

Tea terraces Cash crops such as tea provide a vital source of revenue for communities in the Himalaya. These fields are situated high in the remote Annapurna Conservation Area, and the terraces also help counteract erosion of the mountain slopes.

Early Kingdoms of the Himalaya: The political and cultural history of the region to 1700

GEORGIOS T. HALKIAS

'In a hundred ages of the gods, I could not tell of the glories
of the Himalaya.' (FROM THE *PURANA*S ['ANCIENT (LORE)'])

The Himalaya range, a crescent of mountains and valleys, forms a geological continuum traversed by the Indus River, in the western Himalayan regions of Ladakh and Baltistan, and the Tsangpo/Brahmaputra flowing from southern Tibet to the region known as Eastern Himalaya. The climate is, on average, arid because of the high altitude, which prohibits the cultivation of rice and wheat and leaves barley as the only cereal crop that will grant yields. Traditionally, yak and sheep husbandry, and trading, have been life-sustaining activities for many highland communities. The relationship of the Himalayan residents to their natural environment governed the social and economic functioning of their communities, their public institutions, aesthetic sensibilities, and unwritten customs concerning the ecological use of water, flora and fauna.

Despite the rugged topography of this imposing mountainous range that posits a geopolitical barrier between the southern plains of India and the vast steppelands of Central Asia, it has been susceptible to migrations and conquests because of strategic mountain passes that have facilitated trade across the Himalaya. Population movement has been a continuing phenomenon and the cultural variations visible today across the western, central and eastern sectors are the outcome of multidirectional migrations (from the north, south, east and west) of people of different linguistic and cultural backgrounds and ethnic origins who have settled in and ruled over these regions at different times.

Indic people from the south brought their Indo-Aryan civilization and language, and their predominantly Hindu caste-based faith, which is mainly represented in the foothills. From the north, peoples of Tibetan ethnicity or tradition established their distinctive form of Buddhist culture and related forms of governance all along the borders with the Tibetan Plateau. Far to the west, Afghan–Iranians established Islamic faiths, customs and laws in Kashmir, Baltistan and Kargil, and to the east, Burmese and a variety of minority tribal peoples brought a mix of traditions, languages, crafts and folk practices.

These Himalayan polities were historically in contact with each other and subject to shifting regional powers. Their political history has been varied and complex, bearing witness to an extravagant variety of languages and dialects, oral and scriptural traditions, religions and beliefs. The seclusion of the region and the long periods of

Place of veneration An image of a deity, probably the wrathful Yama, at the Muktinath Temple in Dhaulagiri, Nepal. The temple is a place of veneration for both Tibetan Buddhists, who regard it as sacred to the *dakinis* or 'sky dancer' goddesses, and for Hindus, who worship the god Vishnu there in the form of ammonites called *salagrama-shila*s.

THE SACRIFICIAL TEMPLE OF THE WRATHFUL GODDESS KALI

kilometres (12 miles) from Kathmandu, capital of Nepal. Considered to be one of the country's most important Hindu temples, this nefarious site is devoted to the goddess Kali in her aspect as Dakshinkali, depicted with matted hair, open inflamed eyes and drunk on the blood of her dead victims strewn across the battlefield. Masses of Hindu devotees from Nepal and India, holding offerings of flowers, coconuts and rice, visit the temple grounds, which are regularly filled with the smoke of incense and burned offerings and the ominous sound of bells (left) ringing. It is said that as many as 3,000 animals are slaughtered to Kali every week – their cut throats spraying hot blood onto stone statues of the deity. Kali's followers believe that the goddess is pleased by sacrificial blood and that she will reciprocate by delivering them from misfortune and fulfilling their wishes for secular success in the world.

Hidden down a hill amid thick vegetation, Dakshinkali temple is situated outside the village of Pharping, 20

hibernation during the harsh winters allowed considerable time for the development and refinement of indigenous systems of knowledge, like traditional medicine that relies on Himalayan herbs, animal products and minerals, and the development of arts and superior crafts in wood and bamboo carving, metalwork, silver and gold jewellery, and the weaving of shawls, carpets and rugs. Himalayan architecture and art has its own distinct and indigenous styles shaped by the natural environment and by Tibetan, Indian, Nepali, Persian and tribal cultures whose influence can be discerned in public festivals, traditional customs and ceremonies, music, songs, dances, local food and intoxicants made of barley, rice and millet.

From fantastical tales to mountain kingdoms

Early references to the Himalaya can be found in Sanskrit epic literature, stone inscriptions, dynastic genealogies and some epigraphic material, all of which reveal an ongoing political and cultural exchange between the Himalayan foothills and the Ganges basin. There are also old accounts of the Himalaya in Tibetan, Persian, Chinese, Central Asian and Greek sources. In the Greek and Roman worlds the Himalaya were renowned for their 'gold-digging ants' mentioned by Herodotus, the fifth-century BC Greek historian, who wrote 'of a people who dwell northward of all the rest of the Indians'. These northerners, who 'are more warlike than any of the other tribes' are sent forth to 'procure the gold' that is carried by 'great ants, in size somewhat less than dogs, but bigger than foxes'. Given the age-old commercial links between India and the Mediterranean basin, the Greeks came to know of the gold-mines of western Tibet and the trade in the precious metal across the border into

the Himalaya. This may explain oral histories upheld by atypical communities in the Himalaya who trace their descent back to Alexander the Great, but more likely to fortune-seeking Macedonian soldiers transplanted in Central Asia after Alexander's campaigns in the fourth century BC. The description of 'great ants' digging gold is a seemingly fantastical tale that actually had a basis in reality: to the marmots (*Marmota himalayana*) that can be found in the Himalaya's high-altitude deserts digging deep burrows.

The diverse origins and development of Himalayan Buddhist kingdoms and Hindu principalities cannot be forced into a common historical frame. Himalayan communities preserve their own local histories, social dynamics and cultural variation mediated by ethnicity, trade and migration, and the relationship between societal and ecological features. The peculiar geography of the high mountains dictated an administrative subdivision into as many units as there are fertile valleys and areas, strictly confined to local regions of sufficient agricultural or commercial importance as to make them capable of maintaining viable political entities. With a few exceptions, state formations were small and regional, because neither the population nor the economic resources allowed for the growth of larger political units. When territorial gains occurred during the Tibetan empire in the seventh to ninth centuries AD, and from the sixteenth century with the Namgyal dynasty in Ladakh, they did not last long, falling prey to contesting trading interests or internal fragmentation.

Buddhist monasticism

The highland communities of the Himalaya have been shaped, both socially and politically, by Tibetan Buddhist institutions, media and agents since the times of the

Tiger's Lair Paro Taktsang, known as the 'Tiger's Lair', or 'Tiger's Nest', is a Buddhist temple complex sited precariously on a cliffside in Bhutan's upper Paro Valley. It is said that the Buddhist sage Padmasambhava flew here on the back of his consort Yeshe Tsogyal, who he transformed into a tigress for the journey.

Tibetan empire. Charismatic Buddhist masters could wield considerable influence as religious advisors to the monarchs, who were in turn expected to support the Buddhist community (Sangha) and establish monasteries.

Much like the economy of other borderlands, the commercial routes were shaped by the physiography of the land, comprising valleys, rivers, lakes, glaciers and mountain passes, while cross-border trade relied on the cooperation between communities. The distinct features of the environment also influenced the erection of Tibetan Buddhist monasteries, which were built as forts on hills at strategic locations or along wealthy trading routes – artistically acclaimed examples include Tabo and Alchi in the western Himalaya.

The economic standing of monasteries was often comparable to that of the aristocratic class because many monasteries owned large estates, which were cultivated by villagers who gave the monks a share of their crop. Some, like the monastery of Hemis in Ladakh, held regular religious and tributary missions to Tibet that were also trading enterprises. Hence, monasteries played a significant role in the enlistment of labour, the extraction of agricultural and herding revenues, and the regulation of the trans-Himalayan trade between India, Nepal, Tibet and Central Asia in bulk commodities such as salt, borax, brick tea, cotton cloth and copper, as well as the commercial traffic in more precious items like musk, gold dust, precious stones, furs, nutmeg, sandalwood and Chinese silks and brocades. Cross-border trade was vital to the consolidation of Himalayan kingdoms from the seventh century onwards and contributed to the formation and contestation of political alliances between regional polities. For much of the year, separated by sparsely populated

ATITSE MONASTIC HERMITAGE

Along with Buddhist monasticism, asceticism gained the support of householders and nobles, and played an important role in helping to maintain Tibetan Buddhism in the Himalaya. There are numerous hermitages in the Himalaya, which are usually tucked away in isolated valleys and peaks where Buddhist saints or masters may have meditated in the past. Nesting a few hundred metres above the driveable road that connects Kargil with Leh, the twelfth-century hermitage of Atitse (left) is one of the oldest in Ladakh and belongs to the Drikung (Kagyu) school's Lama Yuru monastery. Having been spared destruction in the fifteenth century, allegedly through miraculous intervention when invading Muslim forces plundered and destroyed many Ladakhi monasteries, Lama Yuru represented the boundary line between Muslim and Buddhist areas until the eighteenth century. The original name of Lama Yuru was Yungdrung tharpa ling, which means 'the site of the liberating swastika surrounded by water'; it dates to the pre-Buddhist Bon religion of the region, and an old myth that the sacred site was once an island in a big lake that was populated by indigenous serpent-beings known as *nagas*. It is said that the great Indian Buddhist saint and yogi Naropa (1016–1100) underwent a strict meditation retreat in a cave that is now part of the complex of Lama Yuru.

and impassable highlands, the Himalayan monarchies remained largely independent of one another and isolated from the major political developments to the south and north until well into the twentieth century.

Western Himalaya: the Tibetan sphere and a fusion of faith

The westernmost area of the Himalaya, comprising Ladakh, Spiti and Lahaul, flourished as vital gateways for international and domestic trade that connected the Indo-Gangetic plain with western Tibet and Central Asia from as early as the Kusana empire in the first to third centuries AD. Ladakh and Baltistan fell subject to the expansion westwards of the Tibetan empire (seventh to ninth centuries AD), but it was not until the tenth century that Nyimagon, a royal descendant of the last Tibetan emperor, Langdarma, settled and ruled independently in this area of western Tibet. After Nyimagon's death, his dominions of Upper Ladakh, Zangskar, Spiti, Guge and Purang were divided up between his three sons. Palkigon is regarded as the founder of the kingdom of Ladakh, which reached its most glorious phase during the Namgyal dynasty from the early sixteenth century onwards. Spiti, with its impressive Kyi, Dhangkar and Tabo monasteries, and Lahaul, the 'Land of Glaciers' featuring the Gandola, Gemur and Kardang monasteries, shared a political, religious and trading history with the kingdom of Ladakh. In 1630, King Senge Namgyal (reigned [r.], 1616–1642) of Ladakh annexed the famous kingdom of Guge, which had existed for 600 years, and adjoining regions. He built his capital in a nine-storey fortress-palace that looms over and dominates the town of Leh, which lies at its foot. In

Illustrated Buddhist canon
An extraordinary handwritten version of the Buddhist *Kanjur* with fine lettering in gold, copper and lapis lazuli attests to the past affluence of the monastic community of Basgo in Ladakh. The legitimacy of monarchs in Ladakh and other Himalayan Buddhist kingdoms was based on their role as supporters and protectors of Buddhist centres such as this one.

TINGMOSGANG PALACE-FORT

The fortified palace of Tingmosgang (above), perched breathtakingly on a rock wall more than 3,000 metres (9,840 feet) above sea level, was built as his capital by King Dragpa Bum of Ladakh sometime in the fifteenth century. Although a devout Buddhist, he married a Muslim princess from Kashmir and had a son with her who bore the half-Tibetan, half-Muslim name of Drungpa Ali. Many of the Buddhist kingdoms in the Himalaya preserved in some respects the politico-religious traditions of the ancient Tibetan empire. The origins of the dynasty known as Namgyal, which means 'Victorious', go back to Dragpa Bum's grandson Bhagan. In the past it was not uncommon for there to be inter-religious marriages both among the laity and between Buddhist kings from Ladakh and Muslim princesses from Kashmir and Baltistan, challenging present-day stereotypes of cultural homogeneity and religious exclusivity.

Tingmosgang surrounds an old temple that dates to the time of its founder. The temple is dedicated to the cult of Maitreya, the 'Awaited Buddha', who is depicted in a life-size statue seated on a royal throne. The old murals, which once adorned all the walls of the sanctuary, stand witness to the vicissitudes of time, for it was here that the Treaty of Tingmosgang was signed in 1684, demarcating the borders between Ladakh and Tibet. Some traditions do not seem to change, such as the appeal of the Tibetan varieties of Buddhism practised throughout these parts of the Himalaya. Several kilometres from the palace-fort of Tingmosgang the winding road leads to the secluded Tsarkarpo hermitage, which is constructed around a water-filled oasis with a small cave said to be impregnated with the blessings of the 'Lotus-Born Guru', the Tantric master Padmasambhava. This hermitage belongs to the Drikung, an offshoot of the Kagyu, which is one of the four main schools of Tibetan Buddhism and the one that dominated the religious and cultural history of Ladakh.

Prayer wall The 'mani-wall' in Muglub, Ladakh, is composed of stones carved with prayers by passing pilgrims in areas influenced by Tibetan Buddhism (opposite). The name derives from the mantra *Om Mani Padi Hum* ('Hail to the Jewel in the Lotus'), an invocation with which many of the stones are inscribed.

1684, Senge's successor, King Deden Namgyal (r. 1642–1694), having lost the Tibet–Ladakh–Mughal War of 1679–1684, was forced to cede his western territories to Lhasa and to appease Muslim-ruled Kashmir by building the Jama Masjid mosque in Leh. This war heralded the political decline of one of the oldest and most powerful of all Himalayan Buddhist kingdoms.

Over the centuries, Indians, Central Asians, Baltis, Mongols, Mughals and Tibetans have traded and fought in the western Himalaya. Linguistic affinities between the dialects spoken in Ladakh and Baltistan with those in the northern and eastern Tibetan regions of Amdo and Kham, and a shared epic tradition of the exploits of the pan-Tibetan culture hero Gesar, attest to an all-pervasive influence of Tibetan civilization across the Himalayan massif. The Tibetan forms of Buddhism practised in these regions belong to the Mahayana, or 'Great Vehicle', with a rich variety of Vajrayana ('Diamond-Thunderbolt Vehicle') rituals and practices. The arrival of Tibetan Buddhism in the western Himalaya marked the decline of the pre-Buddhist religion of Bon that prevailed in the Zhangzhung empire that ruled over these areas. Remnants of old traditions of animism once prevalent in the area, like the cult of the ibex and the worship of sacred trees, gave way to the erection of Buddhist relic monument *stupas*, prayer-inscribed *mani*-walls and architectural *kankani*. Himalayan religious art, however, is not limited to Buddhist temples ornate

EMPIRES AND KINGDOMS: MONGOLS, MUGHALS AND LADAKHIS

The Himalayan Buddhist kingdoms controlled access to the high mountain passes and remained relatively independent of Hindu and later Muslim domination because of their historical, religious and political ties with Tibet and their strategic position in the trans-Himalayan trading flows between the Indian subcontinent and Central Asia. Nevertheless, relations with their co-religionist Tibet were not always easy. On 7 July 1679, in order to regain control of the trading routes and resources in western Tibet (an area occupied nearly half a century earlier by the famous king of Ladakh, Senge Namgyal), the fifth Dalai Lama, Lobsang Gyatso (1617–1682), ordered a punitive military expedition against Ladakh. Gaden Tsewang, a Mongol prince, was asked to lead the Tibetan expedition. King Deleg Namgyal held out against the Tibetan–Mongol forces for three years at the impregnable fort of Basgo. When he was unable to withstand the siege any longer, he appealed to the Mughals for assistance and received reinforcements from Kashmir and Baltistan. However, because of a clandestine agreement between the Tibetans and the Mughals, Ladakh was eventually defeated and reduced to less than half of its former territory. After the Tibet–Ladakh–Mughal War of 1679–1684 the king of Ladakh was forced to sign one treaty with the Mughals and another with the Tibetans at the palace of Tingmosgang.

At Phyang monastery the protector deity Mahakala ('Great Time' or 'Great Black') is depicted wearing a

Mongol military helmet (below), a reminder of the Mongol involvement in Ladakh. In a small, dark chapel devoted to Mahakala at Phyang one may find, among exquisite Buddhist murals and life-size Tantric statues, Mongolian shields and weapons dating to the Tibetan–Mongol invasion of the eastern Himalaya.

BUDDHISTS, SIKHS AND HINDUS: THE SACRED LAKE OF REWALSAR

The religions of Hinduism, Sikhism and Buddhism meet at the shores of Lake Rewalsar (above), also known as Hridalayesh (which means 'Lake Abode of the Master'). It is a mid-altitude lake, 1,360 metres (4,462 feet) above sea level, and it is sacred to the god Shiva. It is here that Shiva taught the great sage Rishi Loma, who beheld visions of the Hindu pantheon and attained the blessings of longevity. On special days associated with Shiva, Hindu pilgrims enter the lake to purify their sins.

The lake takes its name from Rewal, the son of King Reva who ruled over the northwestern Himalayan kingdom of Mandi in what is now the Indian state of Himachal Pradesh.

The tenth and last Sikh Guru, Gobind Singh (1675–1708), came to Mandi, killed Yaksha, the arch-enemy of Rewal, and united 22 Himalayan principalities against the Mughal Emperor Muhammad Aurangzeb (r. 1658–1707). To atone for their wrongdoings Sikh pilgrims visit the *gurdwara*, built in memory of Guru Singh, who resided near the lake.

To Tibetan Buddhist pilgrims, Rewalsar is known as Tso Pema ('Lake of the Lotus'), in reference to the famous eighth-century Tantric master Padmasambhava, who is credited with the transmission of Tantric Buddhism in Tibet. Reverence for him is ubiquitous throughout the Himalaya and there are numerous sacred places and pilgrimage sites associated with Padmasambhava, not just in Tibet, but in Nepal, Bhutan, Sikkhim and across the westernmost parts of the Himalaya. The landscape bears the marks of major episodes in Padmasambhava's life: Rewalsar itself is said to have been formed around a pyre set by the king of Zahor to punish Padmasambhava for courting his daughter, Princess Mandarava. Although the pyre burned for many days, the 'Lotus-Born Guru' emerged victorious on a floating lotus in the form of an eight-year-old boy. To commemorate this event, Tibetan monasteries are built around the lake and a gigantic copper-plated statue of Padmasambhava, nearly 40 metres (130 feet) tall, overlooks the water.

with murals, statues and illustrated manuscripts, but also comprises iconography, symbols and motifs drawn from Hinduism and Islam. There are different strands of Hinduism in the Himalaya, with many temples and sacred sites dedicated to the Hindu pantheon and especially to the worship of Shiva, who is said to have spent many years meditating in the Himalaya. At the Triloknath Vihar, 50 kilometres (30 miles) from Keylong, the capital of Lahaul, the main statue of the shrine has six arms and is worshipped by Buddhists as the *bodhisattva* of compassion, Avalokitesvara, and by Hindus as Lord Shiva, while both communities participate in each other's religious activities.

Central Himalaya

The central Himalaya area may be roughly divided into the Indian regions of Garhwal and Kumaon (both in modern-day Uttarakhand), which are populated mainly by Hindus, and north-central Nepal, which is culturally Tibetan. People in the foothills comprise a variety of subgroups, which share basic cultural patterns but show local variations in their dialects, system of castes, art and architecture, dress and ornamentation, and marital ceremonies. At Gangotri, the last town on the upper Ganges, pilgrims from the foothills come to pray to Shiva and the goddess Ganga, and historically many gurus, yogis and swamis lived here practising meditation and asceticism. Trade with Tibet was an important undertaking for all Himalayan communities. Buddhist Newars from Nepal's Kathmandu Valley led caravans across the perilous Indo-Tibetan frontier and over the centuries many of them settled in the cities of Lhasa, Shigatse and Gyantse, forming a Nepalese 'trade diaspora'.

In Nepal, Hinduism and Buddhism coexist side by side and it is only in the border regions, within the administrative districts of Mustang and Dolpa, that religious art and architecture is dictated purely by Tibetan Buddhist standards. Mustang, formerly known as the kingdom of Lo, is populated by ethnic Tibetans who preserve many elements of traditional Tibetan culture, including polyandry. Lo played a vibrant role in the trading of salt, tea, yak tails and wool, grains, musk and spices between Tibet, Central Asia and India before it was annexed by Nepal in the eighteenth century. The one-time kingdom of Dolpo, which is predominantly Bon today and was ruled for some time by neighbouring Lo, also traces its foundation to the times of the Tibetan empire. Dolpo remained virtually independent of Hindu domination until well into the twentieth century.

Bhutan and the Indian highlands

There exist and will always be different perceptions of the Himalaya, some recorded by its neighbours, and others told by foreign visitors, Jesuit and Moravian missionaries, traders, invaders and Western explorers who passed through these regions. There are also the various outlooks of the local people, the Bhutias, Gurkhas, Lepchas, Monpas, Nepalis and other tribes who have inhabited these regions for generations. In the eastern Himalaya, roughly comprising the kingdom of Bhutan and the Indian areas of Sikkim, Arunachal Pradesh and Darjeeling, there are local beliefs about the elusive abominable snowman, the yeti, and of 'hidden valleys' known as *beyul*, tucked away

Sacred *stupa* In Nepal, Bhutan and Tibet *stupa*s, which were originally to house relics of the Buddha, are known as *chorten*s. This one, with its associated prayer flags, is situated in the Punakha Valley near Chimi Lhakhang Temple, founded in 1499 by Drukpa Kuenlay, a nonconformist Buddhist *lama* and master known as the 'Divine Madman'.

in the Himalaya, which may offer physical and spiritual protection for those who need them. The *beyul* fuel the imaginations of devoted Tibetan Buddhists, who envisage them as 'pure lands', or blessed sites untainted by humanity and prophesied in the Buddhist scriptures. Some *beyul*, such as Pemako and Khembalung, have actually been discovered, while more await discovery.

At times history and legend coexist, as in the case of Thangtong Gyalpo (1385–1464), the region's greatest architect, artist and engineer, who pioneered iron chain bridges in the Himalaya and retains a venerable status in local folk memory. Tibetan Buddhists identified and domesticated places in the local topography, assimilating much from local Bon beliefs. Sacred locales, be they mountains, lakes, caves, rivers, streams or trees, populate the religious geography of the Himalaya and in pre-Buddhist times the glacier-covered mountains were venerated as the ancestors of the region's different indigenous peoples. Today, many natural sites are important Buddhist pilgrimage destinations, such as the 'Tiger's Lair' (see illustration, page 25) in Paro, Bhutan, where the great saint Padmasambhava is said to have meditated in a cliff-cave with his consort Yeshe Tsogyal, and the 'burning lake', a pool in Bhumthang district where Pema Lingpa dived in with a lamp and discovered a treasured text hidden centuries earlier by Padmasambhava.

Bhutan did not emerge until long after the collapse of the Tibetan empire and the subsequent struggle among rival Tibetan Buddhist schools for patronage in the twelfth and thirteenth centuries. Following Bhutan's unification in the early decades of the seventeenth century, under the rule of the *chogyal* ('Buddhist-king') Ngawang

THE *LAMA* AND THE TAKIN

The takin (*Budorcas taxicolor*), a single species of its genus, is a hybrid-looking mammal of the Bovidae family. This unusual-looking bovine, with an unmistakeable affinity to goats and other hoofed mammals, is a compact, powerfully built herbivore. It is classified as 'vulnerable to endangered' in some areas due to hunting, poaching and the destruction of its fragile natural habitat.

The Bhutanese takin (*Budorcas taxicolor whitei*) is one of four subspecies of its kind that occupies an important role in Bhutan's religious history. It is said that the Buddhist patron saint of Bhutan, the *lama* Drukpa Kuenlay (1455–1529, depicted left), known as the 'Divine Madman' for his unconventional behaviour, was asked by his devotees to perform a miracle. Before granting them their wish he requested that they bring him a whole cow and a goat to eat. Having devoured both, leaving only the bones, he stuck the goat's head on the remains of the cow. To everyone's amazement, upon his command the animal came to life, ran to the meadow and began to graze.

The takin is the national animal of the kingdom of Bhutan. They graze and browse in the forested valleys of this eastern Himalayan kingdom during the summers, while in the winters they search for grass in the Alpine zones. A small population of protected takin is found at the Motithang Takin Preserve, near Thimpu.

Namgyal who had fled Tibet in 1616, the kingdom was organized into a dual system of government with *dzong*s, or fortresses, built to serve either a secular or a spiritual purpose: acting as units of civil administration with a protective garrison or as temples and offices to accommodate monks of the Drugpa school of Buddhism.

Bhutan is the only Himalayan kingdom that is now independent just as it was in the past. The Buddhist kingdom of Sikkim had to call on Tibet a number of times for military assistance in order to stave off Bhutanese incursions. Nevertheless, Sikkim, which means 'Hidden Valley of Rice', a stronghold for the Nyingma school of Tibetan Buddhism, enjoyed relative autonomy from 1642 onwards, when the first *chogyal*, Puntshog Namgyal, founded a hereditary princely line of Tibetan ancestry.

Further to the east, bordering with Bhutan, lies the Indian state of Arunachal Pradesh. Hindu influence in art and culture can be discerned in the foothills as early as the tenth century AD and the connection in Indian mythology of the Brahmaputra River with the Hindu god Brahma must have been an ancient source of inspiration for Hindu pilgrims. However, the many tribes and their local histories make it difficult to reconstruct a political and social history of the area.

To the north of the Brahmaputra River, the Monpa people populate the highlands, and although they are followers of Buddhism, animistic and shamanistic rituals and practices are widespread in the region. Many Buddhist temples and monasteries are under the control of Tawang monastery, one of the largest Buddhist establishments in India. It is a matter of great pride among the Monpas that the sixth Dalai Lama (1683–1706) was born into a Monpa family in Tawang region.

Fusion of faiths The extremely mixed nature of religious belief in the Himalaya is demonstrated by this syncretic pilgrimage to Gosaikunda in Nepal's Trisuli Valley. The pilgrimage combines elements of shamanism, Buddhism and Hinduism, and takes place on the shores of Gosaikund Lake during the August full moon.

3

Early Travellers and Adventurers:
The Himalaya to 1815

STEWART WEAVER

The Himalaya has been a place of spiritual pilgrimage since at least the middle centuries of the second millennium BC, when nomadic clans of Indo-European origin began migrating across the Iranian Plateau and over the Hindu Kush into India, bringing with them their own Vedic pantheon of gods and goddesses, to whom they assigned a mythic home in the mountains. Mount Kailas, a relatively modest trans-Himalayan peak in western Tibet, is particularly revered among Hindus as the seat of Lord Shiva (perhaps because of its close proximity to the source of all three of the subcontinent's great rivers: the Indus, the Ganges and the Brahmaputra). But many of the mountains have divine associations and have drawn pilgrims of all faiths from time immemorial. Sadly, few ancient pilgrims left written accounts of the mountains, but from the ancient Vedic texts we get at least some sense of how deeply they revered them. 'In a hundred ages of the gods I could not tell thee of the glories of Himachal, where Shiva lived, and where the Ganges falls from the foot of Vishnu like the slender thread of the Lotus flower,' runs a well-known verse in the *Skanda Purana*. 'As the dew is dried up by the morning sun, so are the sins of mankind by the sight of Himachal.'

Pilgrim's end The Chinese Buddhist monk Xuanzang (c.596–664) is shown returning home after his long pilgrimage to India in search of sacred texts. The journey took him through most of the Central Asian mountain ranges, including the Tian Shan where he encountered 10-metre (33-foot) snowdrifts. His accounts of the Himalaya are fanciful – he claimed the passes were so high that birds could not fly and had to traverse them on foot.

Pilgrims and missionaries

The arrival of Buddhism in China in the first century AD proved a stimulus to trans-Himalayan travel a few centuries later, when a number of the faithful felt drawn to India in search of their religious heritage. Of these, the earliest known was Faxian (Fa Hsien), who in AD399 set off from his home in Ch'ang-an (today's Xi'an) on foot westwards across the trackless Taklamakan Desert and then south across the Pamir Mountains to the kingdom of Peshawar in today's Pakistan. His record of his journey through the Pamirs, what he called the Tsung Ling Mountains, does not elucidate his precise route but leaves no doubt as to its terrors:

These mountains are covered with snow both in winter and summer. They shelter ven-
omous dragons also, which, if once provoked, spit out their poison. Scarcely one person
out of ten thousand survives after encountering the various difficulties which oppose
their advance—the wind, and the rain, and the snow, and the driving sand and gravel.
. . . Steep crags and precipices constantly intercept the way. These mountains are like
walls of rock, standing up 10,000 ft. in height. On looking over the edge the sight be-
comes confused, and then, on advancing, the foot loses its hold and you are lost. At the
base there is a stream called the Sin-to (Indus). Men of old days have cut away the cliff

ALEXANDER THE GREAT

The first Europeans to travel in the Himalaya were the soldiers of Alexander the Great, whose eagerness to rule the entire known world took him through the Khyber Pass – the traditional route of invasion through the mountains of the northwest – and into India (below) as far as the Beas River in 326BC. Alexander probably never ventured beyond the hilltop fortress of Aornus (Pir-Sar) in today's Swat district of Pakistan, but the existence of the town of Sikandrabad in the mountainous Hunza Valley suggests some contact with adventurous Greeks. 'Skardu', the name of the staging village for K2 on the Gilgit Road in Baltistan, allegedly recalls 'Iskandaria', a Balti rendering of 'Alexander', and local legend attributes the barge by which the early K2 expeditions crossed the Indus at Skardu to the Macedonian prince – it is 'Alexander's Barge'. The revolt of Alexander's army in 325BC forced his quick withdrawal from India, and in the end this much-vaunted 'invasion' amounted to little more than a passing raid. Nevertheless, the excavations of the Indian Archaeological Survey in the 1920s proved the widespread Alexandrian presence in the mountain regions and lent the Himalaya a Hellenistic gloss that captivated the imaginations of early, classically educated mountaineers.

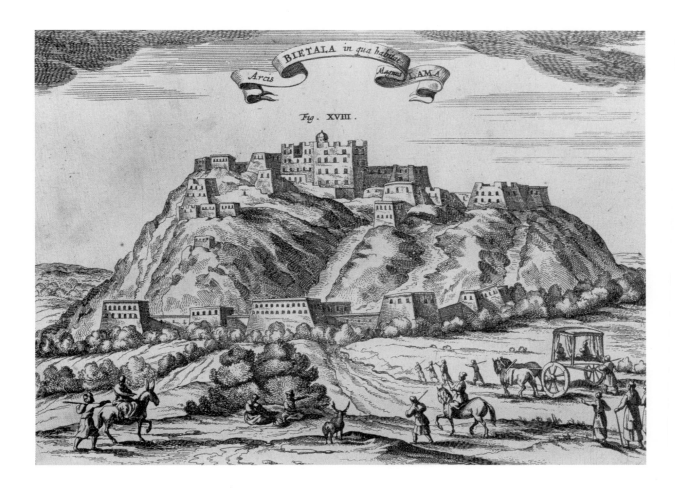

so as to make a passage, and have carved out against the rock steps for descent, amounting altogether to 700 in number. Having passed these, there is, suspended across, the river, a bridge of ropes, by which travelers pass over it.
(From *Travels of Fah-Hian and Sung-Yun, Buddhist Pilgrims, From China to India (400 A.D. and 518 A.D.)*, translated by Samuel Beale, London, 1869.)

From Peshawar Faxian made his way east into the plain of the Ganges, where he lingered for many years before making his way home by sea. Not quite two centuries later, his compatriot and fellow pilgrim Xuanzang (Hsuan Tang), inspired by a dream of scaling Sumeru, the sacred mountain at the centre of Buddhist cosmology, undertook an even more epic, 16-year journey through much of Central Asia and India, including the forbiddingly mountainous regions of Kashmir and Nepal. 'The roads are steep and dangerous, the cold wind is extremely biting, and frequently fierce dragons impede and molest travellers with their inflictions,' Xuanzang wrote, perhaps a touch fancifully. His precise routes through the mountains are impossible to reconstruct from his writings – which were in any case unknown in the West until the late nineteenth century – but he is said to have been the first traveller on record to visit all the mountain ranges of south-central Asia, from the Pamirs to the Himalaya, with the possible exception of the Karakoram.

The great Venetian traveller Marco Polo crossed the Pamirs from Balkh to Kashgar and may have skirted just north of the Karakoram en route to China in 1272 or 1273, but his famous *Travels* devotes all of four pages to this portion of his journey

Potala Palace This engraving, published by the Dutchman Athanasius Kirchner in his *China Illustrata* in 1667, is based on accounts Kirchner received from the Austrian Jesuit Johann Grueber, who had visited Lhasa in 1661. For many in the West it was the only visual representation available of the great palace of the Dalai Lama until the advent of photography.

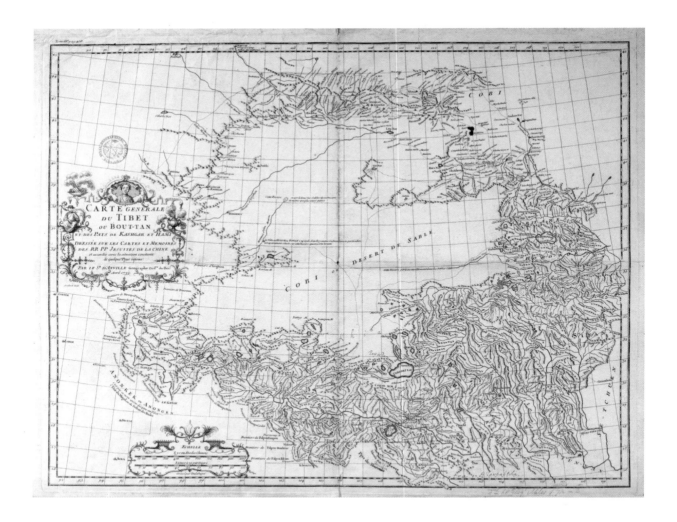

In the mid-eighteenth century the most widely available map of the Himalaya was the one published in 1735 by the French geographer D'Anville as part of his *Description de l'Empire de la Chine*. Unfortunately his information on the Himalaya was derived from a survey sent out by the Kangxi emperor in 1705–1717 and many of the river courses shown in the mountains are completely wrong.

and just one generic description of surpassingly high but otherwise unidentifiable mountains. The first Europeans really to penetrate and come to grips with the mountains were Jesuit missionaries drawn north from the Portuguese enclave of Goa by persistent (and false, as it turned out) reports of Christian communities in Tibet. In 1603, Brother Bento de Góis, accompanied a trading caravan from Lahore to Kabul and thence through the Pamirs to Yarkand, thus becoming the first known European to travel overland from India to China. The first Europeans to cross the Himalaya proper were Father Antonio de Andrade and Brother Manuel Marques, who set out from Agra in March 1624 and four months later reached Tsaparang on the upper Sutlej River by way of the perilous (5,486-metre/18,000-foot) Mana Pass in Garhwal. Andrade established the first Jesuit mission in Tibet the following year and it briefly flourished, drawing a succession of priests over the Mana and later the Rohtang Pass, which connects the Kulu and Lahaul valleys over the outer Himalayan Pir Panjal range. To the east, meanwhile, two Portuguese Jesuits, John Cabral and Stephen Cacella, had crossed the mountains by way of the Chumbi Valley and the Tang La, or Tang Pass, and established a second mission at Shigatse on the Tsangpo that survived until 1631. Thirty years later, Johann Grueber, an Austrian Jesuit, and the Belgian Albert d'Orville travelled overland from Beijing to Agra by way of Lhasa and Kathmandu. Crossing the Nepal Himalaya where they did, between the great peaks of Shisha Pangma and Cho Oyu, they were almost certainly the first Europeans to see Mount Everest and evidently the last to be unmoved by it: nowhere in his diary does Grueber make even briefest mention of the mountains, an interesting commentary in itself on seventeenth-century (or Jesuit) sensibility.

Early surveyors and emissaries

With the lapse of the Jesuit missions after 1720, the initiative in Himalayan exploration passed to the soldiers, surveyors and ambassadors of the British East India Company. Founded by royal charter in December 1600, the 'Governor and Company of Merchants of London', as it was then formally known, established its first trade enclave in India at Surat on the Tapti River in 1612. Initially, it had no interest in territorial aggrandizement; it was in India on sufferance of the Mughal emperor simply to trade for spices and textiles. Over time, however, as Mughal authority waned and trade rivalry with the French increased, the East India Company found itself drawn into local dynastic struggles from which it usually emerged with surrogate governing authority. The date often taken to mark the dawn of 'British India' is 23 June 1757, when Colonel Robert Clive defeated the army of Siraj-ud-daula at the mango grove of Plassey and established the East India Company as the ruling power in Bengal. Calcutta, the modest trading post established by Job Charnock on the Hooghly River in 1690, became from 1772 the capital of British India, the seat of the governor-general, and the essential northern vantage point from which over time the British were to explore, comprehend and ultimately control the Himalaya.

Before leaving India in 1767, Robert Clive appointed Captain James Rennell of the Bengal Engineers to the post of surveyor-general of Bengal, an appointment often taken to mark the foundation of the Survey of India. Rennell's brief was to map all East India Company territory in the administrative region of British India known as the Bengal Presidency, which he did mainly by compiling the route surveys of, for instance, such military officers as Captain George Kinloch, who led a small expedition

In disguise A painting of William Moorcroft and Hyder Young Hearsey, who crossed into western Tibet in 1812 disguised as Hindu *sadhu*s. They made many valuable discoveries and followed the Ram Ganga to its source east of Nanda Devi. On their way back they were imprisoned several times, both by the Tibetans and by Gurkhas.

in aid of the Malla ruler of Nepal when his territory was invaded by the Gurkhas in 1767. The expedition suffered the first serious setback to British arms in Asia, but Kinloch did return with helpful sketches of the borderlands of south-central Nepal. Rennell himself did little surveying in the field, but he travelled north as far as the border with Bhutan, glimpsed the snow-covered peaks to the north and guessed that they were 'among the highest mountains of the old hemisphere' (assuming, as all Europeans did in those days, that the Andes of the 'new hemisphere' were the highest in the world). Such a suggestion would eventually pique the scientific curiosity of the Survey of India, but for now the British remained more interested in what lay beyond the mountains than in the mountains themselves, and in May 1774 Warren Hastings, the first governor-general of India and one determined to extend the reach of British influence in Asia, sent the 28-year-old Scotsman George Bogle on a mission to Tibet, charged with studying the geography of the country and assessing the overall prospects for trade.

Accompanied by an army surgeon named Alexander Hamilton and a small retinue of Bengali servants – not one of whom had ever before seen snow – Bogle made his way first through the Assam Himalaya to the fortress monastery of Taschichodzong, the seat of the government of the Deb Raja of Bhutan. After three months of diplomacy, having finally secured permission to enter Tibet, he proceeded west and then north through the Chumbi Valley, that famous break in the Himalayan rampart between Sikkim and Bhutan that would later prove the high (although roundabout) road to Everest for the early British climbing expeditions. Out of the valley the great holy peak of Chomolhari rose 'almost perpendicular like a wall', Bogle wrote in some astonishment, while off to the west he could just glimpse the high mountains of Sikkim, among them Kangchenjunga, the third-highest mountain in the world (which Bogle described somewhat incongruously as 'the snowy hill seen from Dinajpúr and other plains in Bengal'). From the Chumbi Valley, Bogle and Hamilton crossed the 4,572-metre-high (15,000-foot) Tang La, thus becoming the first Britons to cross the Himalaya onto the Tibetan Plateau. Barred from entering Lhasa, where the Dalai Lama was still in his minority, they made their way instead to Shigatse, where Bogle took a Tibetan wife and won the trust and friendship of the sixth Panchen Lama, Lobsang Palden Yeshé, then ruling as regent in the Dalai Lama's stead. Bogle won little in the way of commercial advantage for the East India Company, however, and nine years after his empty-handed return Hastings sent a second emissary to Shigatse, this time his aide-de-camp and cousin, Samuel Turner. Bogle and Turner were intrepid travellers and astute cultural observers, but neither had been accompanied by a trained surveyor, and apart from identifying the Tsangpo River with the Brahmaputra in Assam, their missions added little to geographical knowledge of the Himalaya. When James Rennell published the second edition of his *Map of Hindoostan* in 1788, everything north of the outer foothills remained *terra incognita*, a wide space filled with randomly drawn lines of generic and abstract mountain ranges.

The veil of obscurity that lay especially heavily over the central Himalaya lifted briefly in 1792, when the Gurkha rulers of Nepal appealed to Calcutta for help against a Chinese-backed Tibetan incursion from the north. Lord Cornwallis, Warren Hastings's phlegmatic successor as governor-general, declined to send troops but did send a diplomatic mission under Colonel William Kirkpatrick to mediate the dispute. By the time Kirkpatrick arrived in the Kathmandu Valley in 1793, the fighting had ended, along with the need for his mediating services, but he and his escort lingered for three weeks, which was long enough to justify Kirkpatrick in later composing his *Account of the Kingdom of Nepaul*, the first such account by any European visitor

A REGION OF DREADFUL DESOLATION

The last of the priestly pioneers of Himalayan travel was the Italian missionary Ippolito Desideri (1684–1733), who travelled from Srinagar in the Vale of Kashmir to Leh, in the trans-Himalayan region of Ladakh, by way of the Zoji La in May 1715. Widely considered the first of the great explorers of Tibet, Desideri was also the first European to enter at all sympathetically into the study of Tibetan language and culture. But he was no lover of the mountains, as his account of his crossing of the Zoji La makes painfully clear. The mountains were, he wrote:

... the very picture of desolation, horror, and death itself. They are piled one atop of another. And so close as scarcely to leave room for the torrents which course impetuously from their heights, and dash with such deafening noise against the rocks as to appall the stoutest traveler. Above and at their foot the mountains are equally impassable; you are therefore forced to make your way about half-way down the slope, and the path, as a rule, is so narrow as barely to leave room for you to set down your feet; this .... A false step, and you are precipitated down the abyss with the loss of your life, or at the least with broken limbs, as befell some of our fellow-travellers. Were there bushes you might cling by them, but these mountains are so barren that neither plants nor even a blade of grass grows thereon. Would you wish to cross from one mountain to another, you must pass over the foaming torrents between, and there is no bridge, save some narrow, unsteady planks, or some ropes stretched across and interwoven with green branches. Often you are obliged to take off your shoes in order to get a better footfall. I assure you that I shudder now at the bare remembrance of these dreadful episodes in our journey.

It is clear that in 1715 the romantic appreciation for mountain glory had yet to take hold of the Western imagination; the Himalaya was a desolate and fearful obstacle to be crossed out of missionary necessity, perhaps, but otherwise to be strenuously avoided.

to that fabled land. Accompanying it was also the first sketch-map of the route to Kathmandu, the work of Lieutenant John Gerard, a member of Kirkpatrick's military escort and later Adjutant General of the Army of Bengal.

Tibetan annoyance at this show of Anglo-Nepalese friendship, together with rising Chinese influence in Lhasa, led to the closing of the Tibetan frontier to the British: apart from an occasional trespasser, no Briton would again cross the Tang Pass onto the Tibetan Plateau until Francis Younghusband reopened Anglo-Tibetan relations at gunpoint in 1904. For their part, the Nepalese briefly tolerated a British resident at Kathmandu between 1801 and 1803, thus affording the surveyor Charles Crawford a tantalizing glimpse of the surrounding mountains, which were, he was convinced, 'of vast height', perhaps as high as 6,100 metres (20,000 feet), he thought, above his stations of observation. Such a suggestion caused a stir of interest in both military and scientific circles, but Crawford had neither the time nor the means to confirm it. In 1803 the resident withdrew from Kathmandu, Crawford's drawings and survey journal were both unaccountably lost, and the veil of obscurity once again descended on the central Himalaya. Not until 1950 would foreign travellers return to the Kosi region of eastern Nepal that Crawford had crudely begun to survey in 1802.

In India, meanwhile, East India Company aggression against the Maratha Confederacy had by 1805 extended British territory as far north as Delhi, and where the army went, the surveyors inevitably followed. Robert Colebrooke, Rennell's successor as surveyor-general of Bengal, took to the field in 1807 determined to find the sources of the Ganges. From Patna in Bihar he pushed up the tributary Gogra and Rapti rivers to Gorakhpur, where he took his first series of observations of Nepal Himalaya. He then pushed northwest to Pilibhit in the sub-Himalayan region of Rohilkhand. From here, having taken a second series of observations of mountains that were, he now felt confident, 'without doubt equal, if not superior, in elevation to the Cordilleras of South America', he meant to proceed surreptitiously into Garhwal-Kumaon, then still part of the kingdom of Nepal. But in early 1808 he went down with malarial dysentery and sent his assistant, Lieutenant William Webb of the 10th Regiment of Bengal Native Infantry, to survey the sources of the Ganges in his stead.

Accompanied by Captain F.V. Raper (also of the 10th Bengal) and the colourful Anglo-Indian mercenary Hyder Young Hearsey, Webb followed the Dhauli Ganga tributary as far as Tapoban, where he climbed the (3,658-metre) 12,000-foot Kuari Pass and became the first European to behold the entire Kumaon Himalaya. Everything he saw convinced Webb that these were the highest mountains in the world, but he had no hard evidence until 1810, when he fixed the mountain known to him as Dhaulagiri from four survey stations in the plains and came up with the staggering height of 8,187 metres (26,862 feet). He was accurate to within about 20 metres (67 feet). But back in Europe, where experts stubbornly persisted in believing that the Andes were the world's highest mountains, Webb's findings were generally dismissed as the fevered imaginings of the East. Not until George Everest brought the Great Trigonometrical Survey to the north in the 1830s would the pre-eminent stature of the Himalaya finally be put beyond dispute.

In December 1808, shortly after William Webb's pioneering foray into Garhwal, the English veterinary surgeon William Moorcroft arrived in Bengal as the East India Company's new superintendent of stud. Finding the equine stock in a lamentable state, he set off on a 2,400-kilometre (1,500-mile) journey to the outer reaches of British India, buying horses, gathering information, and generally acquainting himself with the peoples and places of the frontier. He returned to Bengal convinced that the answer to the company's stud problems lay beyond the mountain passes, and in April

1812 he set off again, on dubious authority and in the company of Webb's old friend, Hyder Young Hearsey. Disguised as Hindu *sadhu*s, the two men crossed into Kumaon and traced the Ram Ganga to its source east of Nanda Devi. Finding no breach in the mountain rampart there, they retraced Webb's route up the Dhauli Ganga and crossed the 5,068-metre (16,628-foot) Niti Pass into the Gartok region of western Tibet. There they found few horses but plenty of valuable pashmina wool and, more interesting still, evidence of a recent Russian presence in the region. Preoccupied as they still were by the Napoleonic menace, the British had little anxiety to spare as yet for the tsar, who was, after all, for the moment an ally. Still, Moorcroft's discovery of Russians in the trans-Himalaya did not go unnoticed in Delhi or Calcutta, and it would not be forgotten. Meanwhile, barred from venturing farther into Tibet, Moorcroft and Hearsey returned to India as they came, but not before becoming the first Englishmen to follow the ancient pilgrim road to Manasarovar, the sacred lake at the foot of Mount Kailas where worship and adoration of the mountains had begun, many centuries before.

DRAWINGS
Illustrative of the 3 feet
THEODOLITE
Constructed for
The H. E. India Company
by
Mess.ᵗˢ Troughton & Simms.

Surveyor General's Office, Calcutta 1874.

4

Surveying the Himalaya 1815–1892

STEWART WEAVER

In 1814, ostensibly provoked by Gurkha encroachments on its territory, the East India Company went to war against the kingdom of Nepal and seized the mountain province of Garhwal-Kumaon, thus bringing a complete north to south (Tibet to India) cross-section of the Himalaya under direct British rule for the first time. Even before the war had ended, John Anthony Hodgson was named surveyor of the northwest mountain provinces and started to explore the valleys west of the Kali River, which was now the effective border with Nepal. Four years later, his successor James Herbert established the first Himalayan surveyor's base-line at Saharanpur and began to calculate the heights of the peaks, one of which, Nanda Devi, came in at the startling (and almost accurate) figure of 7,848 metres (25,749 feet). (The modern measurement is 7,816 metres/25,643 feet.) No one, as yet, had any thought of climbing such peaks, but in 1830 G.W. Traill, the first deputy commissioner of Kumaon, crossed the Great Himalayan axis between Nanda Devi and Nanda Kot by way of the difficult snow-bound pass that still bears his name. For its time, this was a notable 5,395-metre (17,700-foot) ascent, and according to local legend it so aroused the wrath of the goddess Nanda that she struck Traill snow-blind and would not relent until he made a repentant offering at the temple dedicated to her in Almora.

Of all the early British travellers in the western Himalaya, the most intrepid was Godfrey Thomas Vigne, a one-time solicitor turned sportsman cum artist, who turned up in India in 1834 and spent the better part of the next four years exploring the remote valleys of Kashmir, Ladakh and Baltistan. His motives were obscure, as were his precise routes and itineraries, and more than one historian has guessed that he was a spy in the pay of the East India Company. If so, he was an unusually protean one who spent as much time hunting, painting, writing and botanizing as he did exploring, but his achievements as a mountain explorer were nevertheless notable. Besides opening up the Vale of Kashmir to European admiration, he crossed the high passes east of Nanga Parbat, the western buttress of the Great Himalayan axis, and so 'discovered' the Karakoram, which he explored as far as the snout of the Chogo Lungma Glacier. His classic *Travels in Kashmir* (1842) is not only the first comprehensive account of the northwestern mountain region, it is also the first to appreciate the mountains in romantic terms. As Ian Cameron has said, Vigne was 'the first European to see the mountains as we see them today, not as an inanimate barrier, but as a manifestation of nature at its most magnificent'.

Surveying tool An elevation drawing of Sir George Everest's theodolite carried by him in 1830–1843 during the Great Trigonometrical Survey of India, which had begun in 1802. The theodolite was used by James Nicolson to measure the height of the peak that would later be named Mount Everest, and to establish that it was the highest in the world.

SCIENTIFIC TRAVELLERS

DR. HOOKER COLLECTING PLANTS IN THE SIKKIM HIMALAYAS.
From a picture by the late Frank Stone, A.R.A.

His main interests were botanical (here, left, he is depicted collecting plants), but Hooker was an amateur geologist as well, and his famous *Himalayan Journals* (1854) contain some of the first and still most compelling descriptions of 'Chumulari', 'Kinchin-junga', and other notable peaks of the eastern Himalaya. Although no surveyor, Hooker spent enough time making maps to arouse the suspicions of the Raja of Sikkim, and in November 1849 he was seized and detained at Tumlong, north of Gangtok. The East India Company secured his release by threatening invasion, and then annexed a portion of southern Sikkim just for good measure, thus bringing the British Raj that much closer to the battlements of Kangchenjunga.

After Hooker, the most prominent scientific explorers of the Himalaya at mid-century were Hermann, Adolf and Robert Schlagintweit, three Bavarian brothers who came to India in 1854 to undertake a study of the Earth's magnetic field. From Calcutta, Hermann went east to Assam and explored the valley of the Brahmaputra River. Adolf and Robert, meanwhile, made their way to the central Himalaya in Kumaon, where they made a climbing attempt on what they thought was Kamet but was probably Abi Gamin, the nearest adjoining peak to the north. As far as anyone can tell, this was the first sporting ascent in the Himalaya, the first attempt to get to the top of a mountain just for the sake of it, and not surprisingly it failed, although not before the Schlagintweits and eight courageous porters had spent ten nights above 5,182 metres (17,000 feet) and reached an estimated height of 6,778 metres (22,239 feet), a record that stood for nine years.

Of the many naturalists who travelled hard on the heels of the surveyors in the Himalaya, the most important was Joseph Dalton Hooker (1817–1911), friend and protégé of Darwin, who went out to India in 1847 and spent the better part of the next two years in Sikkim and eastern Bengal.

Servants of the map

In India, meanwhile, the Great Trigonometrical Survey was proceeding steadily north from Madras towards the mountains along the 78th degree of longitude. It was dangerous, expensive and painstaking work, but by the time George Everest retired as superintendent of the survey in 1843, he had brought the 'Great Arc of the Meridian' to its terminus at Dehra Dun and begun the several subsidiary surveys that finally made possible the definitive measurement of the eastern Himalaya from the late 1840s. When Kangchenjunga came in at 8,586 metres (28,169 feet) above sea level, it was thought surely to be the highest mountain in the world – but only briefly, for in November 1847, Andrew Waugh, Everest's successor as superintendent, had spotted from a prominence outside of Darjeeling a shy and indistinct summit that he suspected might be even higher. For now he simply called it 'gamma' and left it to his assistants to take its bearings from various angles over the next few years. By 1850, 'gamma' had become 'Peak XV' and the focus of much excited attention in Calcutta.

INDEX CHART
TO THE
GREAT TRIGONOMETRICAL SURVEY
OF
INDIA

But not until March 1856 would the survey formally fix its height at 8,840 metres (29,002 feet) above sea level (only about 8 metres/26 feet short of its true height of 8,848 metres/29,029 feet) and designate it the highest mountain in the world. What then to call it? Although the Great Trigonometrical Survey is obviously implicated in that minute elaboration of knowledge by which the British took possession of India, chain by chain, its officers and surveyors were normally scrupulous in adhering to local names for topographical features. Only when Waugh's exhaustive search for a native appellation for Peak XV came up empty did he presume to name it in honour of his predecessor, George Everest.

By the mid-nineteenth century, huge tracts of the once-proud kingdom of the Punjab, including Kashmir, had fallen to the British or their puppets and thus lay open to exploration and survey. Neither the British surveyors nor their native assistants were mountaineers in the conventional sense of the term. They carried no ice-axes, they wore no crampons, they knew nothing of Alpine rope or points of belay. Even

Survey sheet The index chart for the Great Trigonometrical Survey of India, made in 1870, four years after the survey's completion. By triangulating from the known heights of peaks that had been surveyed, Everest and his team were able to create a framework of triangulation covering much of the Himalaya and to fix the height of the mountains.

River of ice The Baltoro Glacier in the Karakoram is one of the longest sheets of ice in the subpolar regions, at some 58 kilometres (36 miles) in length. It is also comparatively fast-moving, advancing up to 2 metres (6.5 feet) in a single day. It was first surveyed by Henry Haversham Godwin-Austen in 1861.

so, for the purposes of science they lugged their theodolites and heliotropes to very considerable heights, to the 5,000–6,000-metre (16,400–19,700-foot) summits, even, of the outer mountains, where they would sometimes camp for weeks, cold, exhausted and hungry, waiting for the clear line of sight on which all their intricate trigonometrical calculations depended. And it was from one of these summits above the Vale of Kashmir that in 1856 Lieutenant Thomas George Montgomerie of the Royal Engineers spotted at a distance of 225 kilometres (140 miles) two commanding peaks of the Karakoram and, not knowing what else to call them, marked them down for the moment as 'K1' and 'K2'. K1 turned out to have a local name and as per survey custom went on to the maps as 'Masherbrum'. But K2 had none that the British could ever find, and thus K2 it remained, in cryptic cartographic homage to the unsung climbers of the Survey of India.

The outbreak of the Great Mutiny in 1857 brought sporadic violence to Kashmir, but the survey continued under the notable leadership of Henry Haversham Godwin-Austen, soldier, explorer, artist, geologist and the greatest mountaineer of his day. By this time the British had identified the Karakoram as the logical northern frontier of Kashmir – the logical border, that is to say, between British India and the unknown hinterlands of Central Asia. Godwin-Austen's task was to make known this border, to establish it and put it on the map. He had no authority actually to cross the Karakoram, but in 1861 his explorer's enthusiasm got the better of him and accompanied by some 60 porters and assistants he ventured up the Panmah Glacier as far as the Muztagh, the formidable 5,486-metre (18,000-foot) ice-bound pass over the Karakoram, just 32 kilometres (20 miles) west of K2. He next proceeded east up the Braldu Valley to the snout of the Baltoro Glacier. Just beyond lay the innermost sanctum of the Karakoram, a vast canyon of rock-strewn ice and snow that enfolds ten of the world's 30 highest mountains.

Godwin-Austen was the first European to ascend the Baltoro, the first to measure and map its course, the first to climb on the monumental spires and buttresses that enclose it. He never set foot on K2, but from the summit of an outlying spur of Masherbrum he saw it clearly enough to fix its position and establish that its glaciers drained south to the Indus – a notable discovery that in the minds of the British put the world's second-highest mountain securely within their Indian sphere of influence.

Happily, a late-nineteenth-century effort to impose the name 'Mount Godwin-Austen' on K2 foundered, and Everest remains the only great Himalayan peak to suffer such colonial indignity. Maps still recognize the glacier that flanks K2 to the east as the 'Godwin-Austen Glacier', however, in postcolonial tribute to the greatest of the Karakoram surveyors. No such feature honours the memory of William Henry Johnson, a contemporary of Godwin-Austen who rose through the ranks of the survey to become Montgomerie's assistant in Kashmir, yet in simple mountaineering terms his were arguably the most notable achievements of these years: by 1862 he had placed nine triangulation stations above 6,100 metres (20,000 feet). Of these, four remained the world's highest for the next 60 years. As an Indian-born, humbly educated civil assistant who had never been to England, Johnson hardly existed in the intensely status-conscious eyes of the British Raj, and thus his remarkable climbing achievements went all but unnoticed. But at least we know his name. Climbing along with him (and with all the other Britons, or 'sahibs' as they were referred to by Indians, of the survey) were unknown numbers of native assistants, the humble *khalasi*s, paid about six rupees a month to lug the essential signal poles and theodolites to rarefied heights unimaginable in Europe. The famous story that attributes the world's height record to one such *khalasi*, said to have carried a signal pole to the 7,030-metre (23,064-foot) summit of Shilla in 1860, has, alas, been discredited (at least insofar as the mountain turned out to be only 6,111 metres/20,048 feet high). But it ought to be recalled anyway, in recognition of the considerable mountaineering achievements of these anonymous servants of the map without whose tireless assistance Godwin-Austen and company would have achieved nothing.

The *pundits*

In July 1863, a Muslim traveller named Abdul Hamid left Leh, the capital of Ladakh, for the fabled city of Yarkand in what the British then called Chinese Turkestan.

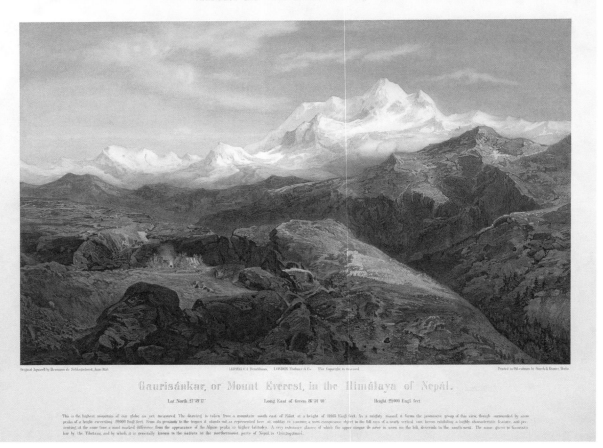

Gaurisánkar, or Mount Everest, in the Himálaya of Nepál.

Lat North 27°59'17"   Long East of Green 86°54'40"   Height 29,000 Engl feet

This is the highest mountain of our globe as yet measured. The drawing is taken from a mountain south-east of Tibet at a height of 11,695 Engl feet. As a mighty massif it forms the prominent group of this view, though surrounded by snow peaks of a height exceeding 20,000 Engl feet. From its proximity to the tropics it stands out as represented here at midday in summer, a most conspicuous object in the full sun of a nearly vertical sun, hence exhibiting a highly characteristic feature, and presenting at the same time, a most marked difference from the appearance of the Alpine peaks in higher latitudes. A very extensive glacier, of which the upper cirque de névé is seen on the left, descends to the south west. The name given to it by the Tibetans, and by which it is generally known to the natives in the northernmost parts of Nepal, is Chingopamari.

Everest watercolour A view of Everest from Darjeeling painted in 1856 by Hermann Schlagintweit, one of three German brothers commissioned by the East India Company three years before to conduct a 'Magnetic Survey' of the Himalaya. Schlagintweit suggested the name Gaurishankar as the local name for Everest, but he had in fact misidentified Everest with another peak some 58 kilometres (36 miles) distant.

Although dressed as a simple *munshi* (teacher or learned one), Hamid was in fact a clerk in the Survey of India who had been trained in the use of sextant and compass and sent over the mountains to gather topographical and political intelligence for the British. He was the first of the '*pundits*', as they came to be known (from the Sanskrit word *pandita*, meaning a learned person), native explorers attached to the survey for the purposes of espionage along the Himalayan frontier. By this time, the British had staked out an empire in India that roughly corresponded to the line of the mountains and closely abutted in the northwest on Chinese and Russian Central Asia. Russophobia was at its height, and government officials in Calcutta wanted desperately to know what was going on in the ill-defined kingdoms beyond the mountain passes. So, unable to travel there inconspicuously themselves, for many years they recruited and trained Indian subjects to what Kipling famously called the 'Great Game' – that is the strategic contest of influence and intrigue in the Himalayan regions in the late nineteenth century.

The idea of employing Indians as explorer-spies was Thomas Montgomerie's. When surveying in Ladakh in 1860, Montgomerie had noticed that natives travelled freely through areas forbidden to Europeans and thought they might therefore be put to the work of clandestine exploration. The recent mutiny had created an atmosphere of racial mistrust in India, and Calcutta initially greeted the idea of native spies with wary scepticism. But the failure in quick succession of two British-led attempts to enter Tibet in 1861 and 1862 eventually settled the issue in Montgomerie's favour.

The next year, he recruited Hamid, taught him the rudiments of route surveying, and dispatched him over the mountains inconspicuously equipped with sextant, compass, thermometers, watches, a lantern for reading instruments by night, pen and ink, and two small notebooks.

Alas, having survived an arduous crossing of the Karakoram Pass and a severe winter in Yarkand, Hamid died of wild rhubarb poisoning while on his way back to Leh. Montgomerie nevertheless declared the experimental expedition a success and the survey now took up the clandestine exploration of Central Asia in earnest. From the village of Milam in Kumaon, Montgomerie recruited two cousins, Nain Singh and Mani Singh, and brought them to the headquarters of the Survey of India at Dehra Dun, where they learned the subtle art of distance measurement by rosary-bead and prayer wheel before setting out on their remarkable careers as itinerant spies. Nain Singh set out from Kathmandu and crossed the Himalaya in 1865, surveying as far east as the forbidden city of Lhasa. Two years later, he crossed the Mana Pass out of Badrinath and undertook the first systematic survey of western Tibet. In 1873, he joined T. Douglas Forsyth's famous mission to Kashgar, an elaborate affair that featured six military officers, several scientists, four Indian surveyors, 350 porters and 550 pack animals. The purpose of the Forsyth mission was to establish friendly diplomatic relations with Yakub Beg, the recently self-proclaimed emir of Kashgaria. In this it largely failed. Yet it successfully provided cover for a great deal of clandestine travel in the trans-Himalaya and was, in scale and overall style, the prototype of those future mountaineering expeditions that awkwardly combined military surveillance, scientific research and climbing pure and simple.

The trekking arm of empire

The fifth and final journey of Hari Ram to Nepal and Tibet in 1892–1893 was the last known exploit of the Indian *pundits*. The Great Game was not over. In fact, with the Russian annexation of the ancient trans-Caspian city of Merv in 1883 and the subsequent Anglo-Russian standoff at the Afghan village of Pandjeh in 1885, it had entered its decisive phase. But with the fall of William Gladstone's Liberal government in 1886, the British no longer felt obliged to play the game by stealth or in secret. The hour of the 'Forward Policy' of open confrontation had arrived, and on the Himalayan frontier it became manifest in the oddly diminutive person of Francis Edward Younghusband.

Soldier, explorer, geographer, brigand, patriot, mystic: Younghusband was, as one biographer puts it, 'the last great imperial adventurer', and he more than anyone evokes the colonial context in which Himalayan mountaineering developed. Born in the Punjabi hill station of Murree in 1863, he was the son of Major-General John William Younghusband and the nephew of Robert Shaw, the British political agent at Yarkand. Following the customary rite of passage through English boarding school and the Royal Military College, Younghusband took a commission in the 1st (King's) Dragoon Guards and returned to India, where he soon won a

Pundit's equipment The compass and Tibetan prayer wheel used by the *pundit* Nain Singh for his survey of the Tsangpo Valley in Tibet. During his near 2,000-kilometre (1,240-mile) journey Nain Singh took measurements in secret all the way, and his work enabled this accurate map of the Tsangpo to be published in 1874.

Mountain approach A view of Nanda Devi, taken from 3,200 metres (10,500 feet). The 7,816-metre (25,643-foot) peak is surrounded by a ring of mountains, and the difficulty of access into the inner sanctuary around the mountain meant that serious attempts at climbing it were not made until the 1930s.

reputation as an eager, adventure-seeking officer with a tendency to hive off into the unknown. Yet he was also an introspective romantic with a sympathetic interest in Eastern spirituality, and together these two qualities – his adventurism and his mysticism – compelled him continually towards the mountains. How he came to the notice of the intelligence branch of the British Army in India is unclear, but in May 1885, in the immediate aftermath of the Pandjeh incident, he was summoned to Simla to undertake the revision of the military gazetteer of Kashmir and then sent off on what ultimately became an epic, 19-month journey across Central Asia, from Manchuria and Beijing to Kashgar and Yarkand and then south over the Karakoram to Kashmir. It was all highly original, pioneering stuff, but the highlight for posterity was the crossing of the Karakoram, for here Younghusband eschewed the conventional caravan route over the Karakoram Pass and crossed the Muztagh, the difficult, high-altitude pass just west of K2 that had defeated Godwin-Austen in 1861. He thus became the first European to see K2 from the north, and, more significantly still, with no mountaineering experience or equipment he and his Balti guide managed what the great Swedish explorer Sven Hedin later described as 'the most difficult and dangerous achievement in these mountains to date'. However limited its value from a strategic or scientific point of view, this crossing of the Muztagh opened an era in the history of mountaineering and confirmed Younghusband in his self-appointed role of Himalayan ambassador to the West.

In 1889 Younghusband returned to the Karakoram to investigate recent tribal raids on trade caravans and to counter Russian and Chinese overtures towards the rogue Kashmiri dependency of Hunza. Although an Anglo-Russian Boundary Commission had settled the Afghan frontier along the Hindu Kush in 1885, the Kashmiri frontier along the Pamirs and the Karakoram remained hopelessly ill-defined, from the British point of view, and vulnerable to unfriendly incursion. In 1888 a minor frontier war had led to the permanent establishment of a British agency at the strategically sensitive crossroads of Gilgit, some 160 kilometres (100 miles) north of Srinagar. Younghusband's job now was to extend the Gilgit Agency's control north and east through the mountains. Accompanied by a small escort of men from the 5th Gurkha Rifles, he crossed the Karakoram Pass out of Leh and undertook the first systematic exploration of the trans-Himalayan Shaksgam Valley. He then moved west towards the Pamirs, crossed the Mintaka Pass into Hunza, and followed the Hunza Valley south past Rakaposhi to British-administered Gilgit. What precisely he accomplished by all this mountain roaming is difficult to say. Younghusband

Karakoram party Francis Younghusband, with George Macartney, Henry Lennard and Richard Beech, on his mission to Kashgar in 1885–1886. During the arduous trip, in which Younghusband discovered the Sarpo Laggo Glacier and the Aghil mountain range, he had to sleep in the open, without fires, to avoid being seen by hostile Hunza raiders.

simply was, as one biographer has said, 'the trekking arm of empire in the border zones of British India, Russia, China, and Afghanistan'. Moreover, he was the figure in whom the political and strategic exigencies of the Great Game inspired a spiritual and artistic appreciation of Himalayan travel for its own sake. Younghusband was not, himself, truly a mountaineer of the Himalaya; he did not aspire to the summits. But his well-known mountain journeys between 1886 and 1891, besides contributing to the essential preliminary 'pacification' of the border country, were the direct inspiration, in 1892, for the first large-scale Himalayan mountaineering expedition: that of Sir William Martin Conway to the Karakoram.

THE LAST OF THE *PUNDITS*

From the point of view of mountain exploration, the last and most important of the pundits was Hari Ram, of whom little is known other than that he was a Hindu of Kumaon who entered the service of the Survey of India in 1868. Three years later, he left Darjeeling in the guise of a physician, passed through Sikkim and over the Tipta La to Shigatse in Tibet, and then moved eastwards across the Tibetan Plateau to Tingri, later the staging town for expeditions to the North Face of Everest. From here, he followed the Bhote Kosi over the hair-raising Thong La, 96 kilometres (60 miles) west of Everest, where at one point the path consisted of slabs of stone laid over iron pegs driven into the vertical wall of the chasm more than 450 metres (1,500 feet) above the river. In January, he arrived safely in Kathmandu and returned thence to Darjeeling, thus achieving the first known circuit of the Everest group. Two years later, from his home village of Pithoragarh in Kumaon, Hari Ram crossed the Kali on a single rope span and traversed northern Nepal from west to east as far as the Kali Gandaki, the tributary torrent that cleaves the mountains between the Dhaulagiri and Annapurna massifs. And in 1885 he returned from a long retirement to lead a furtive expedition up the Dudh Kosi to the Solu Khumbu region of northeastern Nepal, where he lingered for a month before braving the Nangpa La, a high glacial pass over the Himalayan crest between Cho Oyu and Gaurishankar. Although he could not see Everest off to the east, at 24 kilometres (15 miles) he was nearer to it than any trained observer to date, and the route survey he brought back constitutes the crude foundation of all subsequent British efforts to comprehend the Everest region.

5

The Opening Phase 1891–1918

AMANDA FABER

Although there had been a few isolated expeditions earlier in the nineteenth century, it was the advance of British control into the foothills of the Himalaya in the 1870s and 1880s that made climbing for pleasure properly feasible. Experienced climbers brought techniques they had learned in the Alps but found that they were not enough for the even larger scale of the Himalaya. Greater understanding of the effects of altitude and a proper appreciation of the contribution that could be made by local people, in particular Nepalese Sherpas, led gradually to success. By the end of this era, ambitions were starting to turn to Everest.

Naturalist and geologist Joseph Hooker had visited the Himlaya in 1847 and the German Schlagintweit brothers had travelled to the mountains as early as 1855. Other travellers such as William W. Graham and Francis Younghusband had blazed trails in the late 1880s. However, it was (Sir William) Martin Conway who laid the template for future expeditions when in 1892 he led a multi-skilled party to the Karakoram.

Martin Conway and the birth of the modern expedition

Conway had several Alpine seasons under his belt by the time he left Cambridge, and as a distinguished art historian was perfect 'old school' Alpine Club material. His expedition was funded mainly by his wealthy stepfather-in-law, who was convinced once Conway had obtained support from *The Times*, which agreed to print his dispatches, and scientific sponsorship from the Royal Geographical Society (RGS).

Turned down by the highly regarded Albert Mummery, Conway chose the brilliant and forthright Oscar Eckenstein as his climbing partner. Matthias Zurbriggen, a first-rate guide, and, less conventionally, the first expedition artist in the Himalaya, Arthur David (A.D.) McCormick, were in the group that left Europe. In the Himalaya they were joined by the ebullient Lieutenant Charles 'Bruiser' Bruce and four members of his regiment, the 5th Royal Gurkha Rifles (Frontier Force): Amar Singh, Karbir Thapa, Parbir Thapa and Harkbir Thapa.

Trekking into Srinagar on 3 April, the expedition headed towards Gilgit, where they planned to climb Rakaposhi (7,788 metres/25,551 feet) but the sight of its avalanche slopes dissuaded them. After further exploration of the Bagrot and Hunzar valleys they took the Hispar Glacier to the inner Karakoram.

On arrival in Askole, Conway dramatically sent Eckenstein home. A personality clash seems to have been at the root of the decision, but Eckenstein had also been ill and frustrated at spending 'two and a half months in the mountains without making a single ascent of importance'.

Photographic high Cathedral Peaks soar to the clouds in the Trango Towers in this beautiful photograph by Vittorio Sella, who accompanied the Duke of Abruzzi on his 1909 expedition to K2. Sella's uncle had founded the Italian Alpine Club and his father published the first Italian language treatise on photography. Vittorio combined both these interests to become a noted Alpine photographer and then to produce the finest early shots of the Himalaya.

In early August 1892 Conway travelled to the head of the Baltoro Glacier (perhaps following in the steps of Roberto Lerco who had visited in 1890). Here the group found a glacial junction, which Conway named Place de la Concorde (today known as Concordia). Around them was an amphitheatre of breathtaking peaks including K2 (8,611 metres/28,251 feet), Bride Peak (now named Chogolisa, 7,654 metres/25,111 feet) and the Gasherbrum group with Hidden Peak (Gasherbrum I) at 8,068 metres (26,469 feet). Zurbriggen perfectly summed up the view: 'They don't know what mountains are in Switzerland!' Conway was in raptures:

Here, indeed, was a highway into another world with which man had nothing to do. It might lead into a land of dragons, or giants, or ghosts. The very thought of man vanished in such surroundings, and there was no sign of animal life. The view was like seen music.

Conway needed a first ascent. On 10 August they climbed a minor summit, which Conway named Crystal Peak (6,252 metres/20,511 feet), to survey the area. From here he spotted the perfect target: 'It was…the most brilliant of all the mountains we saw…. And now, in the dim dawn, smote upon our delighted eyes…with one consent we cried out. "That is the peak for us."'

Himalayan pioneer Martin Conway (1856–1937) was the first to mount a large-scale mountaineering expedition into the Himalaya. He had been interested in climbing since childhood and in 1881 published the *Zermatt Pocket Book*, a printed guide to the Alps. He used his Alpine experience and the services of the noted Alpine climber Oscar Eckenstein to make 16 climbs over 4,877 metres (16,000 feet), including a first ascent of the modest Crystal Peak, during his 1892 expedition to the Karakoram.

On 25 August the group donned Eckenstein's crampons (see box, opposite) to climb the ridge leading to the mountain that Conway named Golden Throne (Baltoro Kangri, 7,312 metres/23,989 feet), and which was by most Himalayan standards disappointingly tame. Instead of reaching the summit they found themselves facing it across an impassable gap. Conway remained upbeat, naming their stopping point 'Pioneer Peak' and rounded his barometer reading up from 6,889 metres (22,601 feet) to over 7,010 metres (23,000 feet) – although it has subsequently been measured at 6,499 metres (21,322 feet). His claim to have reached a new world altitude is questionable; there is evidence that Atacama Indians of South America had climbed to similar heights hundreds of years before and William W. Graham may have climbed Kabru (7,394 metres/24,258 feet) in 1883. Nevertheless, Conway was euphoric: 'All recognised that the greatest we were going to accomplish was done and that henceforth nothing remained for us but downwards and homewards.' He had met several of his scientific, botanical and surveying objectives. The expedition book – a first – and a lecture tour helped secure him a Royal Geographical Society Founder's Medal in 1905. Posterity would judge him kindly. Nevertheless, in terms of climbing, his expedition was a relative failure. It was clear that conquering one of the great Himalayan peaks would require a greater degree of single-mindedness.

Albert Mummery and the first mountaineering tragedy

In 1895 Albert Mummery led the first serious mountaineering expedition to one of the great Himalayan 8,000-metre (26,246-feet) peaks. Driven by a passion for exploration and one of the best Victorian technical climbers, he was undone by his failure to recognize the scale of the Himalaya and its accompanying dangers.

THE INVENTIONS OF OSCAR ECKENSTEIN

Although the full-foot crampon had emerged at the end of the nineteenth century, with a six-point version in 1876 and then a ten-point version from Austria in 1884, British climbers still preferred nails hammered into their boots to help them grip on steep ice and snow.

In 1908 Oscar Eckenstein drew up plans for a new ten-point crampon, which reduced the need to cut steps in the ice and snow. It was regarded as cheating by members of the Alpine Club and other purists, who thought it made climbing too easy; but the flat-footing – or 'French' – technique required when using crampons, in which climbers kept as many crampon points in contact with the snow and ice as possible, led to faster and bolder climbing. The Italian climber Henry Grivel made Eckenstein's design commercially available in 1910; and later his son Laurent introduced two front-points.

Ice-axes around this period usually had a shaft that was around 120–130 centimetres (47–51 inches) long. Eckenstein developed a short version that could be used with one hand on steep sections. It had a blade length of 18 centimetres (7 inches) and a shaft of around 84 centimetres (33 inches). Perhaps as a result of Eckenstein's poor relations with the Alpine Club, it was initially unpopular with other climbers, including Martin Conway.

Mummery first visited Switzerland in 1871 and for the next ten years pioneered new Alpine routes. His first ascent of the Zmutt Ridge on the Matterhorn achieved particular notoriety. Another climber, William Penhall, had started out on the route with his guide but turned back in bad weather. Ignoring the 'fierce squalls of wind', Mummery and his guide started to climb and, in what was seen by some as an ungentlemanly move, used Penhall's ice-steps. That – or the then unacceptable fact, in the social circle from which most Alpinists were drawn, that the family had a tanning business – may have been what led the Alpine Club to reject his application for membership in 1880. It only relented eight years later, following Mummery's trip to the Caucasus (where he summited Dykh Tau at 5,204 metres/17,074 feet).

Granted a permit to enter Kashmir, the so-called 'Three Musketeers' of Mummery, Professor J. Norman Collie and Geoffrey Hastings left for Srinagar in June 1895 to climb Nanga Parbat, which was only 129 kilometres (80 miles) to the north and, at 8,126 metres (26,660 feet), the ninth-tallest Himalayan peak.

Approaching the mountain by its South Face, towering 4,600 metres (15,092 feet) above the Rupal Valley, the expedition made two reconnaissances into the Diamir Valley. On both Mummery tried to take what he thought would be shortcuts to avoid the Mazeno Pass and his misjudgments resulted in long, freezing treks on very little food. The first time, they returned to a small welcoming committee consisting of Conway's former companion, Charles Bruce, by now a major, with two Ghurkas, Raghobir Thaba and Goman Singh. To celebrate their safe deliverance the men drank all their Bass pale ale. After the second, they were reduced to eating barely cooked meat in a shepherds' camp, and fell asleep where they sat.

A few days later Bruce reluctantly rejoined his regiment. Hastings returned to the village of Astor, for provisions, while Mummery, Collie, Raghobir and a local Lor Khan prepared for the summit attempt. Collie now suggested they were out of their depth and even Mummery wrote, 'The peaks are too big and too high for real hard climbing'. Nevertheless, he proceeded with his plan to ascend the three 'Mummery

White death An avalanche cascades down the slope of Nanga Parbat. Albert Mummery's companions in his 1895 attempt on the peak believed that it was such an event that killed the climber on his descent. In 1937 a German expedition on the mountain was hit by an avalanche that killed 16 people, one of the highest death tolls in a single incident in the annals of Himalayan mountaineering.

rock ribs' that broke up the icefall at the top of the Diamir Glacier, in order to reach the snowfield above and from there traverse to the summit. During the first two weeks of August the expedition successfully established camps. Then, on the 18th, Mummery, Collie and Raghobir set off for the first camp. When a bad stomach forced Collie to return, the other two pressed on, climbing the very difficult rock rib as avalanches fell around them. Bruce later commented that this was 'some of the most daring mountaineering that has ever been accomplished'. The remaining pair spent the next night in the camp on the second ridge and then before first light carried on up the final rib towards the snowfield. The climbing was very hard but was easing out. At almost 6,100 metres (20,000 feet) Raghobir collapsed, having gone without food for 48 hours. They were forced to descend.

Dissuaded by Collie from any further attempt, Mummery decided to abandon this plan in favour of a snow route on Nanga Parbat's northern Rakhiot Face. This would have meant that the main camp needed to be taken around the mountain, and in Bruce's words, 'Mummery loathed that kind of work'. Instead, he decided to cut over, with Raghobir and Goman Singh, the 6,227-metre (20,430-foot) Diamir Gap, setting out on 24 August.

Three days later, Collie and Hastings arrived in the Rakhiot Valley after bringing the main camp around the mountain. When they looked up at the Diamir Gap, it was obvious to them that there was no way down. They believed Mummery and his companions would have been forced to turn back. With Collie's leave nearly over, Hastings led the search by pushing up the Diamir Valley as far as he could. He found nothing. It seemed Mummery and the others must have been hit by an avalanche.

Collie had started back. However, when he heard that Mummery had not been found he rejoined Hastings and on 16 September the two went back into the valley. Winter had arrived and Collie wrote:

The avalanches were thundering down the face of Nanga Parbat… they at least spoke with no uncertain voice and bade us be gone. Slowly we descended, and for the last time looked on the great mountain and the white snows where in some unknown spot our friends lay buried.

The climbing suffragette

The Conway and Mummery expeditions demonstrated the prevailing attitude that saw the Himalaya as the preserve of British men. It would be challenged by an American woman pioneer: Fanny Bullock Workman. Wealthy, tough and driven by what she called her 'mountain ego', Fanny Bullock Workman was a popular but perhaps uncompromising character who made eight trips to the Himalaya with her husband, Dr William Hunter Workman, and set a female altitude record. Fanny's husband had introduced her to climbing in New Hampshire and the Alps. He was a surgeon 12 years her senior, and when he retired early (from stress) the couple put their daughter Rachel into boarding school and went travelling.

The Workmans discovered the Himalaya in 1898 when they travelled to Ladakh during a cycle trip to escape the heat of the plains. Reaching the Karakoram Pass and having been captivated by the mountains, they arranged for tents and mountaineering equipment to be sent from London that September. The resulting attempt on Kangchenjunga ended after ten days just outside Darjeeling, but they were smitten by the prospect of further climbs.

The following year saw the Workmans in Kashmir, climbing peaks around Askole and the Shigar Valley, modestly naming one Mount Bullock Workman and another Siegfried Horn (in memory of their dead son). In 1902 and 1903 they explored the 50-kilometre (30-mile) Chogo Lungma Glacier, 'correcting' the Survey of India maps and becoming the first Westerners to reach its head at 5,791 metres (19,000 feet). On the second trip William made the now-disputed claim to have reached just over 7,130 metres (23,394 feet) on Pyramid Peak. Returning to Kashmir in 1906, the pair circuited the Nun Kun massif. Fanny's conquest of the 6,930-metre (22,736-foot) Pinnacle Peak established a new altitude record for women – one that held until 1934.

In their final expeditions in 1911 and 1912 the Workmans surveyed the 70-kilometre-long (43-mile) Siachen Glacier with a highly experienced team of Alpine guides and surveyors. They were by now aged 65 and 54, and these expeditions may represent their greatest achievement, encompassing several ascents and the exploration of glacier tributaries.

The Workmans planned to continue after the First World War but in 1917 Fanny developed heart problems that prevented her from travelling. The couple settled in France, where she died in 1925. Despite his poor health, William lived to 91.

THE MUMMERY TENT

Albert Mummery invented a lightweight tent that was named after him and manufactured commercially by Edgington of London. Made of silk, the tent weighed around 1.5 kilogrammes (nearly 3.5 pounds) and was about 1.2 metres (4 feet) high. Long-handled ice-axes were used as poles in the tent, which was secured by attaching guy ropes to stones. Mummery used his creation on his trip to the Caucasus in 1888 and it was first used in the Himalaya on Martin Conway's expedition. Conway had commented: 'The two Mummery tents weighed together 7lbs, so that at a pinch one man could carry all four – the accommodation for fourteen men for climbing purposes.' Norman Collie was impressed by the tent's versatility, which he said was: '…invaluable for bivouacs on the mountains or in places where impedimenta can only be packed on men's backs.'

The Workmans were popularizers as well as pioneers. Expeditions were followed by lecture tours and they wrote several expedition books. Nevertheless, their credentials as explorers are discredited. More dependent than usual on a series of European guides to carry bags and cut ice-steps, some of their maps were inaccurate and their routes misleadingly described. They overestimated altitudes, and many of their claims to be the first to travel to particular areas have been challenged and are probably not correct. Poor equipment must bear some responsibility for these shortcomings, but in one area there can be little doubt: Fanny and William had little cultural sensitivity. Next to the term 'coolie' in the index of their books are references to 'greed and laziness of', 'helplessness of', 'misdeeds of' and eight entries for 'trouble with'. For some critics, Fanny's habit of writing her initials and the date in the snow at every new destination marks her indelibly as a prototype adventure tourist.

Himalayan queen Fanny Bullock Workman (1859–1925), the pioneer of female Himalayan mountaineers, poses with a selection of her climbing gear. Ever eager for adventure, Fanny and her husband cycled all the way from Comorin in south India to Srinagar before trekking to Ladakh, prompting seven expeditions into the Karakoram between 1899 and 1912.

Oscar Eckenstein and the first K2 attempt

After being sent home by Conway, Oscar Eckenstein waited ten years before returning to the Himalaya, years in which he observed relative amateurs like the Bullock Workmans claim their Himalayan successes. Nevertheless, the greatest peaks of the Himalaya remained unclimbed. Eckenstein retained the sense of focus that had led to his clash with Conway and, confident in his technical ability, never lacked self-belief. He returned with a determination to climb K2 in 1902.

Eckenstein led an eclectic group: two strong Austrian climbers, Heinrich Pfannl and Victor Wessely; a Swiss doctor, Jules Jacot-Guillarmod; Guy Knowles, a 22-year-old undergraduate who knew little of mountains but who probably provided most of the funds; and, most strikingly, the expedition's deputy leader – the infamous Satanist, Aleister Crowley.

The team arrived in India on 29 March 1902 and headed to Rawalpindi, on their way to the Karakoram. The next day Eckenstein received a telegram forbidding him from entering Kashmir. Whether it was because he was suspected of being a Prussian spy, or that there was a rumour he was going to try for Everest, or, as Crowley suspected, it was Conway displaying 'unmanly jealousy', it was three weeks before he was able to rejoin his group in Srinagar. On 26 May they reached Askole, where tensions started to show. Crowley was insisting he needed to take his library up the glacier, and the two Austrians, fed up with Eckenstein's discipline, were narrowly prevented from attempting to climb K2 alone.

On 15 June they climbed the Baltoro Glacier to Place de la Concorde (Concordia). The following day Crowley examined K2 from the Godwin-Austen Glacier – 'all day and all night' – and saw a way up the Southeast Ridge that he claimed would get them to the top, 'in one fine day'. Although that was over-optimistic, Crowley had identified the route that would eventually be used to climb the mountain.

Eckenstein disagreed. Instead he chose the Northeastern Ridge. On 7 July they moved the base camp 11 kilometres (7 miles) up the glacier. Two days later Crowley claimed he had climbed alone to over 6,706 metres (22,000 feet); he then fell ill and was unable to join the summit attempt. Jacot-Guillarmod and Wessely started out on the chosen route on 10 July, reaching around 6,553 metres (21,500 feet) before concluding it was not feasible (it was only finally climbed in 1978). However, keen to climb something, the men suggested to Eckenstein that they should attempt 'Staircase Peak', to the northeast of K2. At 7,555 metres (24,786 feet) the mountain, now called Skyang Kangri, might have been achievable, but Eckenstein would have none of it. Instead, Pfannl and Wessely now headed for the notch between K2 and Skyang Kangri. They got to around 6,400 metres (21,000 feet) when Pfannl collapsed with pulmonary oedema, forcing his evacuation lower down the mountain.

The expedition now imploded. Perhaps suffering from malaria, Crowley had waved a revolver at Knowles and had consequently been hit in the stomach. Wessely had eaten all the food reserves and was expelled. And the weather had been consistently appalling. Once again, accomplished Alpine climbers had been unprepared for the scale of the Himalaya.

DOUGLAS FRESHFIELD

In 1899 a servant rushed into the lieutenant governor of Bengal's residence in Darjeeling, having seen 'a new star on Kangchenjunga'. A telescope provided the necessary explanation: an enormous bonfire in Jongri was lighting up the night sky. The delighted governor ordered a gun salute in response. He knew that a team, which included photographer Vittorio Sella, whose pictures would go on to inspire future expeditions, aided by his assistant Botta and his brother Erminio Sella, a guide Angelo Maquignaz, Freshfield's friend and surveyor Professor Edmund Garwood, and around 80 porters, had achieved its purpose. Douglas Freshfield, a lifelong explorer, had just led the first successful circuit of the world's third-highest mountain – Kangchenjunga (8,586 metres/28,169 feet).

K2 team Oscar Eckenstein (third from the left), the leader of the 1902 K2 expedition, shown with the rest of his climbing team, Dr Victor Wessely, Dr Heinrich Pfannl, Aleister Crowley, Dr Jules Jacot-Guillarmod and Guy Knowles. Despite the seeming harmony of this picture, the expedition ended in total chaos, with Crowley even menacing Knowles with a revolver.

Aleister Crowley and the 1905 disaster at Kangchenjunga

After the 1902 trip it is hard to comprehend why Jacot-Guillarmod approached Crowley in April 1905 to suggest they attempt Kangchenjunga (8,586 metres/28,169 feet). Crowley, now married with a child and the founder of a new faith he called 'Thelema', agreed to come on condition that he had authority in 'all matters respecting mountain craft'. The disastrous expedition that ensued would cause the unnecessary death of four men and destroy Crowley's reputation as a climber.

Jacot-Guillarmod invited Alexis Pache and Charles Reymond to join Crowley, and on 8 August the expedition left Darjeeling accompanied by around 230 porters. There, Crowley had employed the Italian hotelier Alcesti C. Rigo de Righi as transport officer, commenting later that he was not to know that his 'pin brain would entirely give way as soon as he got out of the world of waiters'.

Crowley had with him the photos, maps and reports from Douglas Freshfield's expedition in 1899. Ignoring Freshfield's recommendation that the best route was the western face of Kangchenjunga, Crowley decided to attempt the mountain from the southwest via the Yalung Face (the route by which the mountain was eventually climbed for the first time in 1955). However, when they reached a camp at nearly 6,250 metres (20,500 feet) the disharmony that had characterized the trip escalated. Jacot-Guillarmod and de Righi, fed up with Crowley's leadership and his brutal treatment of the porters, tried to oust him as leader. After another argument, Jacot-Guillarmod, de Righi and Pache decided to go, with four porters, to a camp lower down. Tragically, one of them slipped and in the avalanche that followed Pache and three of the porters died.

Reymond rushed to help when he heard their cries, but in a callous display of contempt Crowley stayed in his tent. Even more shockingly, Jacot-Guillarmod reported that the next day Crowley went past the avalanche site, 'without even knowing if our comrades would be found'. It was another three days before their bodies were recovered. Back in Darjeeling, Crowley seized the expedition's funds – only agreeing to repay some to Jacot-Guillarmod, who had funded most of the expedition, when he threatened to disclose Crowley's pornographic poems.

Aleister Crowley had been part of the first serious attempts on K2 and Kangchenjunga – two of the three highest mountains in the Himalaya. On both attempts, he was the one who identified the route that would eventually be used in the conquest of each mountain. Nevertheless, for perhaps obvious reasons, he is not now much remembered in the annals of the Alpine Club and Royal Geographical Society (RGS).

ALEISTER CROWLEY – 'THE GREAT BEAST'

Mystic, poet, magician, pansexual and Satanist, Aleister Crowley (1875–1947) experimented with drugs, Tantric Buddhism, astrology, yoga and incorporeality. Labelled 'The Beast' by his Plymouth Brethren mother (an epithet to which he added 'Great'), Crowley's behaviour would lead ultimately to him being called 'the wickedest man in the world' – a notoriety that would earn him a place on the famous album cover for 'Sgt. Pepper's Lonely Hearts Club Band' by The Beatles.

Before leaving Cambridge to focus on the occult, Crowley had climbed widely in Switzerland, Wales and Cumberland. In 1898 he met Eckenstein in the Lake District and found they shared the same iconoclastic contempt for the 'stuffy' Alpine Club. Sixteen years older, Eckenstein became his mentor and shared with him his new 'balance climbing' technique. Crowley 'wondered and worshipped', and commented 'at that very hour … was the very man I needed'. Before parting they made a provisional plan to travel together to the Himalaya.

Longstaff and the Nanda Devi Sanctuary

The British doctor Tom Longstaff met Crowley in Switzerland in 1898, recognizing him as 'a fine climber, if an unconventional one'. Seven years later, in 1905, it was Longstaff's turn to seek success in the Himalaya, when, accompanied by Alexis and Henri Brocherel

THE FIRST USE OF SUPPLEMENTAL OXYGEN ON A MOUNTAIN

Decreased air pressure at altitude results in a reduced supply of oxygen to the body. For example, at the top of Mount Everest there is approximately one-third of the oxygen available at sea level. Supplementary oxygen is commonplace today among climbers in regions above 8,000 metres (26,246 feet) in altitude, where its use reduces risk and improves survival rates, especially during descents.

The 1907 expedition to Trisul was the first to carry oxygen, when A.L. Mumm brought along oxygen generators or pneumatogen cartridges, manufactured by Siebe Gorman and Co. Ltd., normally used in mines.

Mumm thought they might be useful at altitude but the rest of the team showed little interest and he did not get a chance to test them. In Mumm's account of the expedition, *Five Months in the Himalaya: A record of mountain travel in Garhwal and Kashmir*, he records one experiment:

In the interests of science I tried whether a dose from the pneumatogen cartridge would assist me to enjoy a pipe. I think it certainly did; and I found I could smoke with satisfaction for several minutes continuously, which I had not been able to do before inhaling the oxygen; even so, however, it left me rather breathless.

from Courmayeur in northern Italy, he went to the Kumaon Himalaya to explore the southeastern approaches of Nanda Devi (7,816 metres/25,643 feet). After surveying the Pachu Glacier they crossed into the Lawan Valley, where they encountered the ring of mountains – 12 above 6,400 metres (21,000 feet) – that surround Nanda Devi and create the legendary 'Sanctuary'.

On 8 June Longstaff reached a col in the ring at 5,910 metres (19,390 feet), from where he could see a further hidden valley within the Nanda Devi Sanctuary – now called the Inner Sanctuary – accessible by the Rishi Gorge. He was the first person to see it, but was unable to descend into it. The party also reconnoitred the east peak of Nanda Devi but did not have enough food to attempt the mountain. Back in the Lawan Valley the three attempted Nanda Kot (6,861 metres/22,510 feet) but turned around at 6,450 metres (21,161 feet) when the snow became too dangerous for them to continue.

Longstaff was a man of independent means and travelled wherever he wished. He became one of the most prominent British explorers of his time, remembered for his 'pirate beard' that 'blazed red against the Himalayan snows'. In 1907 he joined Charles Bruce and A.L. Mumm in a plan to celebrate the jubilee of the Alpine Club with a reconnaissance of Mount Everest. When the India Office denied them permission, on 'considerations of high Imperial policy', they decided to revisit the Nanda Devi region and attempt Mount Trisul (7,120 metres/23,359 feet). On 12 June, Longstaff, the Brocherel brothers and the Gurkha Karbir Burathoki decided to 'rush the summit', climbing the final 1,829 metres (6,000 feet) from their camp on the Trisul Glacier in ten hours.

This was the first time a climbing party had climbed above 7,000 metres (22,966 feet) and it established a record for the highest summit conquest (Graham's ascent of Kabru, in 1883, aside). The expedition also tried to penetrate the Inner Sanctuary but ran out of time and instead they made a preliminary reconnaissance of the eastern and western approaches of Kamet (7,756 metres/25,446 feet).

In 1909 Longstaff went to the Karakoram. He discovered and crossed the Saltoro

Pass at 5,547 metres (18,199 feet), discovered the Siachen Glacier, and surveyed the unknown mountains of Teram Kangri. During the First World War, Longstaff was sent to Gilgit as an assistant political officer, only to be invalided home in 1917 when he was hit on the head by a polo ball. He recovered and became chief medical officer on the British Everest expedition in 1922.

The Duke of Abruzzi's expedition

Luigi Amedeo Giuseppe Maria Ferdinando Francesco di Savoia-Aosta was the grandson of the king of Italy (Vittorio Emanuele II) and, until his father abdicated in 1873, son of the king of Spain. As the Duke of Abruzzi, he led a charmed and extraordinary life as a vice admiral, a diplomatic envoy, a racing car driver and yachtsman, and a frequenter of the gossip columns for his relationship with the beautiful and wealthy Katherine Elkins. As a mountaineer, he is best known for his attempt on K2 in 1909.

The duke began climbing in the Alps, conquering the Zmutt Ridge with its pioneer Albert Mummery. Inspired, he vowed to give all his free time to mountain exploration. He became known for his trips to the Arctic and the mountains. He was the first to reach the summit of Mount St. Elias (5,489 metres/18,008 feet) on the US–Canada border in 1897, recorded a new northerly point in a failed attempt to reach the North Pole in 1900, and in 1906 climbed the major peaks in Uganda's Ruwenzori range.

Royal mountaineer Luigi Amedeo, Duke of Abruzzi (1873–1933), shown here aged 24 shortly after his return from Mount St. Elias in North America, had already made a mark in mountaineering circles with his expedition to East Africa in 1906 that also established that the Ruwenzori was not the real source of the Nile. Although the Duke of Abruzzi's 1909 expedition to K2 set a height record of 7,498 metres (24,600 feet), the failure to reach the summit bitterly disappointed him.

In 1909 the British authorities gave Abruzzi permission to attempt K2 and to explore the Baltoro Glacier in the British Punjab, clearing the way for what Younghusband called 'the most perfectly organized expedition'. The duke assembled an impressive and harmonious team, including four guides from Courmayeur and three porters, Vittorio Sella as expedition photographer (see box, page 66) and Filippo De Filippi, the expedition doctor (who returned to the Karakorum in 1913). Keen to challenge the altitude record of around 7,285 metres (23,901 feet) set by Carl Wilhelm Rubenson and Ingvald Monrad Aas, Abruzzi knew that if he failed on K2 there were other mountains high enough close by.

On 13 March 1909 around 4,750 kilogrammes (nearly 10,500 pounds) of equipment arrived in Rawalpindi. By 8 May the expedition had reached Skardu, where they saw K2's breathtaking peak for the first time: in De Filippi's words, 'the indisputable sovereign of the region, gigantic and solitary'. From here Abruzzi headed to Askole. After establishing a base camp at 4,877 metres (16,000 feet) near the southern wall of K2, he reconnoitred its four ridges.

The duke first attempted the southeast spur. On 29 May he set out with father and son guides Joseph and Laurent Petigax and a group of Italian and Balti porters. They abandoned the attempt at about 6,200 metres (20,341 feet) because it was too steep for their porters to establish the necessary camps. Naming it the Abruzzi Spur (Ridge), the duke had unknowingly unlocked the eventual route to the summit.

Unperturbed, the expedition made a second attempt up the west side of K2. Progressing slowly up the Savoia Glacier, at constant risk from avalanches and crevasses, the duke and three guides reached an altitude of 6,666 metres (21,870 feet) only to find the way to the northern slopes of K2 blocked by pinnacles, towers and a corniced ridge. Deeply disappointed, the duke called a halt.

Keen for that altitude record and a first ascent, the duke went back to the other side of K2 and set up a camp on its northeast spur in order to attempt 'Staircase Peak', what is now Skyang Kangri, at 7,555 metres (24,786 feet). The attempt was foiled at around 6,705 metres (22,000 feet), first by heavy snow and then by an ice-wall. There was one brief moment of consolation when the weather cleared long enough for the duke to take a photograph of the East Face of K2. It became the cover of the expedition book and was so good it was mistakenly attributed to Sella.

Scientifically, the expedition had been a success. It had completed the mapping of the upper Baltoro Glacier, had made valuable botanical and geological observations and had studied the effects of altitude; while Sella had taken astonishing mountain photographs. All that was required was a climbing record for Italy. Thinking he had only a few good days of weather left, the duke focused on the unclimbed Chogolisa (Bride Peak, 7,654 metres/25,111 feet).

The duke's hopes for good weather proved in vain. The one clear day gave extraordinary views of K2 at sunset, but otherwise heavy snow meant it took eight days to establish camp at 6,335 metres (20,784 feet) on the Chogolisa Saddle. From there the duke made two summit attempts, getting to within around 150 metres (492

The Italian royal mountain
The presence of a grandson of the king of Italy, the Duke of Abruzzi, on K2 in 1909 established an Italian claim to it. Landmarks include the glacier and the saddle, both named by the duke to honour his house Savoia; the De Filippi Glacier named after expedition member Filippo De Filippi, the expedition doctor; and the Abruzzi Ridge (Southeast Spur), which is now the standard route up the mountain. The ridge was used when an Italian party finally climbed the mountain in 1954.

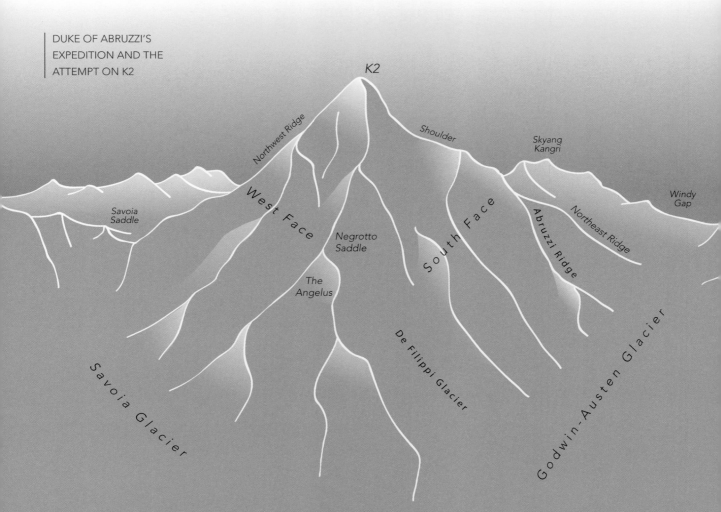

DUKE OF ABRUZZI'S EXPEDITION AND THE ATTEMPT ON K2

K2

Northwest Ridge

Shoulder

Skyang Kangri

Windy Gap

West Face

Savoia Saddle

Negrotto Saddle

South Face

Abruzzi Ridge

Northeast Ridge

The Angelus

De Filippi Glacier

Savoia Glacier

Godwin-Austen Glacier

VITTORIO SELLA

Called by many the greatest mountain photographer of all time, Vittorio Sella (1859–1943) was known for technical perfection and for photographs that inspired 'religious awe' in Ansel Adams.

Sella had travelled with the Duke of Abruzzi before, and he hesitated when the aristocratic mountaineer invited him to join the K2 expedition. While the duke worried that Sella might be tired of his temper, Sella regretted that 'the beauty of the view does not interest him'. Sella relented and the resulting photos are regarded as some of his finest work. He used a tripod and camera combination that weighed 18 kilogrammes (40 pounds), and glass plate negatives that were 900 grammes (2 pounds) each. These were transported in bags that he designed specially.

feet) before thick fog prevented further progress. He descended disappointed, but with an altitude record of 7,498 metres (24,600 feet), which would not be broken until the British team came to Everest in 1922.

Alexander Kellas's high-altitude ascents

The archetypal European climbers in the Himalaya, from Conway and Mummery to Abruzzi, undertook their expeditions with the backing of private wealth. Alexander Kellas, a shy chemist from Aberdeen, was the antithesis of this archetype. He organized eight expeditions to Sikkim, mapping, photographing and practising what he called 'the most philosophical sport in the world'. He also applied his scientific background to become the first person to study the physiology of acclimatization. He would end up spending more time above 6,100 metres (20,000 feet) than any of his contemporaries.

Kellas was more of a hill walker than a technical mountaineer. On his first trip to India in 1907, he trekked for two weeks in Kashmir before heading to Sikkim and the Zemu Glacier. From there, accompanied by two Swiss guides and three porters, he attempted Mount Simvu (Simvo) at 6,812 metres (22,349 feet) and the Nepal Gap at 6,300 metres (20,669 feet) on the North Ridge of Kangchenjunga. Foiled by bad weather, poor visibility and crevasses, Kellas still found it 'interesting enough as an introductory tour': an understatement given his passion for mountains that was to follow.

Kellas returned to the northeast of Sikkim in 1909, accompanied by 62 porters, including several Sherpas. The expedition's successes included the West Ridge of Langpo Peak (6,954 metres/22,814 feet) and the crossing of the Jongsong Pass (6,187 metres/20,300 feet) onto the Jongsong Glacier, but Kellas was forced to retreat from Jongsong Peak (7,462 metres/24,481 feet), and the Nepal Gap again defeated him. Two attempts on Pauhunri were also frustrated by the weather. On the second, they got to within 60 metres (nearly 200 feet) of the 7,125-metre (23,375-foot) summit but were forced to descend in failing light, exhausted by deep snow and freezing winds.

In May 1911 Kellas returned to Sikkim to study weather conditions in the pre-monsoon period. Possibly keen to settle unfinished business he attempted the Nepal Gap for the fourth time and reached the summit save for a small rock wall. Inspired by

Glacier view The Duke of Abruzzi's expedition made its way along the Vigne Glacier, where Vittorio Sella took one of his finest panoramas (known as Panorama P) of the approaches to K2. The peaks visible include Mitre Peak (the prominent white pyramid in the background on the left-hand side) and the Mustagh Tower (further to the right, above the dark triangle in the background). K2 is the dark pyramid on the right, behind the buttress in the foreground.

THE PHYSICAL CONSTRAINTS ON HIGH-ALTITUDE CLIMBING

Alexander Kellas made a huge contribution to scientific research on the effects of high altitude on the body (here, left, with a view to saving energy, Kellas had a villager in Sikkim test out a pulley system). Norman Collie commented that Kellas was 'probably the best authority of the subject'.

Kellas's research began in 1908 in the Alps when he measured variations in human blood's red corpuscle count. Three years later he would conclude that his experience of 'lassitude' at altitude was caused by the impaired production of oxyhaemoglobin. Kellas proposed that acclimatization should be carried out slowly and that breathing should be more frequent. He also suggested climbers should 'camp high and start as early as you safely can'.

His papers, *A consideration of the possibility of ascending the loftier Himalaya* and *A consideration of the possibility of ascending Mt. Everest*, were part of the contemporary debate about whether it was possible to climb Everest without bottled oxygen. He concluded that Mount Everest could be climbed without oxygen provided that the man was of 'excellent physical and mental constitution in first-rate training'.

this success, he crossed the Lhonak Pass at 5,944 metres (19,500 feet) and attempted to reclimb Langpo Peak (6,954 metres/22,815 feet) to take a closer look at the summit of Jongsong Peak.

Kellas's 1911 expedition accomplished an unprecedented ten first ascents above 6,100 metres (20,000 feet). They included Chomo Yummo (6,829 metres/22,404 feet), Sentinel Peak (6,490 metres/21,292 feet) and Pauhunri, which at the time was measured at 7,065 metres (23,180 feet). Everyone believed Tom Longstaff held the summit altitude record from his climb of Mount Trisul in the Garhwal Himalaya in 1907, which he measured at 7,134 metres (23,406 feet). When the height of Pauhunri was revised to 7,125 metres (23,376 feet) and Trisul to 7,120 metres (23,359 feet) it became clear that Kellas had held the record until 1930 (putting aside the possibility that in 1883 William W. Graham had climbed Kabru at 7,394 metres/24,258 feet). Sadly, Kellas never knew this.

Kellas made three further trips between 1912 and 1914, but had to cut the last one short because of the outbreak of war. By now, he had begun to turn his attention to Everest (8,848 metres/29,029 feet). In 1911, unable to glimpse it, he had sent a Sherpa to photograph the eastern side. It was to be the start of a love affair with the mountain, which culminated in his death in 1921 as he journeyed towards it (see pages 73–74).

The Sherpas

In September 1907 two Norwegians, Carl Wilhelm Rubenson and Ingvald Monrad Aas, left Darjeeling to climb Mount Kabru, which they had reconnoitred the year before. It was an ambitious target. Rubenson had done little more than scrambling in Norway and Aas had never climbed a mountain before. They failed to reach the summit but set a new altitude record at 7,285 metres (23,900 feet).

Unconstrained by colonial attitudes, Rubenson and Aas had advocated employing Sherpas as climbing partners – not just as porters for carrying. Rubenson announced: 'It is only to their courage and many other good qualities that we owe our success so far.' Kellas subsequently adopted this philosophy. He frequently relied on Sherpas hired in Darjeeling and publicized the advantages of employing them as both porters and climbers.

After his first expedition in 1907 Kellas became determined 'to return and try climbing with Nepalese coolies who seemed to me more at home under the diminished pressure than my European companions'. After further expeditions he described them as 'first-rate climbers' who with proper training would be able to climb peaks such as Kangchenjunga and Everest. Kellas assessed the performance of the Sherpas empirically. He compared their progress to his own and concluded:

FRANCIS YOUNGHUSBAND

Himalaya at the end of the nineteenth century was Francis Younghusband.. An adventurer, mystic and imperialist, Younghusband became a subaltern in the 1st (King's) Dragoon Guards in 1882. Five years later he established his reputation as the pioneer of Karakoram exploration when he became the first European to cross the Mustagh Pass into Baltistan. It has been called one of the most remarkable journeys ever made: 'When I reached the bottom and looked back, it seemed utterly impossible that any man could have come down such a place.'

In 1902 Younghusband was appointed by the Viceroy of India Lord Curzon to be British Commissioner in Tibet to counteract perceived Russian influence. Once there, Younghusband overstepped instructions and turned a diplomatic mission into a military invasion (pictured left), causing the deaths of around 700 Tibetans at Chumi Shengo in April 1904 (some estimates put the figure as high as 5,000). On 7 September 1904 Younghusband forced a treaty at Lhasa on the Dalai Lama. Although repudiated, the agreement would ultimately give Britain exclusive access to Tibet and in turn to Everest. When leaving Lhasa Younghusband sent Captain Cecil Rawling and his surveyor Captain C. Ryder on a reconnaissance trip to the mountain. They concluded it was climbable from the Northeast Ridge.

One of the key figures in both the continued exploration and the burgeoning British imperial penetration of the

FOCUS TURNS TO EVEREST

While the borders of Tibet and Nepal were closed to foreigners the only access to Everest was by clandestine expeditions. In 1893 Lieutenant Charles Bruce had suggested to Francis Younghusband (then second in command in Chittral) that the two of them should attempt Everest covertly from the Tibet side. Nothing came of this. Curzon, Viceroy of India, had also entered the debate by encouraging Douglas Freshfield to climb Everest in 1899; in 1905 he even offered Freshfield £3,000 towards his expenses. Nevertheless, Bruce's request to launch an expedition to Everest in 1907 was turned down.

In 1913 John Noel disguised himself as 'a Mohammedan from India' while on leave from the East Yorkshire Regiment. He aimed to get as close as he could to the mountain. After a few attempts, he and three guides – Adhu, Achum Bhutia and Tebdo – got to within 64 kilometres (40 miles) before the Tibetans turned them back.

The First World War thwarted the plans for an expedition that were made by the now General Cecil Rawling, who sadly died in action. A month after the armistice, the RGS sent a letter to the Secretary of State for India asking permission to climb Everest, but did not get a reply. Then, on 10 March 1919, Noel gave a lecture at the RGS, entitled 'A journey to Tashirak in Southern Tibet and the Eastern Approaches to Mount Everest'. In it, he spoke about his trip in 1913 and of Rawling's plans. The room was filled with the key Himalayan explorers: Freshfield, J.P Farrar, Younghusband and Kellas, who all supported the idea of an attempt.

When Younghusband took over the presidency of the RGS in June 1919 he took up the matter with the President of the Alpine Club. The enthusiasm was easy to parody. In *Punch*'s 'Himalayans at Play', Sir Francis Oldmead says his route up Everest will be 'up the Yulmag valley to the Chikkim frontier at Lor-Lumi, crossing the Pildash at Gonglam, and skirting the deep gorge of the Spudgyal'. However, Younghusband and the others were deadly serious; all attention was turned to climbing Everest.

At any height up to 15,000 to 17,000ft one could hold one's own with the unloaded coolie and easily beat the loaded man. Above 17,000ft however, their superiority was marked, an unloaded coolie climbing much quicker than myself, and even a moderately loaded coolie going up as fast as one cared to go, up to 21,000 to 22,000ft. Above that elevation a moderately loaded coolie could run away from me, and with an unloaded coolie one had not the slightest chance.

He also studied the Sherpas' diet at altitude, which was mainly vegetarian and supplemented by food found locally, including wild mountain rhubarb, which gave Kellas 'peculiar intermittent throbbing in the cerebella region'. He also noted the Sherpa remedy for suspected frostbite: rubbing feet and putting 'dried grass, of which they carried a small supply, into their boots'.

Outside his scientific research, Kellas forged close friendships with the Sherpas and particularly with Tuny, 'Tuny's brother' and Sony. Kellas experienced auditory hallucinations and according to the biologist J.B.S. Haldane he answered the voices when no Westerners were around and found his Sherpas 'had great confidence in a man who had long conversations with the spirits at night'.

Majestic icescape. The Duke of Abruzzi and guides climbing on the Chogolisa icefall in 1909, photographed by Vittorio Sella. Chogolisa's icy serac fangs endow it with both menace and an otherworldly beauty. The expedition to Chogolisa Saddle set a new altitude record of 7,498 metres (24,600 feet), which was not broken until the British expedition to Everest in 1922. Chogolisa remained unclimbed until 1958 when a Japanese expedition climbed the northeast summit; the southwest summit was climbed by an Austrian expedition in 1975.

6

Himalaya Between the Wars 1919–1939

STEPHEN VENABLES

As the clouds rolled asunder before the heights, gradually, very gradually, we saw the great mountainsides and glaciers and ridges, now one fragment, now another, through the floating rifts, until, far higher in the sky than imagination dared to suggest, a prodigious white fang – an excrescence from the jaw of the world – the summit of Everest appeared. (FROM THE RECONNAISSANCE OF MOUNT EVEREST, 1921, BY C.K. HOWARD-BURY, LONDON, 1922.)

It was 13 June 1921 and from a hill rising above the Tibetan Plateau, George Mallory was seeing for the first time the immense, icy East Face of the world's highest mountain. A well-known Alpinist, at 34 he was the youngest member of the Everest Reconnaissance Expedition, led by Colonel Charles Howard Bury, backed by the British imperial government in India and issued with a rare passport from the Dalai Lama that allowed the foreigners entry to Tibet. The team included seasoned explorers such as Dr Alexander Wollaston and the surveyor Henry Morshead, already famous for his investigation of the Zangbo Gorges in eastern Tibet. Morshead had also climbed the previous year with the other doctor on the team, Alexander Kellas, attempting the unclimbed peak of Kamet in northern India. Kellas probably knew more about high-altitude climbing than anyone else alive. Before the First World War he had climbed three high peaks in Sikkim, including the 7,125-metre (23,376-foot) summit of Pauhunri, accompanied by Sherpas – the people of Tibetan extraction who would become synonymous with Everest. Not only did Kellas have practical experience; as a pioneer high-altitude physician he calculated that on the final climb to the summit of Everest (8,848 metres/29,029 feet), confronted with lung-sapping air pressure just one-third of that at sea level, it should just be possible for a very fit person to ascend more than 90 metres (300 feet) an hour. However, he also postulated that if the terrain were at all difficult, the climber would probably need the boost of supplementary oxygen.

All of that still lay a long way in the future. The job of the 1921 team was to explore the approaches to the mountain and ascertain whether it could be climbed. Just getting there from Darjeeling, trekking up through the steamy jungles of Sikkim, then across the dusty uplands of Tibet, was a gruelling journey of more than 480 kilometres (300 miles). The veteran Scottish mountaineer Harold Raeburn had to return, stricken with dysentery. And then Kellas, aged just 52, weakened by

First base The 1921 Everest Reconnaissance Expedition's camp at Pethang Ringmo in the Kama Valley, to the east of Everest, with the cliffs of Chomo Lonzo overhead. With an approach march of more than 480 kilometres (300 miles) and an ambitious programme of mapping, geologizing and making botanic collections, the expedition was a long-drawn-out affair. Four months passed between setting out from Darjeeling and making a foray onto the North Ridge on 24 September.

Everest and its environs The immediate surroundings of Everest (following page), a three-sided pyramid, showing its three main faces, ridges and glaciers. The 1921 team gave the outliers Tibetan names: Lhotse, meaning South Peak; Nuptse, meaning West Peak; and Changtse, meaning North Peak. The Pethang Ringmo camp is just to the east of the area in the map.

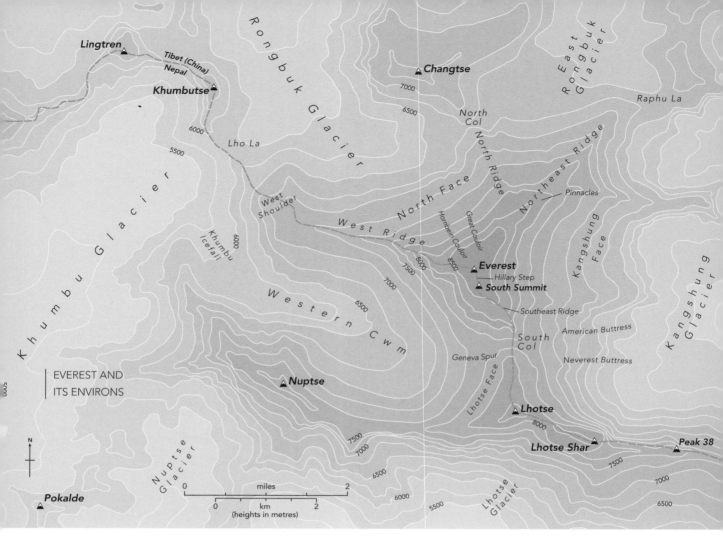

EVEREST AND
ITS ENVIRONS

diarrhoea, developed complications in the thin cold air and died. He was buried near the fortress of Kampa Dzong, only a short way north of the Sikkimese mountains he knew so well.

The rest of the team marched on to Shegar Dzong ('Crystal Fort'), from where for the first time they could discern the pyramid structure of Everest's great North Face, now just 80 kilometres (50 miles) to the south. Over the next few weeks, assisted by Sherpas – who had come with them all the way from Darjeeling – and by local Tibetans, the British 'sahibs' (as they were known to the locals, a polite term meaning the person in charge) unravelled the tangle of ridges and glacier valleys radiating from the summit. They discovered that the mountain was a three-sided pyramid. Its southern aspect lay in the forbidden territory of Nepal, so they concentrated on the north and east faces. The latter, which Mallory had already glimpsed from that distant hill, rose at the head of the beautiful Kama Valley, where local shepherds tended their grazing yaks in flowery meadows. But the 3,400-metre-high (11,155-foot) wall above appeared lethal – huge rock buttresses capped by tottering ice-cliffs, with avalanches sweeping the gullies in between: an approach, Mallory opined in the official expedition report, for 'other men, less wise'.

If Everest were to be climbed it would have to be from the arid Rongbuk Valley on the north side. But how to get onto the North Face itself? Almost by accident, after crossing one of many high snow passes, the expedition stumbled on the upper basin of East Rongbuk Glacier, whence an eminently climbable ice-slope led them to the saddle of the North Col. Mallory cut steps up to the col. From there, at 6,466 metres (21,214 feet), the broad, easy-angled hump of the North Ridge seemed to lead without any obvious problem right up to the Northeast Ridge – the left-hand skyline of the great north-facing pyramid. It seemed that, in addition to mapping a huge tract of previously uncharted country, the expedition had found a potential route to the top of the world. But they were not equipped to climb to nearly 9,000 metres (29,527 feet) above sea level. That would have to wait until the following year.

1922 – the first attempt on Everest

Seven months later, on May Day 1922, Mallory and Morshead were back at Rongbuk, as part of a new team selected by the Royal Geographical Society and the Alpine Club. In charge was General Sir Charles Bruce – the same Bruce who in 1895 had organized Mummery's attempt on Nanga Parbat, and who Younghusband described as: '... a kind of benevolent volcano in perpetual eruption of good cheer. And of such irrepressible fun that no amount of misfortune can ever quell him.'

Under the command of this ebullient Ghurka officer was a mixed team of climbers. In addition to Mallory and Morshead, the group included a very tall, very fit army officer called Edward Norton, an equally fit surgeon called Howard Somervell and one of Britain's most experienced Alpinists, George Finch. In contrast, the leader's nephew, Geoffrey Bruce, had virtually no mountaineering experience at all. Charged with filming and photographing the expedition was Captain John Noel, returning to the Everest region for the first time since his illegal foray of 1913. A 160-strong team of local Tibetans provided the yaks to transport the expedition's supplies on the final stage of the approach from Shegar Dzong, over the Pang La, to base camp near the

Mountain tomb The headstone of Alexander Kellas's grave at the fort of Kampa Dzong (opposite below). The veteran mountaineer and physician had fallen victim to dysentery in the approaches to Everest during the 1921 reconnaissance expedition. His tomb lies in sight of the great peaks of Sikkim, Chomo Yummo, Pauhunri and Kangchegyao.

A well-earned rest Sherpas taking a break on the East Rongbuk Glacier during the 1922 Everest expedition, which employed 40 Sherpas, five Gurkhas, a large number of cooks and Tibetan porters, in addition to the 13 European climbers. During an avalanche on 7 June, seven Sherpas were swept to their deaths.

The 1924 team The members of the 1924 Everest expedition in camp (opposite, below). In the back row (left to right), Andrew Irvine, George Mallory, Edward Norton, Noel Odell and John Macdonald. In the front row (left to right), Edward Shebbeare, Geoffrey Bruce, Howard Somervell and Bentley Beetham.

The north side of Everest This map shows the main routes explored by the British in the early 1920s, including the six camps of the 1924 expedition when Mallory and Irvine made their summit attempt.

Rongbuk monastery. Above base camp, most of the work of ferrying loads was done by Sherpas and Ghurkas.

Nowadays, when 200 or more climbers can reach the summit of Everest in a single day, shepherded up a continuous line of nylon rope, plugged into modern oxygen sets to counteract the deadly thin air, clothed in the finest modern lightweight insulation, planning ascents around satellite weather forecasts, it is sometimes hard to imagine just how different it was for those pioneers in 1922. On the first attempt they hoped to climb in a single day from the North Col to 8,200 metres (26,902 feet). In the end, with all the men – particularly the porters – weakened and chilled by the wind, they had to stop and send the porters back from around 7,620 metres (25,000 feet), where the sahibs pitched the two tents on uncomfortable sloping ledges. Here Mallory, Morshead, Norton and Somervell spent a miserable night, higher than any humans had been before. Sleep does not come easily at 25,000 feet. Nor does the grim business, not yet fully understood in 1922, of forcing enough liquid into one's dehydrated body. This has to be done by melting snow and ice over a stove – usually, in those days, an unsatisfactory arrangement with solid fuel tablets. Despite all that, Mallory, Somervell and Norton managed to get away by 8.00 a.m. the next morning, leaving Morshead, who felt he would slow them down.

Struggling laboriously over the powder snow smothering the sloping rocks of Everest's tilted strata, gasping in the thin air, they reached a point later calculated at 8,225 metres (26,984 feet), before realizing that the summit was way out of their reach. George Finch, following a different route, got slightly higher before he too was

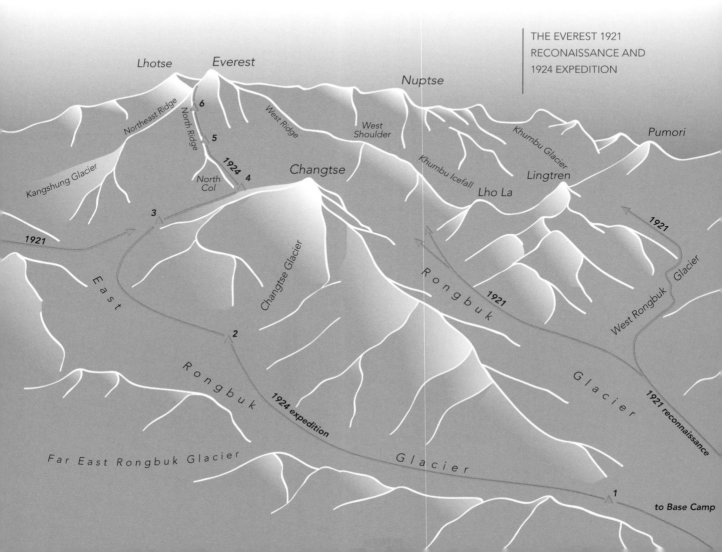

THE EVEREST 1921 RECONAISSANCE AND 1924 EXPEDITION

GEORGE FINCH AND OXYGEN

Unlike most of the early British pioneers on Everest, George Finch had a strong scientific background (he would later become a professor of chemistry at Imperial College London). Practical and creative, he made a prototype down-filled duvet jacket, in contrast to the wool and tweed sported by the rest of the team. Unlike the other sceptics, he was also convinced that the only sensible way to attempt Everest was with the aid of supplementary oxygen. Stuck for two days in a storm at the top camp, he found that regular puffs of bottled oxygen staved off the most debilitating effects of altitude (in his case alternating oxygen with

puffs on a cigarette!). After the storm, he continued with Geoffrey Bruce, now breathing continuously from the primitive oxygen sets then being developed by the Royal Air Force (RAF). Despite Bruce being a total novice, the two men made faster progress than Mallory's party, and established a new altitude record of 8,321 metres (27,300 feet), before Bruce's tiredness forced Finch to make the painful decision to turn round. Mallory was so impressed by Finch's performance that two years later, desperate to finish the job once and for all, he decided to take oxygen on his final attempt on the summit.

forced to retreat. After a few days' recuperation at base camp, the expedition decided to make one more attempt, but on the way up to the North Col a roped party of nine Sherpas was caught in an avalanche and seven were killed. Somervell, in particular, was stricken by a guilty sense of grief: 'Why, oh why could not one of us Britishers have shared their fate?'

The mystery of Mallory and Irvine in 1924

In 1924 the Dalai Lama granted Britain permission for another Everest attempt. As if to atone for the avalanche tragedy two years earlier, Norton, Somervell and Mallory made a lung-busting dash to the North Col to rescue four Sherpas who had lost their nerve on a steep ice-slope. Heroism notwithstanding, the expedition was beset by problems. A sick Charles Bruce had to return to Darjeeling, handing over the leadership to Norton. Cold windy weather persisted, delaying attempts at the summit. But finally, thanks to the efforts of Sherpas Norbu Yishang, Lhakpa Chedi and Semchumbi, Norton and Somervell established a new Camp 6 at an incredible 8,168 metres (26,798 feet). Yet even from this high jumping-off point, they were defeated by the long rightward traverse towards the summit. Somervell simply ground to a halt, photographing Norton as he continued alone towards the tantalizing summit pyramid before reaching a high point of 8,573 metres (28,126 feet) above sea level – an altitude record for oxygenless climbing that would only be beaten in 1978. Norton felt capable of continuing, but dared not risk being caught out by darkness: so he and Somervell retreated to the North Col.

Three days later, on 8 June, a second attempt was made by Mallory and the youngest team member, Sandy Irvine. The pair – unlike Norton – intended to follow the skyline Northeast Ridge. Cameraman John Noel had his telephoto lens trained on the ridge but never saw them. Noel Odell, climbing up to Camp 6, claimed that he *did* briefly see two figures, before clouds closed around them. Two days later, when Odell returned to Camp 6, the tent was still empty and he had to conclude that Mallory and Irvine were dead.

In recent years mountain sleuths have hypothesized endlessly on whether or not the two men reached the summit. All we know for certain, since Mallory's body was found in 1999, with a broken leg and a snapped rope, is that the two men died after a fall, leaving Edward Norton to break the tragic news to their families and lead the sad survivors back to Darjeeling.

Sikkim and attempts on Kangchenjunga

Western exploration of the Himalaya has always been at the whim of political circumstance. During the interwar years the British, with their imperial clout, had a monopoly on access to Tibet, and therefore Everest. In the quest for the highest peaks, other Western nations had to settle for slightly lower – but not necessarily *easier* – summits. In 1929, one year after its founding in Darjeeling, the British-run Himalayan Club received a letter from Germany asking the club to help a team of young Munich climbers led by Paul Bauer: 'They

Up Kangchenjunga
The 1929 and 1931 German expeditions to Kangchenjunga, led by Paul Bauer, attempted this fearsomely knife-edged spur on the east side of the mountain, in Sikkim. The attempt in 1931 ended when Hermann Schaller and a Sherpa fell to their deaths on the Zemu Glacier.

want to test themselves against something difficult – some mountain that will call out everything they've got in them of courage, perseverance and endurance.'

The immense, five-peaked complex of Kangchenjunga, the world's third-highest mountain provided just the challenge they needed. Entry to Nepal was out of the question, so Bauer's only option was in Sikkim: the East Face – one of the biggest, steepest, most dangerous faces in the world, and still unattempted to this day. However, there was a possibility of a route to the side of the face, up the crest of the Northeast Spur – a Baroque concoction of crystal towers, cupolas and gargoyles, perched above huge precipices. Up this dizzy ice-roof the Munich men hacked their way, sometimes tunnelling right through those towers which they could go neither over nor round. Slowly they established a classic chain of camps and snow caves up this most unclassic route, completely redefining the art of snow- and ice-climbing, eventually, on 3 October, reaching about 7,400 metres (24,278 feet), close to the spur's junction with the North Ridge.

Then they were pinned down by a five-day storm. Afterwards they were stretched to the limit just getting down the spur – slithering, sliding, fighting for their lives against the constant smothering snowslides, working selflessly to help Ernst Beigel, whose feet were badly frostbitten. Then they fought on down towards the Tista Valley, struggling through torrential rain and landslides until, at last, as Bauer recalled afterwards, 'dishevelled, dead-beat, our nerves worn out with the wild struggle against nature, with unkempt beards and covered with mud, we trod with heavy feet into the brilliantly lit dining room of the Lachen bungalow'.

The editor of Britain's *Alpine Journal*, Colonel Edward Strutt, was impressed. A few years later he would fulminate xenophobically against Munich's Eiger candidates, but in 1929 he was more generous, describing Paul Bauer's first Kangchenjunga expedition as 'a feat without parallel, perhaps, in all the annals of mountaineering'. Bauer returned in 1931. This time his team almost reached the top of the Northeast Spur, but were defeated by a final, lethally loaded, avalanche-prone slope of snow. In 1936 Bauer led a third expedition to Sikkim, but this time to tackle some of the lower satellites of Kangchenjunga, including the ethereally beautiful Siniolchu (see illustration, page 10). The ascent of this 6,888-metre (22,598-foot) summit by Günther Hepp, Adolf Göttner and Karl Wien, was a tour de force of 'Alpine-style' climbing – moving in a single push up the mountain, bivouacking ad hoc, en route, in the open.

Munich maestro Paul Bauer, leader of the futuristic Kangchenjunga attempts, photographed in 1936 during a later expedition to Nanga Parbat.

Garhwal – the 'small is beautiful' approach

Frank Smythe had an ambivalent relationship with the world's very highest peaks. He was very strong at high altitude, did well on Kangchenjunga in 1930 and would in 1933 equal Norton's record on Everest, but he found the huge, cumbersome expeditions deemed necessary on these giant peaks to be uncongenial. He wrote: 'The ascent of Everest has become a duty, perhaps a national duty, comparable with attempts to reach the poles, and is far removed from pleasurable mountaineering.'

For pleasure he chose Garhwal in the United Provinces of northern India (now Uttar Pradesh and Uttarakhand) – a gorgeous region where India's highest peaks tower above verdant gorges, whose rivers form the many tributaries of the holy Ganges, sacred to Hindus and Buddhists. During the Raj this region was reasonably accessible to British explorers, and in 1907 Tom Longstaff had created a new record here with his ascent of Trisul. Now, in 1931, Smythe set his sights on the higher summit of Kamet, which had eluded Kellas and Morshead in 1920. Although he took just five fellow British climbers, they were supported by ten Sherpas from Darjeeling. Prominent among the sahibs was

FUTURE EVEREST LEADER IN SIKKIM

In October 1937 a fine expedition to Sikkim was carried out in lightweight style by Reggie Cook and John Hunt. Among the climbs they made was an attempt to reach the North Col of Kangchenjunga. The pair concluded that there was no reasonable route from this side, but 42 years later the mountain *would* be climbed from the North Col, although approaching from the other side. John Hunt would go on to lead the first ascent of Everest in 1953. Among the famous Sherpas on this 1937 expedition, Pasang Dawa Lama almost reached the summit of K2 in 1939 and went on to make the first ascent of the world's sixth-highest peak, Cho Oyu, in 1954; Pasang Kikuli was less fortunate on the same 1939 K2 expedition, sacrificing his life when attempting to rescue Dudley Wolfe, a sick American marooned high up at Camp 8.

a young coffee planter from East Africa, Eric Shipton, who had recently made the second and third ascents of Mount Kenya by difficult new routes. For him the chance to visit the Himalaya was a dream come true. He loved the whole experience and was in the first party to reach the summit of Kamet, with Smythe, Romilly Holdsworth and Sherpa Lewa. Two days later the climb was repeated by a local porter, Kesar Tsing, with St. John Birnie and Raymond Greene, the expedition doctor. Not only had seven members of the expedition reached the top: at 7,756 metres (25,446 feet) it was the highest summit yet attained by mankind.

The Nanda Devi Sanctuary in 1934

Eric Shipton took to the Himalaya like a duck to water. Above all else it was the exploration – the diversity and mobility and the delicious surprise of unlocking the landscape's secrets, rather than merely 'bagging a summit' – that appealed most to him. Two years after Kamet, while roaming through Tibet and Sikkim in 1933, on the way home from an attempt on Everest, Shipton realized that this mountain vagabondage was something he could continue all his life, provided he kept things simple and operated on a minimal budget. So, having served his apprenticeship, he now decided to organize his *own* expedition in 1934. He would return to Garhwal for the entire summer season and see whether he

could solve the outstanding mountaineering problem in the region – one that had eluded many previous visitors, including his leader on Everest, Hugh Ruttledge: he would try to penetrate the great ring of high peaks surrounding the twin summits of Nanda Devi, the mother goddess peak sacred to Hindus.

In Kenya Shipton had got to know another coffee planter and keen mountaineer called Bill Tilman. It was Tilman who had partnered him on the formidable West Ridge of Mount Kenya and on several pioneering climbs in Uganda's Rwenzori Mountains. Despite huge differences in personality – Tilman a famously taciturn misogynist; Shipton a loquacious romantic – both men shared a taste for simplicity bordering on the spartan, and an insatiable appetite for exploring wild country. They had formed a brilliant partnership, so Shipton invited Tilman to join him on his Nanda Devi project. Once in India they were joined by three Sherpas – Angtharkay, Kusang and Pasang Bhotia – whose resilience, loyalty and good humour would be vital to the expedition's success.

All previous attempts to reach the Nanda Devi Sanctuary had foundered in the deep gash of the Rishi Gorge, which was the only real breach in the ring of surrounding peaks. Arriving before the monsoon in May the team made the most of reasonable weather, pushing up the narrow cleft, until they were forced high up onto the retaining walls, scrambling precariously above a drop of nearly 1,000 metres (3,280 feet), relaying loads over sections that amounted to real rock climbing rather than merely trekking.

By keeping baggage to a minimum and dispensing with the need for local porters, who would have baulked at the difficulties, they were able to get through to the Nanda Devi Sanctuary, where they were delighted to find herds of ibex and other wild goats grazing in the idyllic high meadows.

After climbing to three high cols on the rim, they returned down the Rishi Gorge. Undaunted by the arrival of the monsoon, they then turned their attention to the Arwa and Gangotri valleys, whose stupendous granite peaks would attract some of the world's top climbers at the end of the twentieth century. Then Shipton, Tilman and their three retainers made a very hard crossing between the Badrinath and Kedarnath valleys and found themselves descending a fearsome gorge, which entailed some detours and river crossings so time-consuming that they ran out of food and had to live off bamboo shoots, cooked over smoky fires amid torrential rainfall. When the weather improved in the autumn, they returned to the Nanda Devi Sanctuary to complete their survey, ascertaining that the mountain could probably be climbed by its South Ridge. As if that were not enough, Shipton concluded his campaign with the first ascent of 6,802-metre (22,316-foot) Maiktoli with Angtharkay and Kusang, before the whole team exited the area by the difficult Sunderdhunga Col.

First Ascent of Nanda Devi in 1936

Shipton's brilliant success in 1934 prompted the Himalayan Committee in London to make him the leader of a reconnaissance expedition to Everest in 1935. Tilman, naturally, was part of the team. The following

A forbidding face
The North Face of Kangchenjunga was attempted by Günter Dyhrenfurth's international expedition of 1930, which included Englishman Frank Smythe (opposite, below). The mountain was finally climbed in 1955 by the Southwest Face, in Nepal, a route first attempted by Aleister Crowley in 1905.

Rock rest Bill Tilman takes a precarious rest on a rock outcrop on Nanda Devi during his 1936 ascent of the mountain. When he and his summit partner Noel Odell reached the top, Tilman's initial euphoria was followed by melancholy. As he later wrote, he had 'a feeling of sadness that the mountain had succumbed, that the proud head of the goddess was bowed'.

year Shipton returned to Everest, somewhat reluctantly, for another full-scale attempt. This time Tilman, who sometimes had difficulty acclimatizing to altitude, was not invited.

The Himalayan Committee may have rebuffed Tilman, but that didn't stop a group of Americans asking him to lead a proposed Anglo-American expedition that had set its sights on Kangchenjunga. When Tilman arrived in Calcutta in 1936, as both leader and advance scout, he was told by the imperial government that his expedition could not have a permit. 'Like most oracular pronouncements,' he wrote afterwards, 'no reasons were given.' Ever phlegmatic, Tilman accepted the alternative on offer – the peak he had reconnoitred two years earlier: Nanda Devi. As he made his way several hundred miles northwest to Garhwal he realized that the bureaucrats' obstruction was actually a godsend: at 7,816 metres (25,643 feet) above sea level, Nanda Devi's main summit was some 770 metres (2,526 feet) lower than Kangchenjunga, so the team stood a much better chance of actually getting up the mountain.

The biggest problem was reaching the start of the climb. The Rishi Gorge had been hard enough with just a lightweight team in 1934. This time, getting eight climbers, high-altitude porters and several weeks' supplies up the gorge was a logistical nightmare and the expedition nearly foundered when half the local porters deserted. Tilman eased the problem by ditching any food he deemed not to be strictly 'nutritious'. According to one of the Americans, Ad Carter, that meant leaving behind the only edible rations.

Minor food gripes notwithstanding, the Anglo-American pioneers were a harmonious bunch. The American team had been selected by Charles Houston, a luminary of the legendary Harvard Mountaineering Club, who would later lead two attempts on K2. The British contingent included the Everest veteran Noel Odell.

Once they had reached their base camp in the Nanda Devi Sanctuary, the eight climbers started work on Nanda Devi's rocky South Ridge (see map, page 171). With the usual vital support of Sherpas, they took turns breaking trail and carrying loads to make a series of camps, one of them just a single tent with its outer edge hanging over the precipice. The top camp was a more spacious platform at 7,300 metres (23,950 feet). Modest by nature, Tilman proposed that Odell represent the British on the final push to the summit. Charles Houston was selected to represent the Americans, but he suddenly came down with violent stomach cramps, so Tilman took his place. They set off at first light on 29 August 1936.

Afterwards, sitting in his study in North Wales to write up the expedition, Tilman captured beautifully the tragic-comic purgatory of life at extreme altitude:

> It was bitterly cold, for the sun had not yet risen over the shoulder of East
> Nanda Devi and there was a thin wind from the west. What mugs we were to
> be fooling about on this infernal ridge at that hour of the morning! And what was the
> use of this ridiculous coil of rope, as stiff as a wire hawser, tying me for better or for
> worse to that dirty-looking ruffian in front! Such, in truth, were the reflections of at
> least one of us as we topped a snow boss behind the tent, and the tenuous nature of
> the ridge in front became glaringly obvious in the chill light of dawn.

They moved very slowly, at first on pleasantly sound rock, but then on deep snow, 'like trying to climb cotton wool', where every step 'cost six to eight deep breaths' and 'on top of the hard work and the effect of altitude was the languor induced by a sun which beat down relentlessly on the dazzling snow, searing our lips and sapping the energy of mind and body'.

They were rewarded at 2.00 p.m. when they emerged onto a long, broad ridge of snow, with nothing more above it:

> Odell had brought a thermometer and no doubt sighed for the hypsometer.
> From it we found that the air temperature was 20 degrees F, but in the absence
> of wind we could bask gratefully in the friendly rays of our late enemy the sun … After
> three-quarters of an hour on that superb summit, a brief forty-five minutes into which
> was crowded the worth of many hours of glorious life, we dragged ourselves reluctantly
> away, taking with us a memory that can never fade and leaving behind 'thoughts
> beyond the reaches of our souls'.

At 7,816 metres (25,643 feet) above sea level, considerably higher than Kamet, this was the highest summit yet attained: not bad for a man who was deemed unsound at altitude.

Everest resumed – the 1930s

Nine years after the disappearance of Mallory and Irvine near the summit of Everest, the Dalai Lama gave permission for a new British expedition to return to the mountain. Among Hugh Ruttledge's team of 1933 was the brilliant young rock climber, Jack Longland, who excelled himself escorting a team of Sherpas down from Camp 6 in

TENZING NORGAY

In the spring of 1935 when Shipton was hiring Sherpas at the start of the long approach march to Everest, he was taken by the winning, eager smile of a young man called Tenzing Norgay and signed him on. Although Tenzing came to be known as a Sherpa, he was actually born in Tibet, at a camp in the Kama Valley beneath the Kangshung Face of Everest, where his parents were tending their yaks in the summer grazing grounds. Later the family crossed the Nangpa La to Nepal and settled in Solu Khumbu, home of the Sherpas. Tenzing subsequently left home and travelled to Darjeeling to seek work as a climbing porter, hence his meeting with Shipton.

The two men bumped into each other again in 1936. Disappointed after another failure on Everest, on his way home Shipton diverted to Garhwal to join a survey party led by Gordon Osmaston and was delighted to find Tenzing on the team. Seventeen years later he was equally delighted when the news came through that Tenzing, through sheer determination and force of personality, had become one of the first two people to reach the summit of Everest.

a blizzard. Frank Smythe and his Kamet companions, Shipton and Greene, were also on the team, as was Shipton's partner on the second ascent of Mount Kenya, Percy Wyn-Harris. On this Everest attempt it was Wyn-Harris who found the ice-axe Irvine had dropped or put down, high on the North Face, on the day he died. With Lawrence Wager, Wynn-Harris reached Norton's high point, less than 300 metres (984 feet) below the summit, as did Frank Smythe; but the final steep, precarious slope on the far side of a gully called the Great Couloir eluded them.

Shipton found the scale of the whole enterprise distastefully profligate and in 1935 he led a 'reconnaissance' for one-tenth of the cost of the 1933 expedition. He was asked to assess conditions during the monsoon. Not surprisingly, his team of six climbers did not get high on Everest itself. However, in a campaign of wide-ranging exploration – perhaps unequalled in Himalayan history – they did make first ascents of 26 more modest peaks.

In 1936 another full-blown attempt was made, again under Ruttledge's leadership, but it was thwarted by bad weather, with deep snow clogging the North Face. The final interwar expedition was led by Bill Tilman in 1938. One member of his team, Peter Lloyd, did useful work testing and improving oxygen equipment. However, he received little encouragement from the leader, who declared:

> *My own opinion is that the mountain could and should be climbed without [oxygen], and I think there is a cogent reason for not climbing it at all rather than climb it with the help of oxygen … If man wishes gratuitously to fight nature, not for existence or the means of existence but for fun, or at the worst self-aggrandizement, it should be done with the natural weapons.*

Many would applaud those sentiments. However, when the Everest campaign was renewed after the Second World War such ethical niceties would be swept aside in the increasingly urgent quest to claim the ultimate mountaineering prize.

The Hidden Peak
Gasherbrum I was given its nickname by Martin Conway in the 1890s, but the first serious attempt to climb it was made by Günter Dyhrenfurth's 1934 International Himalayan Expedition. The 8,068-metre (26,469-foot) peak, the 11th highest in the world, was finally climbed by Nicholas Clinch's American expedition in 1958. Clinch described it as 'a long walk in the sky'.

Karakoram – repeated rebuffs on the highest peaks

Of all the great mountain ranges of Central Asia none matches the Karakoram for sheer scale and austere grandeur. Before the building of modern roads, any expedition into this mountain desert, where the greatest glaciers outside the polar regions feed the mighty Indus River, was a huge undertaking. Small wonder that attempts on the Karakoram's highest summits were all rebuffed.

Perhaps the most ambitious project was Günther Dyhrenfurth's International Himalayan Expedition (IHE) of 1934. To help fund the expedition he took a team of actors and film-makers in addition to the climbers who were to attempt Gasherbrum I, or Hidden Peak, one of the four 8,000-metre (26,246-foot) peaks that dominate the head of the immense Baltoro Glacier. The expedition had made little headway before it was stopped by a violent storm that, further south on Nanga Parbat, killed eight members of a German expedition. However, the route on Gasherbrum I that the German Hans Ertl and the Swiss André Roch attempted – the IHE Spur – would, many years later, be the line by which the mountain was eventually climbed.

In 1935 James Waller led a British attempt on Saltoro Kangri, further east in the Karakoram. This massive, complex peak towered over the Bilafond La, which Fanny Bullock Workman and Dr William Hunter Workman had crossed en route to the Siachen Glacier 23 years earlier. Waller's small team of relatively inexperienced climbers had first to find a feasible route up the mountain, then attempt it in the face of the storms that so often hamper work in the Karakoram. They made a spirited attempt under the 'climbing leader' John Hunt, who would lead the first ascent of Everest 18 years later.

Three years later Waller returned to the Karakoram, this time leading an attempt on Masherbrum, the peak that had first been surveyed as K1. After several weeks forcing a winding route up the south side of the mountain, Jock Harrison and Robin Hodgkin reached a point at about 7,700 metres (25,262 feet), quite close to the summit, before strong winds forced them back to Camp 7 at about 7,500 metres (24,606 feet). Already frostbitten, at dawn the next day the pair had to abandon the camp when it was buried in an avalanche. Wading down through a blizzard, they failed to make Camp 6 and spent a miserable night in a crevasse. The rest of the team then had to abandon all the gear and it took them three days to escort the two climbers – now badly frostbitten – down to base camp. Harrison subsequently lost all his toes and most of his fingers; Hodgkin also lost parts of most of his fingers.

K2 – a fiercer challenge than Everest

On the night of 17 July 1938, while Jock Harrison and Robin Hodgkin's camp on Masherbrum was being buried by snowslides, American climbers on the far side of the Baltoro Glacier were sitting out the same storm at Camp 5 on the world's second-highest mountain, K2. Their leader Charles Houston had cut his teeth in the Himalaya in 1936 on Nanda Devi with Bill Tilman. For this much more daunting objective he selected a compact team of just six American climbers, supported by six Sherpas. They decided to tackle the complex ribs and buttresses of the Southeast Spur, identified as a likely route in 1909 by the Duke of Abruzzi, and now known as the Abruzzi Spur.

In comparison to the sprawling mass of Everest's North Face nearly 1,300 kilometres (800 miles) to the east, the Abruzzi Spur, despite offering the line of least resistance on K2, is a formidably steep, unforgiving proposition. Even today, festooned with fixed ropes and wire-ladders, the key passage up House's Chimney, first led by Bill House in 1938, remains a formidable obstacle, reinforcing modern climbers' respect for the pioneers.

Charles Houston was an inspirational leader. Building on his Nanda Devi experience, he chose his team very carefully, avoiding big egos, emphasizing the comradeship of the rope and – in acknowledgment of the fact that this was a much harder and potentially more dangerous mountain than Everest – always putting safety first. He recognized that on this steep, complex terrain, it would always be difficult, if not impossible, to retreat during one of the inevitable Karakoram storms. He insisted, wisely, on moving very methodically up the mountain, stocking camps with ample reserves of food and fuel, and always keeping members of the team close together.

His team succeeded in pushing up what would become the classic route on the mountain, placing seven camps as they did so. From the top camp Houston and Paul Petzold reached the broad snowy whaleback called the Shoulder, at about 7,925 metres (26,000 feet). Although Petzold pushed on a short way towards the final steep pyramid, both men felt too exhausted and over-extended to continue. Houston ordered the whole team to descend to base and safety before a prolonged storm swept over the mountain, ruling out further attempts.

Masherbrum An aerial view of Masherbrum towering over the Baltoro Glacier. The easier far side of this 7,821-metre (25,659-foot) peak was attempted by a British expedition in 1938 that almost ended in disaster. The mountain was finally climbed in 1960 by the Americans George Bell and Willi Unsoeld.

The American expedition to K2 in 1939 could not have been more different. Fritz Wiessner, its leader, had made his name as a brilliant rock climber in the eastern Alps and had taken part in Wili Merkl's Nanga Parbat expedition in 1932. Now on K2, Wiessner pushed beyond the Shoulder, accompanied by a reluctant Pasang Dawa Lama, and succeeded in climbing up the very difficult rocks flanking the icy Bottleneck Couloir. The two men had reached a height of about 8,370 metres (27,460 feet), just one rope length short of the easy snow-slopes leading to the summit, when darkness fell. Pasang refused, not unnaturally, to contemplate a bivouac in the open, so they descended, losing both pairs of crampons in the process. Amazingly, they tried again the next day, this time by the couloir. But without crampons it proved impossible.

Wiessner's personal feat ranks among the most remarkable pieces of climbing ever achieved at extreme altitude, but his leadership style seems to have been cavalier. While he and Pasang Dawa Lama were battling for the summit, one of his team members, Dudley Wolfe, was simply left at Camp 8, too exhausted to go higher. On their return Wiessner and Dawa Lama got Wolfe down to Camp 7 but during the subsequent drama – which involved a series of catastrophic misunderstandings, including the inexplicable stripping of lower camps – Wolfe was left at Camp 7. Back at base camp, Wiessner dispatched teams of Sherpas to climb all the way back up. On one occasion they reached Camp 7, only to find that Wolfe was too weak to move. On the final gallant attempt at a rescue, Pasang Kikuli, Pasang Kitar and Pintso all

Fairy idyll The 1932 German-American Nanga Parbat expedition approaches the Fairy Meadow, offering a spectacular view of the higher ground beyond. The lush greenery bedecked with flowers was given its nickname by the German climber Wili Merkl in 1932.

disappeared. They were never seen again, but Dudley Wolfe's remains were discovered 54 years later, at the foot of the Abruzzi Spur, in 1993.

Nanga Parbat – the Naked Mountain

The quest to attain the world's highest summits between the wars can be interpreted as a minor final flourish of Western imperial ambition in Asia: Britain assumed a monopoly on Everest, American climbers rose to the challenge of K2, while the French tried Gasherbrum I. The Germans, under Paul Bauer, made gallant attempts on Kangchenjunga, but the mountain that became most inextricably linked to German identity was Nanga Parbat, or Diamir – the Naked Mountain. This giant, sprawling mass of rock and ice, rising in the world's greatest single elevation from the gorge of the Indus, became an all-consuming obsession for German mountaineers, and one that would continue way beyond the Second World War.

During his attempt on the mountain back in 1895, Albert Mummery had chosen the western Diamir Face. When the Munich climber Wili Merkl led the first German attempt in 1932, he decided on the northern Rakhiot Face. After the long, hot, dusty approach, base camp was sited idyllically among pine trees in the almost surreally picturesque Fairy Meadow. But the face above them was a gigantic glacier sprawling at just the kind of moderate angle to amass lethal quantities of avalanche-prone snow. The route zigzagged laboriously through this minefield, eventually traversing across the flank of the subsidiary Rakhiot Peak towards the high ridge of the Silver Saddle.

Merkl's first attempt petered out at about 7,000 metres (22,965 feet), but he returned in 1934 with a bigger, stronger team, lavishly equipped and carrying the full blessing of the new Nazi regime. The Germans were assisted by a large team of experienced Sherpas and on this occasion they were able to push on, and on 6 July an advance party reached the Silver Plateau at 7,830 metres (25,689 feet). Although the summit was some 296 metres (971 feet) higher, the horizontal distance was 1.5 kilometres (just under a mile).

Many years later Hermann Buhl would discover just how difficult that long connecting ridge was, but the 1934 team never got that far – and many of them never returned to base camp. On the night of 6 July 16 men were at Camp 8, above the Silver Saddle, but there was no one else manning the camps between them and Camp 4, 1,500 metres (4,921 feet) lower down and 4 kilometres (2.5 miles) distant. That night a storm swept in from the west. The storm continued all the next day and by 8 July the men were half buried as the tent poles snapped under the weight of new snow.

The ensuing retreat became a rout. Peter Aschenbrenner and Erwin Schneider made it down to Camp 5, but in the process they became unroped from three Sherpas

Fateful climb Wili Merkl is shown on the slopes of Nanga Parbat during the 1934 expedition that would end in his death. The attempt was hampered from the start by a lower than expected snowline compared to the 1932 reconnaissance. Stormy conditions that lasted more than a week led to the deaths of six Sherpas and three Germans, the worst Himalayan climbing tragedy to date.

and abandoned them to their fate. The other men did not even reach Camp 7 and had to spend a night in the open. The following day Uli Wieland collapsed and died just 5 metres (16 feet) from the tents. The storm continued and by 15 July, despite gallant attempts by Sherpas from below to wade up through chest-deep snow and rescue their comrades, six Sherpas were dead, including one called Galay, who had chosen to remain with the leader, Wili Merkl, who had collapsed below the Silver Saddle (see map, page 126). A third German, Wilo Welzenbach, died at Camp 7.

That grim tragedy was eclipsed three years later when the Germans returned to Nanga Parbat and 16 men, asleep at Camp 4, were wiped out by a massive avalanche of ice. As if to avenge the slaughter somehow, Paul Bauer led a fourth German expedition in 1938. The frozen corpses of Merkl and Galay were found near a prominent tower called the Moor's Head, but this expedition was also defeated by the weather.

In 1939, for the fifth attempt, Peter Aufschnaiter took a predominantly Austrian party that included Heinrich Harrer, who had taken part in the first ascent of the North Face of the Eiger the previous summer. The party concluded, correctly, that a route up the Diamir Face, although technically harder than the Rakhiot Face, would be shorter, more direct and probably safer. They were just applying for permission to make a full attempt in 1940 when the Second World War broke out. Before they could return to Europe, Aufschnaiter and Harrer were interned as aliens. Their subsequent escape from a British prison camp resulted in an extraordinary adventure, including some quality map-making by Aufschnaiter and a bestselling memoir by Harrer called *Seven Years in Tibet*.

Formidable Sherpas Pasang Dawa Lama (opposite) on the 1939 American K2 Expedition, traversing a steep slope typical of the precarious terrain on the Abruzzi Spur. With Fritz Wiessner, Pasang Dawa Lama tackled the hardest climbing achieved so far at that altitude, very nearly reaching the summit. However, during the subsequent retreat, Dudley Wolfe was inexplicably left alone at one of the high camps. He was never seen alive again, and three Sherpas died trying to rescue him. Charles Houston, leader of the previous year's attempt, blamed the 1939 disaster on Wiesnner's leadership. Houston tried and was again unsuccessful in 1953. His account of the attempt was aptly titled *The Savage Mountain* (top).

Blanks on the map – exploring the remotest corners of the Karakoram

While the great set-piece expeditions were locked into desperate, often tragic, attempts on the highest summits, other teams chose to range wider and further, exploring the remoter reaches of Central Asia – in particular the immense glaciers of the Karakoram, expanding on the pioneering work of Vigne, Younghusband, Longstaff, Abruzzi, De Filippi and the Workmans.

The wildest terrain – still barely known today – lay on the north side of the watershed, where huge pinnacled glaciers flow into the Shaksgam Valley. Kenneth Mason explored this area in 1926 for the Survey of India and the Duke of Spoleto continued his work in 1929. Perhaps the most impressive explorers, though, were the Dutch couple, Dr Philip Visser and Jenny Visser 't Hooft. During three expeditions – in 1922, 1929–1930 and 1935 – they surveyed numerous Karakoram glaciers, all the way from Shimshal in the west to the Saser Kangri in the east.

Eric Shipton's expeditions of 1937 and 1939

It was inevitable that sooner or later Eric Shipton would be tempted by the immense spaces of the Karakoram, a landscape that he later described as having 'a kind of celestial loneliness'. It was at the end of the 1936 Everest expedition, disenchanted with the fruitless struggle, that he decided to turn his attention to the Karakoram.

WILO WELZENBACH

The most talented of all the climbers who died on Nanga Parbat was probably Wilo Welzenbach. He was born in Munich, like so many of the top mountaineers of his day, in 1900, and after qualifying as an architect he worked for the city council. He made a name for himself in particular as an outstanding ice-climber, with groundbreaking first ascents of some of the great Alpine north faces such as the Lauterbrunnen Breithorn.

He tried to get funding for an expedition to Nanga Parbat in 1930, but the German authorities chose instead to back Paul Bauer, who used the funds for his 1931 attempt on Kangchenjunga. When Welzenbach finally got backing for Nanga Parbat in 1932 his employers refused him leave. Wili Merkl, his companion from the first ascent of the North Face of the Grand Charmoz, assumed the leadership instead. In 1934 Welzenbach finally got to go to Nanga Parbat, only to die of exposure and exhaustion at Camp 7.

When they found Merkl's frozen body three years later, in his pocket there was a note, sent down by Welzenbach, pleading for the climbers below to come and rescue him. Alas they never made it. Had he survived and returned home to continue with his Alpine ambitions, he could well have made the coveted first ascent of the North Face of the Eiger.

(Following pages) The savage mountain The North Face of K2 in Chinese Xingiang. All the early attempts on the world's second-highest mountain, at 8,611 metres (28,250 feet), were from the other side in Baltistan. In 1902 Eckenstein and Crowley made a futuristic stab at the Northeast Ridge. Attention then shifted to the Southeast, or Abruzzi, Spur – scene of the disaster when three Sherpas died trying to reach Dudley Wolfe in 1939. His remains were eventually found in 1993. The Abruzzi Spur was completed when Compagnoni and Lacedelli made the first ascent of the mountain in 1954. The Northeast Spur was climbed in 1978, when Reichardt, Ridgeway, Roskelley and Wickwire finally achieved the American dream of climbing K2.

His plan for 1937 was breathtaking in its scope and ambition. He would take just three fellow Europeans, supported by seven Sherpas, to an initial base camp in the Shaksgam Valley on the north side of K2. Equipment would be minimal – just one rucksack each – and food supplies would be frugal but adequate. Bill Tilman and Michael Spender, the surveyor, had been with Shipton on the Everest reconnaissance of 1935. They were joined by the geologist John Auden (like Spender, his brother was a famous poet).

The Sherpa party was led by Angtharkay, Shipton's loyal companion of previous adventures. In his account of the expedition, *Blank on the Map*, Shipton summed up Angtharkay:

In his view, only three grades of humans should be included in a party. Firstly, there is the sahib, who is there to be satisfied. Secondly, there is the Sherpa, without whom no expedition could achieve its pointless objective; and lastly, there is the local porter, a greatly inferior being, whom, unfortunately, it is necessary to employ when the party has more luggage than can be carried by the sahibs and Sherpas.

On this occasion the 'inferior beings' were over a hundred Balti men, employed to get the team and its supplies right over the Karakoram watershed, crossing the Sarpo Laggo Pass to the Shaksgam Valley. Once established in their base camp, the 11 men were felt to be self-sufficient and free to indulge themselves in a wide-ranging bout of exploration. At first they concentrated on the area north of K2, with Shipton and Tilman taking a close look at the Aghil range. Then they worked their way back south, discovering glaciers such as the Crevasse Glacier, on which no humans had trodden before. They worked south to the enclosed basin of Snow Lake, first discovered by Martin Conway in 1892, then split up, with different parties taking different routes back to the lowlands of India.

Shipton and Spender travelled with Angtharkay through Shimshal to Hunza. Arriving from the Shaksgam they were mistaken for Chinese invaders. Once that misconception was put straight they were escorted to the high meadows of the Shimshal Pass and down into the improbable gorge on the far side. Shipton recalled:

> *Evening brought us to the edge of the most fantastic ravine carved out of alluvial deposits by a side stream. Angtharkay remarked, with some truth, that had we encountered it in unexplored country it would have presented an insurmountable obstacle. As it was, a stairway had been engineered through it with astonishing skill, and it was an easy matter to descend the 1,500 feet into this fearsome gorge.*

A couple of days later they were entertained royally in Shimshal village. It was mid-September and Shipton's elegiac account of the final days of the expedition will resonate with anyone who has travelled through that extraordinary country:

> *The world was very lovely, with the gold of the ripe corn and the early autumn colours of the thorn trees framing the deep green of the apple and apricot orchards and the slender Lombardy poplars. The air was filled with the peace and mellow beauty which autumn brings to these high mountain valleys.*

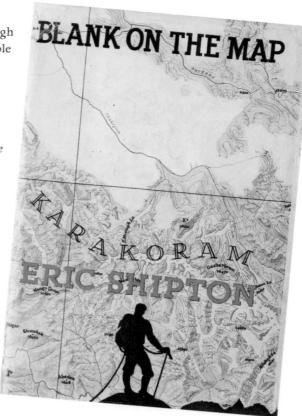

So enchanted was he by the Karakoram that he returned in 1939, this time with a different team, which included the Indian surveyor Faizal Elahi, who was charged with producing a detailed map of the central part of the range. Shipton's ambitions for this second expedition were even grander. The plan, after further explorations around Snow Lake, was to head north in the autumn and overwinter in the Shaksgam Valley, taking advantage of the frozen conditions to travel along rivers that were impossibly flooded in summer, and work gradually east towards the Karakoram Pass, finishing in Leh in the summer of 1940.

Unfortunately Nazi Germany's Adolf Hitler scotched that plan with his invasion of Poland. Shipton was alone, camped on Snow Lake in September 1939, when Scott Russell, the expedition botanist, returned from a resupply trip to announce that Britain was at war. The expedition was effectively over. Talking over the possibilities of an uncertain postwar future, Shipton did mention in passing to Russell that, should Nepal decide one day to open her mountain valleys to foreigners, he would love to return to Everest and explore its southern approaches. But that lay way in the future. For the moment he had to content himself with the retrospective satisfaction of an extraordinary decade of mountain exploration. Summing up that decade in his autobiography, *Upon That Mountain*, he wrote:

> *There are few treasures of more lasting worth than the experiences of a way of life that is in itself wholly satisfying. Such, after all, are the only possessions of which no fate, no cosmic catastrophe can deprive us; nothing can alter the fact if for one moment in eternity we have really lived.*

The unexplored
Eric Shipton – like his companion on so many of his adventures, Bill Tilman – wrote magnificent travel books. The most evocatively titled is *Blank on the Map* (1938), his account of the 1937 Karakoram expedition. With Tilman, John Auden, Michael Spender and seven loyal Sherpas, he explored a vast tract of the Karakoram range and the Aghil range further north, covering much new ground and correcting many of the inaccuracies bequeathed by earlier explorers such as the Workmans. Shipton was one of the first Europeans to see the North Face of K2 (following pages), which he described as one of the most awe-inspiring sights of his career.

7

The Conquest of Everest 1940–1953

MICK CONEFREY

In June 1946 four volunteers entered a decompression chamber at the Naval School of Aviation Medicine in Pensacola, Florida. Operation Everest was underway. Over the next 35 days, the pressure was gradually reduced until it reached one-third of its value at sea level, the same pressure on the summit of Everest. In charge of the experiment was the well-known American mountaineer Dr Charles, or Charlie, Houston, then enlisted. His aim was to investigate the effect of altitude on the human body and how it might affect naval pilots – and mountaineers.

The Second World War had seen significant advances in aviation medicine, but the science of high-altitude physiology was still in its infancy. This was the first experiment of its kind. On day 28 Houston put his volunteers through a series of physical and mental tests. Two of them were incapacitated at an early stage, but two others were able to do a surprising amount of work considering the lack of oxygen.

During the 1920s and 1930s there had been many attempts to climb the high mountains of the Himalaya but no one had ever got to the top of an 8,000-metre (26,246-foot) peak. Some believed that it was physically impossible to survive at such altitudes. Others thought it was possible but only for climbers carrying their own external oxygen supplies. Charlie Houston's findings proved both these ideas wrong, although clearly there was a big a difference between human performance in a warm, relatively well-appointed decompression chamber – in which the participants were fed and watered and even allowed to smoke – and the upper reaches of a very cold, unforgiving mountain.

Operation Everest was an interesting scientific experiment but ultimately it was political rather than scientific developments that finally cleared the way for the decade in which all ten of the world's 8,000-metre (26,246-foot) peaks were climbed. There were two key events: in 1947 India and Pakistan became independent, ending almost a century of the British Raj; three years later, in October 1950, China invaded Tibet and ended 36 brief years of Tibetan independence. The British retreat from Asia and the invasion of Tibet precipitated a third and equally important event: the opening up of Nepal to outsiders.

For centuries Nepal had been one of the most inaccessible countries in the world. Its rulers, a powerful family known as the Ranas, kept its borders locked tight and its hereditary rulers, the Shah dynasty, impotent. Nepalese soldiers were employed by the British Army, and there was a limited amount of trade with Tibet and India, but that was about it. Apart from the British resident in Kathmandu (see page 42), very few Westerners had ever visited Nepal and virtually no one had been allowed to go beyond the Kathmandu Valley.

Rising through the fall One of the Sherpas on the 1953 Everest expedition reaches the final ice-wall at the the top of the Khumbu Icefall. The navigation through the precarious ice pinnacles and shifting crevasses of the icefall was one of the most technically difficult parts of the whole ascent.

In the late 1940s the Ranas changed policy. Fearful of both resurgent communist China and newly independent India, they began to court foreign governments and, as a sign of a new openness, even allowed Western travellers in. When, totally unexpectedly, the Ranas were overthrown by King Tribhuvan, Nepal's hereditary monarch, the process accelerated.

A whole new range of mountains became available to Western climbers.

With the end of empire, British mountaineers no longer enjoyed a privileged position. There were expeditions to Nepal from the United States of America (USA) and Switzerland as well as Britain. At first the Nepalese insisted that there should be some scientific justification to every expedition but before long they relented. In 1949 the American diplomat Oscar Houston, father of Charlie Houston, led a small trek to the Solu Khumbu, the Sherpa homeland. Charlie went along too and so did the famous British climber Bill Tilman, a veteran of several pre-war expeditions.

Leaving Oscar and the older members of the party behind, Charlie Houston and Bill Tilman went as far as the Khumbu Glacier. They climbed a small peak, today called Kala Pattar, and took a photograph of the southern face of Everest and the huge Khumbu Icefall at its foot. Like the British climbers who had glimpsed the Khumbu Icefall from the Tibetan side, they were sceptical that it could ever be climbed, but this was nevertheless a key moment in Everest's history.

A few months later, an event occurred of even greater significance for climbing history: the first ascent of an 8,000-metre (26,246-foot) peak, Annapurna.

Ecstasy and agony on Annapurna

At 8,091 metres (26,545 feet), Annapurna I is the tenth-highest mountain in the world. Before 1950 it had barely been mapped, never mind climbed. In 1949 the Federation Français de la Montagne obtained permission from the Nepalese government to stage an expedition to northeast Nepal to climb either Dhaulagiri or Annapurna. It would only be the second time that French climbers had tackled a Himalayan peak. The only previous expedition, to Hidden Peak in the 1930s, had ended in failure.

The leader of the 1950 French expedition was Maurice Herzog, an engineer from Lyon. Herzog was a decorated war hero and a member of the élite French climbing club, the Groupe de Haute Montagne. The other members of the team were equally formidable. They included three leading guides from Chamonix, the home of European Alpinism: Louis Lachenal, Lionel Terray and Gaston Rébuffat. One-third of the expedition finance came directly from the French government, with the rest mainly from private sponsorship. It was a very patriotic and very hierarchical affair with team members being required to swear an oath of obedience to their leader.

The French team left for the Himalaya in late March 1950, with 3.5 tons of supplies. They had all the latest mountaineering kit including nylon ropes, eiderdown jackets, rubber-soled boots, and some very basic oxygen equipment. In order to get their gear up the mountain, they hired the famous Angtharkay as their sirdar, or head Sherpa, plus six Sherpas. The initial hump to the foot of the mountain was done by 150 porters. Angtharkay had served on several British expeditions of the late 1930s and was a favourite of the well-known British climber Eric Shipton.

After a long approach march they saw Dhaulagiri for the first time on 17 April. It was an awesome sight, even for a group of seasoned mountaineers. Annapurna was not yet visible, the view of it blocked by another huge range of mountains. Maurice Herzog still had not made up his mind which mountain to attempt, so they set up base camp at Tukucha at 2,590 metres (8,500 feet), roughly halfway between the two peaks.

After two weeks, Herzog decided to target Annapurna because they just could not find a viable route up Dhaulagiri. Like many mountaineers before and after him, he worried constantly about the arrival of the monsoon and the heavy snows that would come with it. Although they had brought oxygen sets, ultimately they were not used. When Lionel Terray tried one on for the first time, he almost suffocated. After that, no one bothered.

On 21 May they set up their first camp on the North Annapurna glacier, from which they hoped to hack a route up to the summit. Herzog realized that most direct route would take them up the North Face of the mountain. This was a brave choice because of the risks of avalanche, especially with regular heavy afternoon snowfall but they pressed on and made rapid progress. By the end of May they felt ready to make the final thrust.

Maurice Herzog and Louis Lachenal established what they hoped would be their final camp at 7,400 metres (24,278 feet), just over 600 metres (1,968 feet) from the summit. They were accompanied by two Sherpas, Angtharkay and Sarki. Herzog was very surprised that when it came to it, neither wanted to join them on the summit attempt. As it turned out, this was a wise decision.

At dawn on 3 June the two Frenchmen left camp heading for the top. It was very cold and Lachenal immediately began to worry about his feet, sensing the onset of frostbite. As a professional mountain guide, his climbing skills and his limbs were his livelihood. At one stage he was so concerned that he talked about turning back, but when Maurice Herzog said that he was prepared to go on alone, Lachenal felt unable to leave him. So on they both continued. At 2.00 p.m. they finally reached the summit and entered the history books. Maurice Herzog unfurled a French flag and Louis Lachenal took his photograph, but he was impatient to get down. After a few minutes, they turned around. The ascent had been relatively incident free, whereas the descent was a nightmare.

Maurice Herzog dropped his outer gloves close to the summit and got progressively colder. Louis Lachenal started slightly ahead of him but fell close to their camp and actually slid past it. He was found lying in the snow about 90 metres (300 feet) below the tent. Gaston Rébuffat and Lionel Terray had come up in order to stage a second attempt on the summit, but they were so concerned at the state of Herzog and Lachenal that they immediately abandoned their plans. Lachenal's feet were badly frostbitten – the only way to remove his boots was to cut through the leather.

The next day the four men evacuated their high camp but as they descended the weather deteriorated further, reducing visibility to just a few feet. In a desperate attempt to find the best route Rébuffat and Terray took off their snow goggles but they still missed their next camp. With the weather worsening, the four men climbed into a crevasse and hunkered down for the night. They had just one sleeping bag between them and no food or water.

Things only got worse. At dawn an avalanche hit, burying the boots they had taken off the night before in order to massage their feet. Lionel Terray and Gaston Rébuffat woke up almost completely snow-blind. They were in such a bad way that Herzog and Lachenal had to take the lead: the rescued becoming the rescuers.

When they finally reached base camp, the team doctor Jacques Oudot was shocked to see their condition. Maurice Herzog's hands and feet were almost totally numb. Louis Lachenal's toes had turned black. Fearing that they might develop septicaemia, Oudot began injecting the two men with novocaine, then thought to be effective against frostbite, and penicillin. The novocaine injections, administered to the stomach, were so excruciating that Oudot also had to administer morphine to dull the pain of the treatment.

The march out was a desperate race against time. The monsoon rain had swollen the rivers and made them much more difficult to cross. Herzog and Lachenal, both in desperate pain, were carried on makeshift stretchers. At night Oudot treated their frostbite by cutting off sections of dead skin. When they finally arrived at the rendezvous with their trucks, he amputated four of Maurice Herzog's toes and his little finger. When, a few days later, they transferred to a train, the agony and the grim work continued. Oudot removed Lachenal's toes one by one, operating whenever the train came to a stop.

Towards Annapurna A view from Annapurna base camp towards the South Face of the mountain (opposite, below). Herzog's 1950 expedition tackled the North Face, which involved an arduous search for a break in the mountain range on Annapurna's western flank. Herzog was fortunate to have the hugely experienced Angtharkay (1908–1981, opposite, above) leading his team of Sherpas. The consequences of success, however, were almost fatal for Herzog and here he is seen being carried down the mountain (above) after the effects of frostbite on his fingers and toes rendered him unable to make the descent without assistance.

A historic ascent When the French arrived in the Himalaya in 1950 they were not sure which 8,000-metre (26,246-foot) peak to target: Annapurna I or Dhaulagiri. There were no reliable maps of the area and neither mountain had ever been attempted. Eventually they settled on Annapurna I, because it looked more approachable. Like Mont Blanc, Annapurna is a massif consisting of six major peaks of which Annapurna I is the highest. The ascent of the North Face was surprisingly trouble free, but the descent was a disfiguring ordeal for Herzog and Lachenal.

Back in France, the news of the climbers' success broke on 16 June, prompting a frenzy of headlines. However, to the surprise of everyone, Herzog did not head home straight away. Instead, he went to Kathmandu to fulfil a promise that he had made to the Nepalese king to tell him about their expedition. Meanwhile the others rested up as best as they could.

When the team finally reached Paris on 17 July there was pandemonium at Orly airport. Maurice Herzog was carried aloft from the plane, his hands and feet wreathed in bandages. The press was out in force and the airport thronged with friends and well-wishers who had come to honour France's latest national heroes. When the acclaim had died down and the awards ceremonies were over, Herzog was transported to the American Hospital of Paris at Neuilly-sur-Seine. He arrived in a desperate condition. When the doctors removed the bandages they found his wounded hands and feet infested with maggots.

Herzog was forced to spend almost a whole year in hospital recuperating. When he finally left he had lost all of his fingers and toes. In the meantime he had dictated the most successful expedition book of all time, today estimated to have sold eleven million copies. It turned him into an international celebrity and by far the most famous mountaineer in the world. The book finished, rather enigmatically, with a warning: 'There are many Annapurnas in the lives of men.' He had just inaugurated one of the finest eras of Himalayan mountaineering, but before it could get properly underway, British climbers had to deal with some unfinished business – Everest.

THE ASCENT OF ANNAPURNA I IN 1950

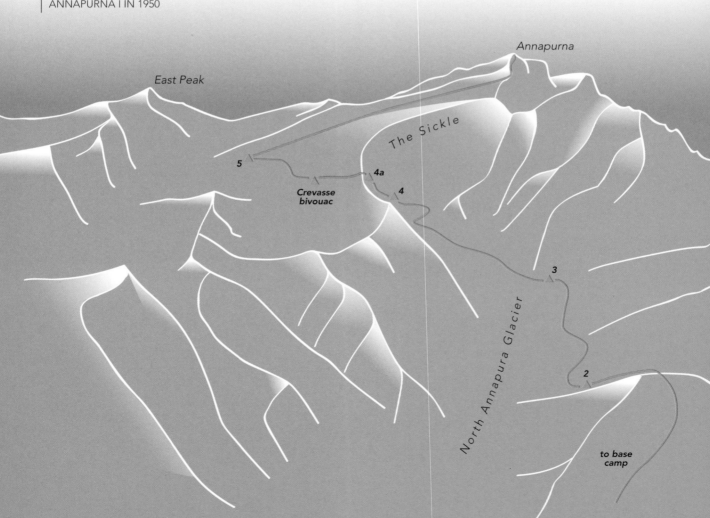

The Everest Reconnaissance Expedition

In early 1951 Mike Ward, a young British climber then completing his national service, approached the Himalayan Committee with a request for help. Made up from the great and the good of the Alpine Club and the Royal Geographical Society, the Himalayan Committee was the successor body to the pre-war Everest Committee. It had inherited a small amount of money from the last expedition and its members were well connected to the British establishment.

Mike Ward proposed to take a reconnaissance expedition to the southern side of Everest to scout possible climbing routes. Fired by the conviction that, because of Britain's long involvement, Everest was 'our mountain', he was incensed at the idea that Nepal was now letting in 'foreign' teams. When he first approached the Himalayan Committee, Mike Ward didn't know anything about the recent Houston expedition to the Solu Khumbu, and had not seen any of the photographs that Bill Tilman had taken of the Khumbu Icefall. The Himalayan Committee agreed to help and Mike Ward began organizing in earnest, assembling a small team of friends and young climbers. It wasn't easy. Wartime restrictions still in force meant that supplies of basics like tents and sleeping bags were limited. Two of Mike's team dropped out, but he persisted. And then something unexpected happened.

In the summer of 1951, Eric Shipton, the doyen of pre-war mountaineers, returned to England. During the war he had worked as a diplomat in China, but had been rudely ejected from his post as British Consul-General to Kunming by Maoist revolutionaries. Although he had no prior knowledge of the Everest reconnaissance expedition he agreed to lead the team. Shipton had some reservations: he thought it unlikely that a viable southern route existed and wasn't sure if he wanted to return to the life of a peripatetic mountaineer. However, the prospect of visiting the Solu Khumbu, the Sherpa homeland, was attractive enough to overcome his doubts.

In September 1951 he arrived in Nepal with Mike Ward and two young British climbers, Bill Murray and Tom Bourdillon. For Eric Shipton, small was always beautiful, but at the last minute he agreed that his party could be supplemented by two New Zealanders who had been climbing in India. It was a decision that would have long-term consequences.

Accompanied by Eric Shipton's old friend and esteemed veteran of the Annapurna expedition, Angtharkay, they spent a month trekking through Nepal to the Solu Khumbu. At Dingla, they were joined by the two New Zealanders – a lawyer called Earle Riddiford and a young climber who spent the winters looking after his father's bee-farm, Edmund Hillary. After much carousing in Sherpa villages, they finally reached the Khumbu Glacier from where they hoped to get a good view of the Southwest Face of Everest.

At first glance, the prospects of finding a good route were not good. The Khumbu Icefall was even bigger and more intimidating than they had expected. Formed at the point where the Khumbu Glacier spilled over a section of very steep ground, the icefall was a deadly maze of crevasses, punctuated by tall towers of ice. On either side avalanches spilled down from the nearby slopes. When Eric and Ed Hillary climbed a tall rib of Pumori, a nearby mountain, in order to get a better look, their expectations were not high. However, to their amazement, when they stopped at about 5,500 metres (over 18,000 feet) and took out their binoculars, they discovered that there was indeed a feasible looking route. The Khumbu Icefall was dangerous from every angle, but if it could be ascended, then the valley that lay beyond it looked relatively easy to ascend. There was a huge slope stretching between Everest and Lhotse. It didn't look easy but Eric Shipton thought it was climbable.

THE ELUSIVE YETI

In November 1951, on their way back from the Everest reconnaissance expedition, Eric Shipton and Mike Ward came across some unusual tracks in the snow. They were large footprints made by a pair of creatures whose feet had four toes and an exaggerated 'thumb'-like digit sticking out to one side. Shipton asked Mike Ward to stand next to the prints and took a series of photographs, using a boot and an ice-axe for size references.

When they consulted their Sherpa, Sen Tensing, he had no doubt of their provenance: they were yeti tracks. Most Sherpas at the time believed in the existence of the yeti, or 'abominable snowman' as it was dubbed in the British press. Murals in local monasteries depicted large, hairy, anthropoids that walked on two legs. Accounts of their behaviour varied. According to some Sherpas, there were two types of yeti: one that preyed on Yaks and another that preyed on humans. Female yetis were said to be slower moving than their mates, on account of their large pendulous breasts.

Back in England, when Eric Shipton's photographs were published in the press, they created a sensation. Were they the first photographs of yeti spoor? According to Shipton's reports in *The Times*, he and Mike Ward had followed the prints down a glacier and noticed places where it looked as if the creatures had leaped over crevasses and used their nails to secure a good purchase on the other side. But in his biography, published many years later, Shipton commented that he had been surprised at all the attention, noting wryly that he had expected the Society for Psychical Research in London to pay more attention to them than the august scientists of the British Museum, who – inspired by Shipton's reports of prints – had organized a yeti exhibition. For several years afterwards, the hunt was on to bring back more proof of the yeti's existence. In 1954 the journalist Ralph Izzard, who had famously tried to gatecrash the 1953 Everest expedition, headed for the Himalaya with Tom Stobart, the well-known cameraman. In spite of several weeks of searching, they did not come back with any more hard evidence.

A few years later Ed Hillary led a further expedition in search of the elusive yeti, but he too failed to come back with anything new. So were Shipton's photos fakes? After all, wasn't he known for his practical jokes? Even if Shipton hadn't faked the prints entirely, had he cleaned them up and enhanced them to make them look more definite?

Today there is some scepticism about Shipton's story, but throughout his life he insisted to his friends that the prints were genuine – and there was corroborative evidence. Mike Ward was with Shipton at the time and a few days later their teammate Tom Bourdillon arrived on the glacier and also saw a long line of prints, although from his description they did not sound quite so definite. Bourdillon wondered if they might not have been made by a bear.

There were no yetis spotted on the Cho Oyu expedition in 1952 or the 1953 Everest expedition, but one of the climbers, Charles Evans, did bring back some hairs, reportedly from a yeti scalp held in a local monastery. Eventually the hairs were given to Scotland Yard and a leading zoologist for analysis. Both concluded that they came from a bear.

The yeti myth is remarkably persistent. More recently, the famous Tyrolean climber, Reinhold Messner, wrote a book in which he claimed to have both fought off and photographed a yeti. He speculated that in fact it was a species of bear, rather than a new creature in its own right. This century there have been several other expeditions in search of the yeti, but as yet no one has produced any solid proof.

They made a first attempt to weave their way through the Khumbu Icefall but when they reached the top, their progress was checked by a steep slope. They tried to climb it but it began to avalanche, almost taking Earle Riddiford with it.

With Mike Ward and the other young British climbers afflicted with altitude sickness, Eric Shipton decided to take a fortnight's break from Everest and explore the territory around it. When they returned, he hoped everyone would be better acclimatized and that much of the loose snow in the icefall might be blown away.

On their return they made a second attempt and managed to get all the way into the Western Cwm before they were halted by a huge crevasse that barred the way to further progress.

Although some of the young climbers wanted to continue, Eric realized that the expedition was now over. They didn't have the time or the equipment to tackle the large crevasse and with winter approaching the days were becoming longer and colder. It had been a much more successful reconnaissance than he had envisaged and he looked forward to returning in the following spring to make a full-scale attempt.

After an exciting return trip in which they had close scrapes with Tibetan border guards and yetis, they finally arrived in Kathmandu in early November. But there was some shocking news: the British would not be coming back to Everest in 1952 because someone else had asked first.

The Swiss expedition of 1952

In 1951 the Swiss Foundation for Alpine Research, a body set up to research avalanches and other mountain phenomena, received permission to send an expedition to Everest. Unlike today, when there is no limit on the number of teams present on the mountain, until the 1970s the Nepalese government only allowed one team at a time. This meant that Eric Shipton and the British would have to wait until 1953.

The Swiss team included some the best known and most respected Alpinists in Europe. Its stars were Raymond Lambert, the famous guide and climber, and André Roch, a noted Alpinist and avalanche expert. Most of the men came from the Androsace, an élite mountaineering club from Geneva. The Androsace had applied to send a team to nearby Cho Oyu, the sixth-highest mountain in the world, but when the Swiss foundation invited them to turn their attentions to Everest, they had no hesitation. For a few frantic weeks, the British Himalayan Committee tried to organize a joint Anglo-Swiss expedition, but ultimately it came to nothing and, ironically, the British ended up going to Cho Oyu instead.

The Swiss flew into Nepal in March 1952 and headed for Everest with 150 porters to carry all their supplies. They made swift work of the Khumbu Icefall, taking a route down the left-hand side, which they nicknamed 'suicide passage', rather than the more central route that Eric Shipton had proposed in 1951. Jean-Jacques Asper, the youngest climber on the team, climbed 18 metres (60 feet) down into the huge crevasse that had stopped Shipton's party, found an ice-bridge and clambered up to the top. He hammered down an ice-anchor, and before long the Swiss had set up a 'Tyrolean Traverse' to ferry men and supplies over into the Western Cwm.

After a rapid ascent, the Swiss got to work on the Lhotse Face, the huge 1,219-metre (4,000-foot) slope below the South Col, the windswept plateau at 7,925 metres (26,000 feet) that lies between Everest and Lhotse. Eric Shipton had felt that the Lhotse Face needed to be climbed in stages, with intermediary camps set up between the top and the bottom but René Dittert, the Swiss climbing leader, tried to prepare a route that could be climbed in a single push. It was a serious mistake.

The Swiss took almost two weeks before they were ready. Ultimately, they found it impossible to ascend the Lhotse Face in a single day and had to improvise a freezing bivouac three-quarters of the way up. Several Sherpas turned back early, so when they reached the South Col they had insufficient tents and supplies to mount an effective assault on the summit. Nevertheless, they were determined to try.

On 25 May Raymond Lambert, Leon Flory and Rene Aubert set off up the Southeast Ridge, the final 900 metres or so (3,000 feet) to the summit, with their sirdar, Tenzing Norgay. Over the last few weeks, Lambert had formed a deep bond with him, the start of a friendship that would last throughout both men's lives. Tenzing could barely speak French and Lambert's English was very limited, but they seemed to have an instinctive rapport.

At 8,310 metres (27,265 feet), they stopped to set up their final camp. They had just one tent, and it was barely big enough for one man never mind four. Reluctantly, but with great generosity, Flory and Aubert turned back and left Lambert and Tenzing to make the final push. They spent an awful night huddled together, trying to keep warm, without sleeping bags or food, except for a few scraps. Worse still, they had no means of producing water, apart from a candle and an old tin.

At first light the following morning Lambert and Tenzing set off, determined to make one final dash for the summit. They had no chance. Their oxygen sets were designed for miners – not for mountaineers operating at high altitude. The valves were so unforgiving that they only released oxygen when a climber was standing still. After four brutal hours, there were still over 305 vertical metres (1,000 feet) ahead of them. Silently, Lambert signalled to Tenzing that it was now time to turn back. They abandoned their tent and stumbled down onto the South Col and into the arms of Flory and Aubert who had stayed high to wait for them. After the first 'assault' party

Nearly there Raymond Lambert and Tenzing Norgay during the 1952 Swiss attempt on Everest. The two men made the first attempt on the summit from the Nepalese side, but were forced to turn back some 150 metres (nearly 500 feet) short of the South Summit. Lambert described the feeling of the final approach as they 'felt our legs grow even heavier and become like lead, while our brains also solidified and lost their faculties'.

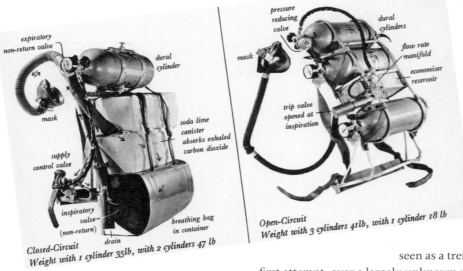

Two circuits Diagrams of the closed-circuit and open-circuit oxygen sets that were developed for the 1953 Everest expedition, which took along with it almost 200,000 litres of oxygen, massively more than the amount the Swiss had in 1952. The closed-circuit sets proved less reliable and Hillary and Tenzing's successful summiting used the open-circuit version.

descended, another group went up to the South Col but they did not even manage to reach Tenzing and Lambert's tent.

When the news reached Europe the Swiss were widely praised. There were claims of a new world record, with Raymond Lambert estimating that they had turned back at 8,595 metres (28,199 feet). Although recent research throws some doubt on this, the expedition was seen as a tremendous achievement. On their first attempt, over a largely unknown route, the Swiss had got high on the mountain and might have even matched Britain's pre-Second World War record.

There was celebration too in the British camp. The Swiss failure meant that Britain still had the chance to seize the greatest prize in world mountaineering in 1953, if they could mount a serious expedition. But in the summer of 1952 the Himalayan Committee, the organizers of the expedition, were far from sure.

Cho Oyu in 1952

While the Swiss had done well on Everest, the British training expedition to Cho Oyu had gone very badly. Its climbers came nowhere near the summit and all in all it was a fractious, unhappy expedition. It was not surprising that Eric Shipton, as team leader, came in for a lot of criticism, much of it behind closed doors.

Looking back now it is obvious that the expectations placed on him were too high. No one had ever attempted Cho Oyu before and even though it was considerably lower than Everest, Cho Oyu was still a very challenging mountain. But it was equally true that Eric Shipton had never quite settled on the 1952 expedition. He didn't like big teams – and didn't like the sense of international competition that now informed what the press were calling the 'Race for Everest'. And although he often seemed to make statements to the contrary, it was obvious that Eric Shipton wasn't very interested in oxygen or any of the scientific aspects of high-altitude climbing. None of those boded well for 1953.

When he returned to Britain in mid-July 1952, against his own instinct and the Himalayan Committee's better judgment, Shipton was invited to lead the 1953 expedition. He accepted the offer, but there followed a summer of intrigue as several members of the Himalayan Committee changed their mind and attempted to find an alternative. It all came to a head at a meeting in early September at which Eric Shipton was invited to take a secondary role in 1953 and hand over the leadership to John Hunt. He could not accept this and resigned from the expedition.

A change of leadership

Eric Shipton's removal caused tremendous disquiet among the 1953 team. One member, Tom Bourdillon, resigned and several others considered their positions.

John Hunt had a lot of work to do getting everyone back on side, but fortunately for the Himalayan Committee they had found someone who was both extremely organized and very charming.

Hunt set about recruiting new climbers and consolidating the powerful core team that Eric Shipton had assembled. Over the next three months, Hunt meticulously planned every aspect of the expedition. Griffith Pugh, a scientist working for the Medical Research Council, acted as Hunt's principal scientific advisor. He helped test and design cold weather clothing – and worked with the team's 'oxygen controller', Peter Lloyd, on the vital question of what type of oxygen set to use.

Each member of the team was allocated a particular sphere of responsibility. George Band, at 23 the team's youngest climber, was put in charge of communications and food; Charles Wylie, the expedition organizer, looked after boots and bridging equipment. Even Ed Hillary, far away in New Zealand, was allocated a particular responsibility – in his case to procure sleeping bags and cooking equipment.

By mid-November, John Hunt was organizing team meetings and setting up research trips to the Alps to test their gear. But there was a problem. Although the expedition treasurer, R.W. Lloyd, continually sent out appeals emphasizing the fact that this was a 'national' expedition that was very important for British prestige, initially little money was forthcoming. The Himalayan Committee had traditionally derived much of its funding from selling the media rights to cover an expedition. However, the long-term partner – *The Times* – refused to commit itself until the results of the second Swiss Everest expedition were known.

In early September, a second Swiss team had gone out to make a further attempt on Everest. It included several members of the spring expedition but was much better equipped. Once again the Swiss hired Tenzing as their sirdar and this time round they also formally made him a member of the team.

The Swiss made quick work of Khumbu Icefall but for the second time their attempt floundered on the Lhotse Face because they insisted on trying to climb it in

Hunt's team The 1953 Everest climbing party of Tom Stobart, Sherpa Dawa Tenzing, Charles Evans, Charles Wylie, Edmund Hillary, John Hunt, Sherpa Tenzing Norgay , George Lowe, Michael Ward, Tom Bourdillon, George Band, Griffith Pugh, Alfred Gregory and Wilfrid Noyce, all of whom are standing, with the rest of the Sherpas seated. Michael Westmacott is not in the picture.

Ice-slopes. Edmund Hillary crosses a precarious ladder bridge over a crevasse on the Western Cwm near Camp 2 during the 1953 Everest expedition (top). Pictured on their way to Camp 2 in 1953 are these Sherpas (opposite, top) carrying loads through the treacherous ice-maze of the Khumbu Icefall.

Science and strength Griffith Pugh performs an alveolar air test on John Hunt (opposite, centre), a procedure for collecting oxygen from the alveoli on the lung's surface, which is used to assess lung function – vital at such high altitude. Edmund Hillary's Sherpa party moves supplies to base camp (opposite, bottom). It was the careful attention to logistics that in the end enabled the 1953 climb to succeed.

one push. Only after a serious accident that left one Sherpa dead and another two wounded did they change their approach and set up intermediary camps. The heroes of the spring expedition, Lambert and Tenzing, were able to reach the South Col for a second time, but even though they were accompanied by a powerful party of Sherpas they found it too cold to make any progress.

Ironically, John Hunt was in Switzerland when he heard the news of the Swiss defeat. In December 1952 he and a small party had flown there to test equipment and clothing at a camp on the Jungfrau Joch. Just before they were due to return to Britain the news of the second Swiss expedition broke. For the British, it was now full steam ahead. *The Times* finally signed up to the expedition and gradually other donations started to come in.

R.W. Lloyd scored a major coup when he persuaded Prince Philip to become the expedition's patron: 1953 was Coronation Year and excitement was growing – in British newspapers there was much talk of a New Elizabethan Age. If Everest could be climbed that summer, it would be the perfect gift to the new queen.

In spite of all the competition with the Swiss, there was also a lot of cooperation. John Hunt and Griffith Pugh visited Zurich and were given advice and practical help from the Swiss Foundation for Alpine Research.

Then, in late February 1953, just before they were due to sail to India, John Hunt fell ill. His doctors discovered that a persistent problem with catarrh was caused by badly damaged nasal cavities. The only solution was to operate, but two weeks before a major expedition was not the ideal moment. At one stage things did not look good, but with characteristic resilience, Hunt pulled through.

Nepal at last

In Kathmandu, Hunt's team camped out in the generous confines of the British embassy. It was a very large group, consisting of 11 climbers, a doctor, a physiologist and a cameraman. Their numbers were later swelled by a journalist, James Morris, from *The Times* sent out to report directly from the mountain. Like the Swiss, the British team hired Tenzing as their sirdar, although they did not formally invite him to become a member of the climbing team.

From the beginning there were small but undoubted tensions between the British and their Sherpa team. There were squabbles over accommodation, the right to keep equipment after the expedition and the size of the loads the Sherpas were expected to carry. Tenzing did not enjoy the same easy rapport with the British team as he had had with the Swiss. The local Indian and Nepalese press were very angry at the exclusive deal *The Times* had to cover expedition news. In response, they played up Tenzing's role, claiming that he would guide the British team to the summit.

When he left Kathmandu in early March, John Hunt was very relieved finally to get into the field. According to his carefully drawn up acclimatization plan, there were several weeks to walk in the Everest area and make training climbs on nearby peaks. For John Hunt, this was a time for team bonding and familiarization with equipment. Several of the climbers had been to the Himalaya before, either on the 1952

Cho Oyu expedition or the 1951 reconnaissance, but there were two new boys —
George Band and Mike Westmacott. As the New Zealander George Lowe remarked in
a letter home, they were a very homogenous group with two Charles, two Toms and
two Mikes. Most had been to public school and almost all had served in the army at
one stage or another.

The Khumbu Icefall and the Lhotse Face

Ed Hillary, now a veteran of three Himalayan expeditions, led the first party into the
Khumbu Icefall. It looked more dangerous than ever with huge new crevasses and
even more pendulous towers of ice, which threatened to totter over at any minute. As
they flagged up a route through, the names they gave to particular sections told their
own story: 'Mike's Horror', 'Hillary's Horror', the 'Ghastly Crevasse' and the 'Nut
Cracker'. Tenzing arranged for logs to be brought up from the Khumbu Valley to be
used as ad-hoc bridges. They had also brought three sections of aluminium builder's
ladder that could be bolted together to help them across the longest stretches.

By the beginning of May they had reached the Western Cwm and had started
to build up stockpiles of supplies and equipment. There were several outbreaks of
'base-campitis', a very unpleasant combination of diarrhoea and a bad throat, but
there were no serious accidents. As the oldest man in the team, and someone who
had just been operated on, it wasn't surprising that John Hunt worried about his
own health. Early on he developed a severe breathless cough. Mike Ward, the team
doctor, thought that it might be pleurisy but Hunt recovered quickly and refused to
take any more than the minimum amount of time off.

On 7 May John Hunt brought the team together to reveal his plan for the final
stages of the expedition, and to nominate the members of the summit parties. It was
a tense moment. Everyone was committed to the idea of teamwork but they were all

ambitious and wanted to play as big a role as possible. In the end his selections were fairly predictable: his deputy leader Charles Evans, would make a preliminary attempt with one of the strongest British climbers, Tom Bourdillon; they would be followed by Ed Hillary and Tenzing a day later. If necessary, there would be a third attempt but Hunt didn't nominate the members of that party. As everyone knew, Hunt had his own ambitions on Everest and would have dearly loved to be on one of the summit teams.

Before any attempt could be made at all, first they would have to climb the Lhotse Face. According to Hunt's plans, they would have to carry roughly 450 kilograms (1,000 pounds) of gear and tents up to its windswept plateau. George Lowe, an expert in cutting steps, was tasked with finding and preparing the route, but from the beginning it went badly.

There was no sign of the monsoon. Then, in mid-May, the weather deteriorated rapidly, with snowstorms most afternoons. To make things worse, the two men allocated to assist Lowe on the Lhotse Face, George Band and Mike Westmacott, both fell ill. Lowe and the Sherpa Ang Nyima did the best that they could, but it was slow work.

John Hunt grew increasingly impatient. He hoped to be ready to stage the first attempt by 15 May, but when that date came they were nowhere near the top. In turn, he sent up Wilfrid Noyce, another strong British climber, and Mike Ward to help George Lowe, but as the days dragged on the New Zealander became increasingly tired.

Hunt was forced to change plan. Instead of waiting for the route to be prepared from bottom to top, he sent up the Sherpa porters and told Wilfrid Noyce that, if necessary he should make a dash for the South Col, with one Sherpa, to prove that it could be done. To give a final boost to proceedings, he allowed Hillary and Tenzing to go up too, to assist and encourage. Wilfrid Noyce and the Sherpa Annalu succeeded, and on the following day Charles Wylie led no less than 15 Sherpas up to the South Col. They emptied their sacks and then rushed down the mountain as fast as they could.

The first attempt

On 22 May Hunt left Advance Base with Tom Bourdillon and Charles Evans, the first summit team. Their ascent up the Lhotse Face was a stark reminder of the difficulties of high-altitude climbing. At different

OXYGEN EQUIPMENT

In the 1920s a fierce debate raged within mountaineering circles about the ethics of using oxygen equipment. Some argued that all 'artificial' aids were by their very nature unsporting. If mountaineering had any value, they insisted, it was in the physical challenge of matching mind, muscle and mountain – without putting any machinery in between. The pro-oxygen lobby dismissed all this. There was nothing wrong, they said, in benefitting from the latest scientific advances. Far from diminishing the sport, oxygen equipment allowed climbers to take on higher and higher mountains. And, they maintained, it was simply impossible for human beings to climb truly high Himalayan mountains without it.

By the early 1950s, the scientific lobby had effectively won the battle. After numerous failures in the 1920s and 1930s, it was taken for granted that portable oxygen equipment was necessary for high-altitude climbing. Some mountaineers still grumbled about the weight and inconvenience of wearing oxygen sets, and others still felt that they got in the way of the pure experience of climbing, but most simply accepted that if they wanted to get to the top of K2 or Everest or Kangchenjunga, they had no other choice.

The equipment available in the early 1950s was far from perfect but it was a significant advance on what had come before. A basic oxygen set consisted of four elements: a carrying frame, one or two oxygen cylinders, a mechanism for regulating the flow-rate, and either a breathing tube or a face mask. The mountaineers of the postwar era benefitted from the work that had gone into improving oxygen equipment for aviators during the Second World War and the Korean War. This resulted in more efficient face masks, along with significantly lighter oxygen cylinders.

In 1952 the British scientist Griffith Pugh conducted the first systematic research into the use of oxygen equipment for climbing, during the Everest training expedition to Cho Oyu. Pugh's aim was to discover the optimum flow-rates for different mountaineering activities. Carrying any extra equipment at high altitude was a significant additional burden to a climber, so in order to overcome the weight penalty, oxygen sets needed to be run at a sufficiently high flow-rate for a climber to feel a clear benefit. However, as Pugh realized, it was futile to run a set at too high a flow-rate because that would mean having to change oxygen cylinders frequently.

Pugh spent a week putting a small group of climbers through their paces on the slopes of the Menlung La. Back in London, after reviewing the data he had gathered, he concluded that the optimum rate for a climber ascending at high altitude was 4 litres per minute. On the descent sets could be run at a lower rate of 2 litres per minute, and at night a rate of 1 litre per minute made a real difference to a climber's ability to sleep.

The 1953 team was equipped with two types of oxygen set. The majority were of the traditional open-circuit design but they also brought some experimental 'closed-circuit' sets designed and built by the British climber Tom Bourdillon and his father Robert.

Climbers wearing a traditional open-circuit set breathed in a mixture of ambient and artificial oxygen. When they breathed out, their exhalations went straight into the atmosphere. Closed-circuit sets used many of the same components as the open-circuit, but their underlying premise was fundamentally different. Climbers wore tight masks that excluded the ambient air and enabled them to breathe pure oxygen from their cylinder. When they breathed out, their exhalations were filtered through a soda lime canister, which broke down the exhaled carbon dioxide and partially recycled it as oxygen. Closed-circuit sets operated at a much higher pressure and used less oxygen, allowing climbers to move faster and further.

But there were downsides: closed-circuit sets were heavy and climbers had to carry spare soda lime canisters as well as spare oxygen cylinders. The chemical processes involved in recycling the carbon dioxide, generated a lot of heat, which could be very unpleasant lower down the mountain. Their tight fitting masks made it impossible to communicate. All in all the closed-circuit sets were more complicated devices, with more valves, more separate elements and more to go wrong.

In 1953 the expedition leader John Hunt decided to try the closed-circuit set on the first attempt, but he opted for the simpler, open-circuit sets for the second. As history shows, it was a wise move.

stages the men's oxygen sets broke down, leaving them feeling very exposed. Erecting their tents in a ferocious gale on the South Col was an ordeal none of them ever forgot. They were so exhausted that they postponed the first attempt until 26 May and spent a rest day preparing their equipment.

For this first attempt Evans and Bourdillon were planning to use the closed-circuit sets that Tom Bourdillon and his father Robert had designed. So far the sets had not performed well, but there was general agreement that they improved with altitude. The task was to climb all the way from the South Col to the summit and back in a single day. Ascending and descending approximately 900 metres (3,000 feet) would not be easy, but Tom Bourdillon was confident that they could succeed. At the very least they would bring back valuable intelligence for the second attempt.

The morning of 26 May began inauspiciously. It took almost two hours to repair a broken valve on Charles Evans's oxygen set. When they finally got away neither man held out too much hope, but as they climbed higher they began to feel the benefits of the closed-circuit set more and more. After passing the skeletal remains of Lambert and Tenzing's tent from 1952 on the Southeast Ridge, they stopped to change oxygen bottles and soda lime canisters. It was a tricky operation but it seemed to go well.

Then after a few minutes, Charles Evans noticed that his oxygen was not flowing properly. Soon it was unbearable. They stopped, but when Tom Bourdillon looked over Charles's set he could find nothing obviously wrong. The damage, it turned out, was to the inside of Charles Evans's soda lime canister. This was a dreadful blow – the first time they had encountered such a problem on the expedition. Amazingly,

South Summit Charles Evans at the South Summit of Everest on 26 May 1953. Problems with his oxygen set probably cost Evans and his partner Tom Bourdillon the final prize of the mountain's main summit.

EVEREST ASCENT
1953

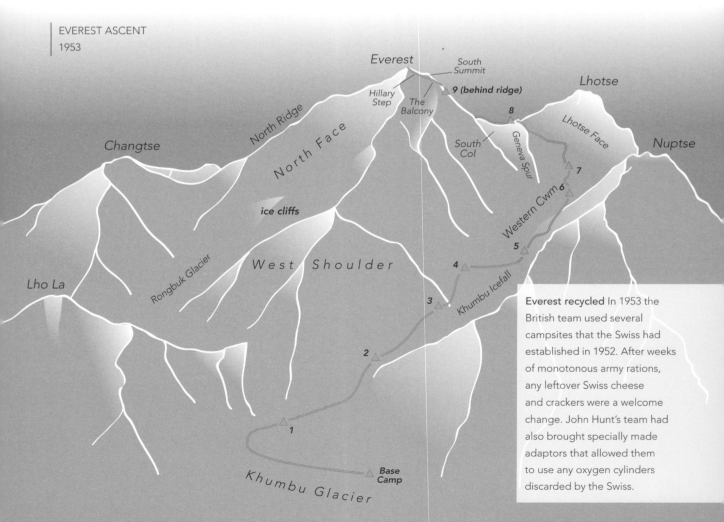

Everest

South Summit

9 (behind ridge)

Lhotse

Hillary Step

The Balcony

8

North Ridge

North Face

South Col

Geneva Spur

Lhotse Face

Nuptse

Changtse

Western Cwm

7

6

ice cliffs

5

Rongbuk Glacier

West Shoulder

4

Khumbu Icefall

3

Lho La

2

1

Base Camp

Khumbu Glacier

Everest recycled In 1953 the British team used several campsites that the Swiss had established in 1952. After weeks of monotonous army rations, any leftover Swiss cheese and crackers were a welcome change. John Hunt's team had also brought specially made adaptors that allowed them to use any oxygen cylinders discarded by the Swiss.

they carried on with Bourdillon in the lead and Charles Evans doing the best that he could behind him.

At around 1.00 p.m. Evans and Bourdillon were spotted, from the South Col below, just cresting the prominent pinnacle on the Southeast Ridge known as the South Summit. The Sherpas let out a huge whoop, thinking that the two men had actually reached the summit itself, but in fact there were still about 90 vertical metres (300 feet) to go.

High on the South Summit, Bourdillon and Evans stopped to take photographs and suck a handful of boiled sweets. As they posed for each other's cameras, they wondered what to do next. By Charles Evans's reckoning they had just enough oxygen to reach the top, but not enough for the return journey.

Tom wasn't so sure. While Charles Evans's oxygen set had been malfunctioning for the last hour, his had worked perfectly. Could he go on alone? This was his third trip to the Himalaya, his second to Everest. He was just a few hundred feet away from the greatest prize in mountaineering.

The two men could not agree but 8,748 metres (28,700 feet) on Everest was no place for a debate. Charles warned Tom that if he continued, he would never see his wife Jennifer again. Tom continued to do his sums. He wanted this to be a rational argument, not an emotional one. He had talked to Jennifer about the risks of climbing. She understood the dangers. There was a big difference, though, between taking a calculated risk and being reckless.

He walked along the ridge to get a better look at the remaining slope. Then he turned around. The first attempt was over – the nightmare was just beginning. Both

Final days Charles Evans and Tom Bourdillon shown on 26 May after their descent from the South Summit (opposite, top left). While Evans and Bourdillon made their attemp, Hunt and Da Namgyal pushed their way up the Southeast Ridge to establish a supply dump (at 8,350 metres/27,395 feet) for Hillary and Tenzing. Hunt is shown enjoying a cup of tea after his return to the South Col (opposite, top right). Hillary and Tenzing (below) are shown at 8,321 metres (27,300 feet) on the Southeast Ridge at around midday on 28 May, on their way up to their final camp.

men stumbled repeatedly on the descent. Whenever one would pull the other off, he would apologize profusely to his partner. Later they joked that they had 'yo-yoed' their way down the Southeast Ridge, but the risks were very real.

On the South Col the other members were getting very anxious. Cloud covered the Southeast Ridge but occasionally it parted for long enough to enable George Lowe to get a glimpse of the descending climbers. He had no way of knowing if the first attempt had succeeded or failed, but he was very worried about the descent. Then, finally, at 3.30 p.m., Tom and Charles appeared on the South Col. Ed Hillary later wrote that when he went out to greet them, they looked like creatures from another planet, covered from head to foot in icicles.

The following day, they had to go down. Tom Bourdillon was in such poor shape that John Hunt reluctantly left his post on the South Col in order to escort him. Not that Hunt was in a very good state himself. On the previous day, while Tom and Charles were making the first attempt, he and one Sherpa, Da Namgyal, had exhausted themselves carrying up the first batch of supplies for Hillary and Tenzing's top camp.

The second attempt

For their attempt Hillary and Tenzing were equipped with the old-fashioned open-circuit oxygen sets. Because open-circuit sets used more oxygen, it would have been impossible to ascend from the South Col to the summit in just one day. Instead, on 28 May Hillary and Tenzing climbed up to an intermediate camp at 8,425 metres (27,640 feet), assisted by George Lowe, Alfred Gregory and Ang Nyima.

They had a rough night, snatching bouts of sleep in two-hour bursts, lying next to each other on an uncomfortable ledge hacked into the slope. The following

Moment of triumph Tenzing Norgay jubilantly waves his ice-axe after he and Edmund Hillary reached the summit of Everest at 11.30 a.m. on 29 May (opposite). Tenzing had attached to his axe the flags of the United Nations, Nepal, the United Kingdom and India. Although Hillary took several photographs of Tenzing, Hillary did not ask Tenzing to take any of him on the summit. The next day (above) they enjoy a mug of tea at Camp 4, where most of the rest of the expedition had been anxiously awaiting news of their success of failure.

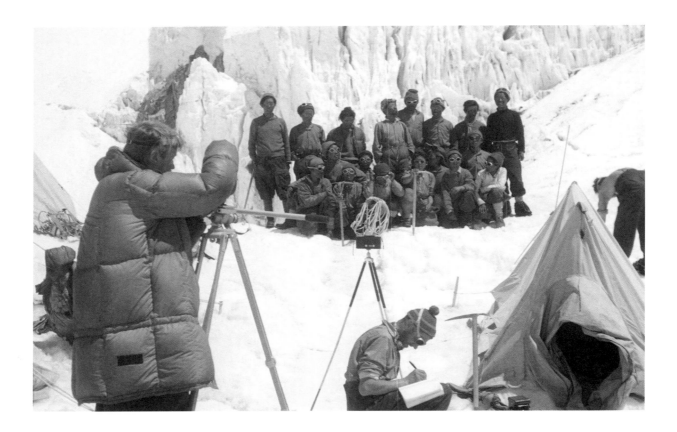

Snow show Tom Stobart
uses a cine camera to film
the Sherpas returning to
Camp 4 from the higher
camps after the summiting.

morning started badly. Ed Hillary's boots were frozen so hard that he had to roast them over a primus stove before he could start. On the positive side, the weather was clear and they were able to get away early.

Like Tom Bourdillon before him, Ed Hillary continually calculated and recalculated how much oxygen he and Tenzing had left as they climbed up the Southeast Ridge. Griffith Pugh had recommended a minimum of 4 litres per minute for climbing, but by Ed's reckoning they just didn't have enough, so they made do with 3 litres. The most dangerous moments came below the South Summit. Whereas Bourdillon and Evans had reached it via a rocky slope, Hillary and Tenzing opted for a different route through heavy drifts of snow. At any moment it felt as if it might avalanche and send them flying thousands of feet down to the glacier below.

Their luck held and they arrived on the South Summit at 9.00 a.m., four hours earlier than Bourdillon and Evans. After a brief pause, they carried on up, having changed their first bottle of oxygen. In front of them lay the final 90 metres (300 feet) of ridge – and Everest's final hurdle: a rock step just a few dozen feet below the summit. They reached it 45 minutes later.

To the left there was a difficult-looking slope about 12 metres (40 feet) high; to the right there was a dangerous looking cornice, hanging down over the Kangshung Face into Tibet. Neither option looked climbable. Ed Hillary took out his camera and began photographing the scene. If this really was the end of their ascent, at least he wanted to bring back the photographs that would prove that they had gotten further than Bourdillon and Evans.

Then he had another look and noticed a small chimney that had formed between the rock face and the cornice. It was just wide enough for him to squeeze into. But would it hold? As Tenzing paid out the rope, Ed Hillary wriggled his way up,

TELLING THE EVEREST STORY

The Everest 1953 expedition received far more coverage in the press and media than any other of the period. Considering that it is the highest mountain in the world – the so-called 'Third Pole' – that was not surprising, but it is also testament to the massive effort that went into covering the story.

Unlike the expeditions of the 1930s, which relied on the leader to provide dispatches, the 1953 expedition had a journalist from *The Times*, James Morris, embedded within the team. He was partnered by a second reporter, Arthur Hutchinson, whose job was to get James Morris's reports back to London as safely and quickly as possible. John Hunt, the expedition leader, was still required to send back dispatches but as the expedition progressed, Morris was responsible for more and more of the coverage.

Under a deal struck by the expedition's organizers, *The Times* had the exclusive right to cover expedition news. It had plenty of competitors, however, both from rival British papers and the local Indian and Nepalese press. In order to keep their dispatches secure, Morris and Hutchinson devised an elaborate code system, substituting words and phrases for members of the team and parts of the mountain.

Expedition dispatches were carried from Everest to Kathmandu by runners. At the outset James Morris did enquire about bringing a radio transmitter but the Nepalese government would not permit it. He was very aware that his runners might be 'knobbled' by the opposition but this never happened. For his final message, announcing the success or failure of the expedition, he opted for a more direct route – sending it to the British embassy from a police radio station at Namche Bazar. Not wanting to send a message that was very obviously in code, for fear that it might offend the staff at the radio station and alert his rivals that something important was happening, Morris came up with a special code – one that would produce a feasible, legitimate-looking message, but which in fact was also encrypted.

On 30 May, when Hillary and Tenzing came down after the first ascent, Morris was lucky enough to be at Advance Base. After a brief interview, he dashed down the Khumbu Icefall with Mike Westmacott, the youngest British climber, and hammered out a radio message and a longer dispatch to be carried by hand all the way to Kathmandu. Waiting runners took these off early on the following day. It was 31 May and Morris realized that there was a very slim chance of getting the news back to England by the Coronation on 2 June.

The coded message travelled from Everest base camp to Namche Bazar, from Namche to the radio station at the Indian embassy in Kathmandu, and finally from there to the office of the British ambassador, Christopher Summerhayes.

The message read: 'Snow conditions bad stop hence expedition abandoned advance base on 29th stop and awaiting improvement being all well!'

But was decoded as: 'Everest climbed on 29 May by Hillary and Tenzing. All well!'

In his excitement, however, Summerhayes misread his cipher sheet and would have sent off a telegram announcing that Tom Bourdillon and Tenzing had made the first ascent, if he hadn't double-checked.

Summerhayes in turn had the message radioed back to London on the afternoon of 1 June. Going from east to west, the time difference was in Britain's favour. After passing through the Foreign Office, the message arrived at *The Times* just in time for the 4.00 p.m. editorial conference. The following day's paper was quickly re-set and an editorial written in which the British triumph on Everest was compared to the achievements of Francis Drake in the reign of the first Queen Elizabeth. *The Times* carried a very small headline in the top right-hand corner of its front page, but other British newspapers were much more effusive – the *Daily Express* ran a huge banner headline all the way across its front page: 'All this and Everest too!'

Most Western papers ran with the theme of a rightful British victory, but there was another side to the press coverage. In India and Nepal there had been resentment from the beginning at *The Times*' monopoly on Everest news. At the end, many chose to tell the story very differently. Instead of a British victory it was played as Tenzing's triumph. According to many local reports, he had guided Hillary to the summit, and according to some he had dragged his partner to the top.

Inevitably the newspaper circulation war created friction and for a period Tenzing was estranged from the others members of the British team. Today, James Morris's timely report is regarded as one of the great scoops of the twentieth century.

Hailing the heroes Although *The Times* had an exclusive deal with the expedition's organizers and broke the news of the first ascent, other newspapers gave extensive coverage to the achievement, such as this *News Chronicle* front page (above), which trumpets the "crowning glory" – an apt metaphor, as news reached London on the day of Queen Elizabeth II's Coronation. The climbers themselves were feted locally and here (opposite) Hillary, Hunt and Tenzing are garlanded with flowers given to them by well-wishers at Banepa, near Kathmandu, Nepal.

digging his cramponed heels into the ice behind him. At any moment the cornice might have broken off and sent him flying, but in the end it held and he reached the top.

He quickly brought Tenzing up and the two men carried on up the final ridge to the summit. Or so they thought. The ridge went on and on, bump following bump, but with no end in sight. Then finally they reached a point where the slope began to decline, and they could see the Tibetan plains receding into the distance. Ed Hillary cut a line of steps up the final hump and they stepped onto the roof of the world.

It was 11.30 a.m. The sky was clear and the view was amazing. They risked turning their oxygen off and found that if they didn't move too much they didn't feel too bad. Ed Hillary took several photographs of Tenzing, standing proudly on the summit, holding his ice-axe aloft, streaming with flags. Then he took photographs looking down on all four faces of Everest, before turning his camera on Makalu. Tenzing was able to see the two most sacred sites for Sherpas: the Rongbuk monastery on the Tibetan side and the Thyangboche monastery on the Nepalese side. He scraped a hole in the snow and buried some small offering to the gods: some sweets and a pencil, given to him by his daughter. Seeing this reminded Ed Hillary of a promise he had made to John Hunt. He took out a small crucifix, given to Hunt by a Benedictine monk, and buried it in the snow on the summit.

Then, after about ten minutes, they turned to descend.

At 4.00 p.m. George Lowe welcomed them onto the South Col with flasks of warm drinks and a relieved smile. He was so excited that he didn't even film their arrival. There was no way to communicate directly with John Hunt down at Advance Base, but Wilfrid Noyce, who had come up to the South Col for a second time to help Hilary and Tenzing down, had agreed to attempt a visual signal. He would take two sleeping bags and arrange them into a T-shape if Hillary and Tenzing had reached the top, lay two bags side by side if they had only got as far as the South Summit or put down a single bag if they had achieved nothing.

Wilfrid Noyce and Pasang Phutar dutifully marched off to the edge of the South Col and lay down in the snow on top of their sleeping bags, arranged appropriately, but it was far too cloudy for them to be seen from Advance Base. After shivering for ten minutes in the wind, the two men retreated, leaving John Hunt none the wiser.

It wasn't until the following morning that Hillary and Tenzing made their way down the Lhotse Face and finally met their leader just above Advance Base. They gave nothing away until the last possible moment. Then suddenly George Lowe smiled and raised his hand – and as John Hunt later described it, for a few moments they all went mad. The relief was immense: there would be no third attempt this season; they would not have to return after the monsoon; finally, they could all go home.

Bringing Everest home

While everyone else was celebrating, James Morris, the correspondent from *The Times*, rushed down the icefall with Mike Westmacott. The following morning a runner left base camp with a brief message to be sent by radio from the nearest town, Namche Bazaar. There was a very slim chance that it might get back to London in time for the Coronation.

A few days later the whole team was down in base camp waiting for the porters who would carry their gear out, when to their amazement they heard over All India Radio that the news of their success had reached Britain and had been broadcast on Coronation Day morning.

As they walked out of the Solu Khumbu, they were greeted with mail runners carrying sacks full of telegrams, newspapers and the first letters of congratulation. John Hunt and Ed Hillary were given knighthoods and Tenzing promised future honours. However, when they reached Kathmandu, a controversy blew up that derailed the celebrations. The Indian and Nepalese press, who had felt excluded from the 'official' Everest story, proclaimed Tenzing the real conqueror of Everest, claiming that he had reached the summit ahead of Ed Hillary. To Tenzing, Hillary and the rest of the team, the whole issue of who was in front was irrelevant, but the press would not let it go. When the party returned to Kathmandu, Tenzing was repeatedly asked to confirm that he was in front. In fact, on the day, Ed Hillary was in the lead, with Tenzing belaying him on a rope a little way below, but

in order to dampen the controversy they released a joint statement saying that they had reached the summit 'almost together'.

The debate died down, but for a brief period it created friction between Tenzing and the other members of the team. When the official expedition book was released in November 1953, it stuck to the 'almost together' formula, though when Tenzing's autobiography was released two years later, it finally put and end to speculation and confirmed that Ed Hillary was a little ahead of his partner.

Back home, the members of the 1953 team were acclaimed as new British heroes. The coincidence of the first ascent and the Coronation created a huge amount of media interest. John Hunt's account of the expedition was a massive success and the team embarked on a long lecture programme that took them from Blackpool to the Belgian Congo. Hunt was always at pains to stress that it was a team effort, but almost inevitably most of the press was devoted to Ed Hillary, with John Hunt a close second.

The media coverage was so great that a large sum of money flowed in to the Himalayan Committee's coffers. This was channelled into a new body, The Mount Everest Foundation, set up to offer financial assistance to mountaineering expeditions. The first significant beneficiary was an expedition set up a couple of years later to Kangchenjunga, led by Charles Evans.

After the successful British ascent Everest was quiet for a couple of years. The planned French and American expeditions of 1954 and 1955 did not take place. Eric Shipton wrote in the press that he hoped that now that the Everest saga was over, the 'real' climbing could begin. John Hunt, too, wondered if attention would move elsewhere, but both men were wrong. Today the slopes of Everest are busier than ever. Since 1953 more than 3,000 climbers have reached the summit. Many of these climbers have come via the Southeast Ridge, the route pioneered in 1953, others have taken new routes. Everest's reputation for invincibility is long gone, but its allure remains strong.

8

The 'Golden Age' 1953–1960

Peter Gillman

O n 16 June 1953 the Austrian climber Hermann Buhl was sheltering from a storm in Camp 3 at 6,150 metres (20,177 feet) on Nanga Parbat. Wind was screaming across the high plateau as the tempest raged into its fifth day. Then Buhl and his companion Walter Frauenberger heard voices. A group of climbers appeared through the murk, bringing both supplies and dramatic news, as Buhl recorded: 'Everest had been climbed!' Buhl was astonished and impressed, as he had not expected the British to succeed. But the revelation that they had reached the summit a few weeks before was 'a great spur to our own endeavours'. Buhl, it is said, toasted the British triumph with a precious bottle of beer, a luxury rare so high on the mountain.

The news came at a crucial moment in the progress of the 1953 German expedition to Nanga Parbat. Approaching from the north, via Pakistan, it had set up its base camp at a height of 4,000 metres (13,123 feet) at the head of the Rakhiot Glacier on 23 May and established Camp 3, intended as the launch point for the summit on 11 June. Since then its plans had been disrupted by the atrocious weather, pinning the climbers down in their camps. As Buhl reported, the British success on Everest brought a timely motivational boost – but it was one that proved temporary. The weather worsened, restricting progress for another two weeks. The expedition began to fragment, creating a division between its supposed leaders in base camp and the climbers at the sharp end out on the mountain. That schism culminated in Buhl attempting the summit on his own and with little support from other expedition members. His bid would rank as one of the greatest endeavours in the history of mountaineering but it contributed to a bitter controversy that sadly tarnished Buhl's achievement.

Nanga Parbat – the German mountain

Just as the British made Everest their preserve, Nanga Parbat was the German mountain – although the first attempt to climb it was made by the eminent British mountaineer Albert Mummery, who died in an avalanche while prospecting for a route in 1895. German teams made four attempts on Nanga Parbat during the 1930s, costing the lives of 26 climbers and Sherpas. It might therefore appear that there was a redemptive quality to the German expedition in 1953. Certainly that was the impression given by its leader, Dr Karl-Maria Herrligkoffer, a 36-year-old physician. Herrligkoffer was the stepbrother of Wili Merkl, who had died on Nanga Parbat in 1934, and he avowed that an ascent would serve as Merkl's memorial.

Ice climb Expedition members at work in the Rakhiot Icefall, the formidable barrier above Camp 1 on Nanga Parbat, where they faced danger from unstable seracs and yawning crevasses. The expedition installed rope ladders on the trickiest sections to assist the Hunza porters in their load-carrying.

There was a quasi-mystical tone to Herrligkoffer's mission statements. Merkl 'rests forever in the bright light of the eternal snows of the mountain', he proclaimed. He invoked military metaphors to declare: 'It is Merkl who mobilises the German forces to mount a fresh assault on the mountain, in order that the death and pioneering work of the four heroes might not have been in vain.' The renowned Alpinist Reinhold Messner was not alone in noting the disturbing historical echoes of Herrligkoffer's call to action.

Controversy beset Herrligkoffer from the start. He was disowned by the German climbing establishment and heavily criticized in German newspapers. Messner later called him 'totally inexperienced yet a master of the arts of propaganda'. He had his admirers, among them the German-Swiss mountaineer Günther Dyhrenfurth, who praised Herrligkoffer's 'great feat' in organizing the expedition 'in the teeth of all opposition'. Herrligkoffer succeeded in finding sponsors and recruiting climbers for his team, including Peter Aschenbrenner, who had been on the 1932 and 1934 expeditions, and Hermann Buhl, the Austrian who was among the outstanding climbers of his generation (see box, page 130).

Herrligkoffer's greatest weakness was to combine a lack of mountaineering experience with an autocratic style that brooked no dissent. Unlike Hunt on Everest, who carried loads to the highest camp, Herrligkoffer led from the rear, spending much of the time in base camp and never going beyond Camp 3. He formally appointed the veteran Aschenbrenner as climbing leader but he, too, issued many of his instructions from base camp and, crucially, was marooned there as the climactic events of the expedition were played out.

Nanga Parbat This map of Nanga Parbat shows the scale of Hermann Buhl's feat. Camp 5 was sited at 6,900 metres (22,638 feet), a daunting 1,225 metres (4,019 feet) below the summit. It took Buhl, climbing entirely alone, 17 hours to cover the 3 kilometres (nearly 2 miles) from the camp to the summit on 3 July 1953 – and another 24 hours to return.

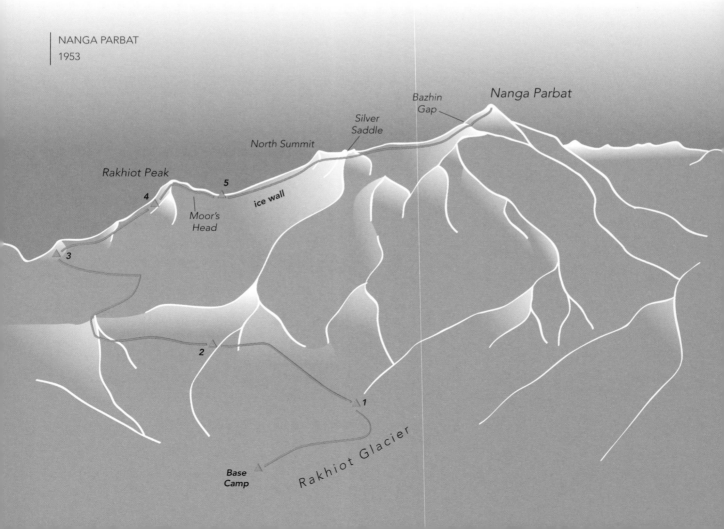

NANGA PARBAT
1953

Nanga Parbat

Bazhin Gap

Silver Saddle

North Summit

Rakhiot Peak

5

4

Moor's Head

ice wall

3

2

1

Base Camp

Rakhiot Glacier

The expedition had the great advantage of following the route established by the pre-war German teams to within 305 metres (1,000 feet) of the summit and set up Camp 3, nominated as the 'assault base', on schedule. Climbing between storms, the lead climbers pitched Camp 4 at the foot of Rakhiot Peak and pushed on to a feature known as the Moor's Head, the site for Camp 5. Then came a further spell of bad weather – relieved only by the news of the British success on Everest – and as the end of June approached Herrligkoffer appeared to lose his nerve. On 29 June he wrote that the weather continued to be bad and morale was proportionately low. He and Aschenbrenner decided to postpone the summit attempt: the lead climbers should return to base while Herrligkoffer devised a new plan of campaign. Aschenbrenner even announced that he wanted to go home.

On 30 June the climbers in Camp 3 emerged from their tents to find the storms were clearing. Buhl recorded that the weather was glorious; the Silbersattel (Silver Saddle), 'gateway to the summit, shone wonderfully above us again'. He and his colleagues were consequently baffled to receive, over the expedition's radio system, demands for them to return to base camp. They were offered a variety of reasons: they needed rest and recuperation; the barometer was falling, portending bad weather; Herrligkoffer wanted to reformulate his plan of campaign; and Aschenbrenner needed 'a proper send-off' as he set off home. Hans Ertl, one of Buhl's companions in Camp 3, responded that, apart from one man who was suffering from acute toothache, none of the climbers intended to come down. Ertl made several requests for support

In camp Expedition members relax for Hans Ertl's camera in Camp 3. From the left, Kuno Rainer, Hermann Buhl, Peter Aschenbrenner, Otto Kempter and Hermann Köllensperger.

(Following pages)
Mountain awe A section of the Diama Ridge, on the Diama, or North, Face of Nanga Parbat. The German expedition of 1953 climbed Nanga Parbat via the Rakhiot Face (see map, opposite), on the far side of the skyline ridge.

THE REMARKABLE HERMANN BUHL

Hermann Buhl's solo ascent of Nanga Parbat – one of the supreme achievements of mountaineering (he is pictured here after that climb) – was fuelled by remarkable qualities of determination, ambition and self-sufficiency. Buhl was born in Innsbruck, in the Austrian Tyrol, in 1924. His mother died when he was four and he spent several years in an orphanage before being cared for an aunt. Considered a frail child, he built his strength when he discovered climbing with the youth section of the Innsbruck Alpine Club. He was enlisted into the German Army in 1943 and after seeing action at Monte Cassino he spent time as a prisoner of war.

After the war Buhl racked up a formidable series of Alpine routes, including the first winter ascent of the Southwest Wall of the Marmolata in 1950, the first solo ascent of the Northeast Face of the Piz Badile in 1952 and an epic four-day ascent of the North Face of the Eiger in the same year, during which he and his partner, Sepp Jöchler, survived stonefall, storms and avalanches.

Despite losing toes to frostbite on Nanga Parbat, Buhl continued pushing Alpine standards, often climbing alone, in the Dolomites and on the Mont Blanc massif. In 1957 he and three colleagues made a daring Alpine-style first ascent of Broad Peak in the Karakoram. Three weeks later Buhl and Kurt Diemberger made an attempt on the Southeast Ridge of the neighbouring peak of Chogolisa, but they were forced to retreat by a storm when only 305 metres (1,000 feet) below the summit. During their descent, Buhl fell to his death through a cornice. Diemberger survived and searched for Buhl with other team members, but his body was never found.

from base camp. As Buhl noted, all were refused: 'That meant a head-on clash; and the clash strengthened our unity.'

The first day of July dawned perfectly, with a cloudless sky. Buhl recorded that he felt in top form – and yet base camp was still instructing the climbers to descend. 'Ertl began to doubt the sanity of the inmates of base camp,' Buhl added. An eight-man team, including three Hunza porters, set off for Camp 4. They reached it at midday and excavated the tents from the snow. Buhl and Ertl climbed another 180 metres or so (600 feet) before returning to Camp 4.

The weather was clear again on 2 July – and still the climbers received another call urging them to descend. This time Walter Frauenberger insisted that they were going for the summit and after half an hour's further argument base camp grudgingly offered its 'blessing' for success. Four climbers and three porters set off from Camp 4, intending to site Camp 5 as high as possible in readiness for a summit bid. But while Buhl, climbing out in front, headed for the Silver Saddle, the porters dumped their loads at a height of 6,900 metres (22,638 feet) – fully 1,225 metres (4,019 feet) below the summit, and with an extra 90 metres (300 feet) of ascent to overcome another dip in the ridge. It was a disturbingly low starting line for a summit bid and there should ideally have been at least one more camp en route, but Buhl concluded there was nothing more that could be done. Because there was only one tent, the two older climbers sportingly withdrew, leaving the attempt to Buhl and Otto Kempter. That night Buhl obsessively rehearsed the ascent route in his mind and was so daunted that he was unable to sleep. Yet he concluded that this was his best chance of making the summit: 'It would just *have* to be possible!'

Buhl set off at 2.30 a.m. on 3 July. Kempter, still in his sleeping bag, stirred as Buhl left the tent. Buhl said he would go ahead and break trail, expecting Kempter to catch him up. Climbing by moonlight, Buhl had to contend with deep snow, a fierce wind and bitter cold. Dawn brought an improvement and at 7.00 a.m. Buhl reached the Silver Saddle. He sat in the snow and took a swig from his flask of Coca tea – a supposedly invigorating beverage Ertl had brought from Bolivia. Ahead lay a mile-long plateau of snow, with Nanga Parbat's subsidiary summit beyond. Buhl had glimpsed Kempter below several times and reckoned he was at least an hour behind. Still believing that Kempter would eventually catch him up, Buhl resolved to press on.

Buhl's decision marked the beginning of an extraordinary ordeal. After the bitter pre-dawn cold, Buhl had to contend with intense heat radiating from the ice and snow. To lighten his load he abandoned his rucksack, stuffing his drinking flask, spare clothes and summit flags into his pockets and slinging his camera across his shoulders. As he crossed the plateau beneath the subsidiary summit, Buhl saw Kempter again and realized he had turned back. At 2.00 p.m. Buhl reached the Bazhin Gap, the notch below the main summit, where he had to lose 90 metres (300 feet) in height. Exhausted and racked by thirst and hunger, he collapsed on the snow. In desperation he swallowed two Pervitin tablets, an amphetamine used by German forces in the Second World War.

In his possibly deluded state, Buhl estimated he needed another hour to reach the crest of the Shoulder, the last feature on the ridge before the summit itself. He was horribly mistaken. He endured a gruelling five hours of climbing, much of it technically demanding, including a hair-raising traverse beneath an enormous gendarme with the Diamir Face yawning thousands of feet below. Finally, crawling on all fours, he reached the top of the Shoulder. His trial was still not over: he spent another hour picking his way among gullies and boulders until, to his joy and relief,

Going solo Buhl is shown (opposite, top) on the northeast flank of Nanga Parbat on 2 July, not long before he and three fellow climbers reached the site of Camp 5, and the day before he made his epic solo ascent. The ordeal of Buhl's gruelling 17-hour climb and his day-long descent is etched in his face in the photograph (opposite, bottom) taken shortly after his return.

there was only a short, easy-angled snow-slope. Shortly afterwards 'nothing went up further, anywhere... I was on the summit of Nanga Parbat'.

The ascent from Camp 5 had taken 17 hours. Buhl recorded that there was no victorious exaltation: 'I was absolutely all in.' He drove his ice-axe into the snow, tied the Tyrolean pennant to his ice-axe and took a photograph. In an epic image, Buhl's descent route along the ridge to Camp 5 is visible, with the peaks of the Hindu Kush and the Karakoram beyond. He replaced the pennant with the flag of Pakistan and took more photographs. The sky was cloudless but then the sun dipped below the horizon and it became bitterly cold. After half an hour on the summit, it was time to descend. Buhl left behind his ice-axe as proof of his ascent and headed down.

It took Buhl 24 hours to reach the safety of Camp 5. His descent was every bit as gruelling as his ascent. Having lost a crampon strap, he clawed his way down towards the Bazhin Gap using one crampon and two ski poles. He had hoped to reach the gap before nightfall, but was compelled to bivouac perched on a tiny ledge, clinging to his ski poles with one hand and to a tenuous hold with the other.

The night was mercifully still and at dawn Buhl continued his descent. Roasted anew by the radiated heat, desperately dehydrated and close to total exhaustion, he suffered from hallucinations, fancying that he could hear voices or was accompanied by another climber. He retrieved his rucksack in mid-afternoon and swallowed a glucose tablet mixed with snow. Gasping for breath, collapsing every few yards, he was spurred on by the sight of Camp 5 below. He stumbled towards the tents and fell into the arms of Ertl, croaking out the words: 'Yesterday was the finest day of my life.' Ertl's photograph, to which the term 'iconic' can for once be accurately applied, shows a man who appears to have aged 20 years, his face blotched and lined, lips barely apart as he struggled in vain to speak.

Three days later Buhl, limping from frostbite that was to cost him several toes, walked into base camp with his companions – meeting, as he told it, 'the coolest of receptions'. This accords with Herrligkoffer's account, which records only that Buhl was welcomed with garlands of flowers presented by the Hunza porters. Herrligkoffer further noted that Buhl had benefitted from 'almost miraculous good luck' with the weather. Later, Herrligkoffer was more forthright, dividing the expedition into two categories: those who had 'sacrificed ambition for communal success' and those who had refused to obey orders – namely Buhl, Ertl and Frauenberger. Reinhold Messner, admittedly no friend of Herrligkoffer, believed he knew the reason for his hostility towards Buhl: Herrligkoffer had dreamed of a collective ascent of Nanga Parbat that would expiate Merkl's death 19 years before. Buhl's solo triumph had violated the visionary spirit of brotherhood Herrligkoffer had invoked and failed to redeem Merkl's sacrifice.

There was a sordid aftermath that included claim and counter-claim in the German courts. After Herrligkoffer published the official account, Buhl retaliated with his own version, contained in *Nanga Parbat Pilgrimage*, prompting Herrligkoffer to sue on the grounds that Buhl had broken his expedition contract. In his account Buhl was defiant, insisting he had been justified to risk making a solo summit bid: 'I was entitled to do so and to say so.' Buhl remains the only climber to have made a solo first ascent of an 8,000-metre (26,246-foot) peak.

Herrligkoffer went back to Nanga Parbat seven times. In 1970 he led an expedition to the Rupal Face, during which Reinhold Messner and his brother Günter, followed by two other climbers, reached the summit. Günter died during his descent and that expedition also ended in bitter controversy and legal action, which flared up once more long after Herrligkoffer's death in 1991.

SEVEN SURVIVORS ON K2

One of the most dramatic episodes in Himalayan history was played out on K2 in 1953. Charles Houston, leader of the 1938 American expedition, returned with an eight-man party in June 1953. By the end of July all eight climbers were at Camp 8 at 7,711 metres (25,300 feet), a short distance below the shoulder of the Abruzzi Spur, and within two days' climb of the summit. But they were trapped by a storm and one of the climbers, 27-year-old geologist Art Gilkey, collapsed in the snow. He was diagnosed with thrombophlebitis, a potentially fatal clotting of the blood. Abandoning their summit attempt, the team embarked on a desperate effort to lower Gilkey down the mountain strapped to an improvised stretcher. In mid-afternoon on 10 August, with the storm still raging, they were strung across the ice near Camp 7 when one climber slipped, dragging five others with him. Their lives were saved when the last man standing, Pete Schoening, held them all on an ice-axe belay. Several climbers were injured, and as they clawed their way to Camp 7 they left Gilkey anchored to the slope some 46 metres (150 feet) away. When they returned in the morning they were horrified to see that Gilkey had disappeared. At first they presumed that he had been swept away by an avalanche. Some came to believe that he had cast himself loose in an act of self-sacrifice, recalling Captain Oates in the Antarctic who walked out into a storm in the hope of boosting his colleagues' chance of survival. Oates's heroism proved in vain; on K2 the seven survivors reached the safety of base camp five days later.

The Italians' bewitching and daunting K2

After the French, British and Germans had climbed 'their' 8,000-metre (26,246-foot) peaks, it was the Italians' turn to enter the fray. Their target was K2, rated by climbers as bewitchingly beautiful and dauntingly difficult, with an epic back-story to rival that of Nanga Parbat. The similarities with the German venture did not end there; even more than in 1953, the Italian expedition of 1954 gave rise to prolonged controversy, again involving one of the most accomplished Alpinists of the day. It raged for more than 50 years and finally brought vindication for Walter Bonatti, who proved to have been traduced beyond reason, even though his near-superhuman feats proved essential to the expedition's success.

Just as Everest was the British mountain and Nanga Parbat the German one, Italians asserted ownership of K2. However, there was less justice in their claim because American expeditions had come closest to climbing the mountain before the Italians. It was the Duke of Abruzzi, the Italian aristocrat, who identified the Southeast Ridge as the most likely path to the summit, and now it is usually referred to as the Abruzzi Spur. He led an expedition in 1909 that was also notable for the photographs taken by the peerless Vittorio Sella. An Italian expedition explored the peak and undertook scientific research in 1929, though without attempting to reach the summit. Americans made their three attempts in 1938, 1939 and 1953, coming to within about 245 vertical metres (just over 800 feet) of the summit in 1939.

When the Italians mounted their expedition in 1954 it was with a sense of national purpose that — as with the Germans on Nanga Parbat — may also have had a redemptive quality following the Second World War. The leader was Ardito Desio, a geographer and geologist who had taken part in the Italian expedition of 1929. In a further echo of the 1953 Nanga Parbat expedition, he was not a climber. He nonetheless proposed that his leadership would be absolute: the expedition would be organized 'along military lines', which included pledging to obey the leader's

Bewitching peak K2 from Concordia, the junction of the Baltoro and Godwin-Austen glaciers on the approach from the south. The 1954 Italian route took the Abruzzi Spur, or Ridge, to the crest of the right-hand skyline, which it then followed to the summit. In 1939 Wiessner's American expedition had come to within around 245 metres (800 feet) of the summit. The Italian summit team found the initial section above that high point immensely difficult but finally they emerged on to easier ground – with 'nothing but blue sky' above them.

orders. During the expedition he issued communiqués invoking nationalist honour – if the climbers succeeded 'the entire world will hail you as champions of your race and long after you are dead'. The British writer and mountaineer Jim Curran noted: 'Mussolini himself could not have put it any better.'

Desio's approach clearly found favour in Italy. The expedition was planned on a formidable scale, requiring 500 porters to carry 13 tons of supplies, including 230 oxygen cylinders, to base camp. The cost was equally daunting: 100 million lira (or around £57,000 – five times the cost of the American expedition the previous year). The Italian Alpine Club, the Italian Olympic Committee and the government-backed National Council for Research all supported Desio.

Desio also showed his ruthlessness in disposing of possible challenges to his authority, or his share of the limelight, when he selected his team. In 1953 Desio made a reconnaissance trip to Pakistan accompanied by Ricardo Cassin, Italy's foremost climber, who had a series of outstanding Alpine ascents to his name. Desio laid down a marker during the trip by flying from one venue to another, leaving Cassin to follow by train. In 1954 Cassin, then aged 45, remained the obvious choice for climbing leader but Desio contrived to have him excluded on medical grounds. The widespread assumption is that Desio did not want a figure of Cassin's eminence on the trip; Cassin said later that Desio wanted him excluded because he was 'a communist'. (Cassin had fought for the Italian partisans against German occupying troops towards the end of Second World War.)

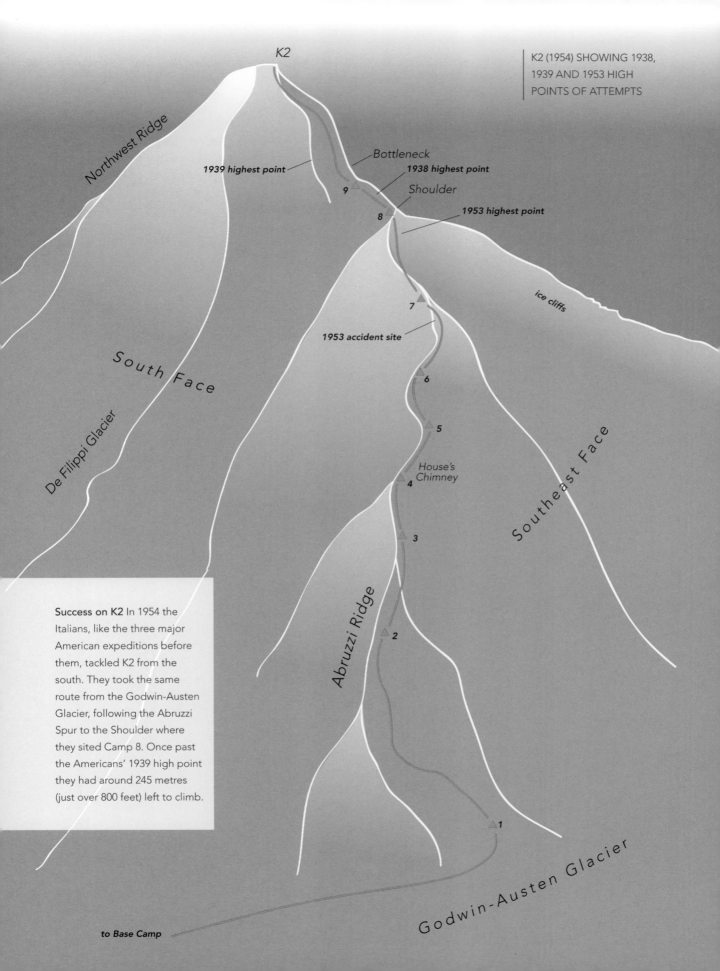

K2

Northwest Ridge

Bottleneck

1939 highest point

1938 highest point

9

Shoulder

8

1953 highest point

ice cliffs

South Face

7

1953 accident site

6

De Filippi Glacier

5

House's Chimney

4

Southeast Face

3

Abruzzi Ridge

2

Success on K2 In 1954 the Italians, like the three major American expeditions before them, tackled K2 from the south. They took the same route from the Godwin-Austen Glacier, following the Abruzzi Spur to the Shoulder where they sited Camp 8. Once past the Americans' 1939 high point they had around 245 metres (just over 800 feet) left to climb.

1

to Base Camp

Godwin-Austen Glacier

In Cassin's place Desio appointed Achille Compagnoni, a ski instructor and professional guide. Among the ten-man team the potential star was Walter Bonatti, who at the age of 24 had posted a series of European climbs that set new standards of technical skill and audacity, including the first winter ascent of the Cima Ovest di Lavaredo in the Dolomites.

The mammoth expedition took a month to travel from Skardu and consolidate its base camp on the upper Godwin-Austen Glacier — a massive encampment, complete with a statue of the Madonna, which Desio dubbed 'the New Italopolis of K2'. Desio reckoned that the expedition was two weeks ahead of what the American team in 1953 had achieved — and he had the advantage of briefings and photographs that the American climbers had sportingly provided. The Italians were also secure in the knowledge that in 1939 the Americans had climbed to within about 245 metres (just over 800 feet) of the summit, enabling them to follow the Americans' tried and tested route. They suffered a setback when an Italian climber died at Camp 2, probably from a pulmonary oedema. They climbed House's Chimney, the most testing part of the Abruzzi Spur, on 30 June and a winch was installed to haul loads to Camp 5 at 6,685 metres (21,932 feet). But for all Desio's planning and exhortations, little of the oxygen equipment was reaching the highest camps. It was not until 28 July that Camp 8 was set up on the Shoulder, the broad hump above the Abruzzi Spur — so far behind schedule that Desio considered abandoning the attempt and returning with a new set of climbers after the monsoon.

Just as on Nanga Parbat, the lead climbers began to call the shots. There was now a select group at or above Camp 7, including Bonatti and Compagnoni, to whom Desio had assigned responsibility for deciding the summit team. Compagnoni selected himself but overlooked Bonatti in favour of Lino Lacedelli, a 29-year-old Alpine guide and ski instructor. Bonatti, it should be said, was suffering a stomach complaint but he was still assigned a key role ferrying the oxygen equipment that Compagnoni and Lacedelli needed for their attempt.

On 30 July the pair set off from Camp 8, heading for a feature known as the Bottleneck where they intended to site Camp 9. Bonatti and a second climber, Pino Gallotti, descended to fetch oxygen cylinders from a cache near Camp 7. There they linked up with three other climbers and all five, laden with cylinders, returned to Camp 8. After two were unable to go further, the remaining three — Bonatti, Erich Abram and Mahdi, a Hunza porter — headed for the rendezvous.

Lacedelli and Compagnoni had told Bonatti that they would site Camp 9 on a snow shoulder beside the Bottleneck. As Bonatti approached the shoulder, he was astonished to see no tent at the expected location. He called out and heard the

Summit standard Achille Compagnoni photographed by Lino Lacedelli, on the summit of K2. Beside him is the ice-axe that the two climbers decorated with the flags of Italy, Pakistan and the Italian Alpine Club. Both men suffered frostbite to their hands, caused in part by removing their gloves to take photographs.

shouted reply: 'Follow the tracks!' At 6.30 p.m. Abram, fearing frostbite, dumped his cylinders and headed back to Camp 8, leaving Bonatti and Mahdi to continue their search as darkness enveloped the mountain. They finally came to a halt and decided to try to excavate a bivouac site. Then Bonatti saw a light higher up and heard another call, this time instructing him to deposit the oxygen and descend. Bonatti called back, urging Compagnoni and Lacedelli to come down and guide them to their tent. There was no reply.

It was that sequence of events, as related by Bonatti, which lay at the core of the bitter controversy that was to engulf the expedition, with claim and counter-claim played out in the media and the courts until the truth was laid bare more than 50 years on. That night Bonatti and Mahdi faced the ordeal of an open bivouac, without a tent or protective clothing. When dawn came they were able to descend; Bonatti was physically unscathed, but Mahdi had suffered severe frostbite. Following amputations to his feet and hands, he was never able to climb again.

Up at Camp 9, around 500 metres (1,640 feet) below the summit, Compagnoni and Lacedelli prepared for their attempt. They first descended to retrieve the oxygen left by Bonatti and Mahdi – and were astounded, they later related, to see Bonatti making his descent, having assumed that he and Mahdi had returned to Camp 8 the previous night. Equipped with the fresh oxygen, they climbed the rocks beside the Bottleneck and had to make a long leftwards traverse below a band of unstable seracs, culminating in a steep 15-metre (49-foot) snow-slope that took an hour to climb. Around this time they passed the high point reached by the Americans in 1939 and finally emerged on easier ground. Shortly before 6.00 p.m. the slope levelled out and they were at the summit.

A bitter experience The 1954 Italian K2 expedition was assailed by strong winds and bitter cold. In the photograph, a group of climbers has just returned to one of the high camps. Lino Lacedelli (centre), one of the successful summit pair, is flanked by Ubaldo Rey (left) and Sergio Liotto (right).

WALTER BONATTI, A SUPREME ALPINIST

Walter Bonatti, the true hero of the Italians' K2 ascent (pictured above, left, with Lacedelli), even though he did not go to the summit, was born in Bergamo, Italy, in 1930. His family was left nearly destitute by the Second World War and Bonatti sought respite through walking and climbing in the limestone peaks of the Grigna massif. Exceptionally talented and ambitious, he soon rose to the fore of Italian Alpinism, and at 19 he and three companions made the fourth ascent of the Walker Spur on the Grandes Jorasses, a totemic route first climbed by the great Riccardo Cassin.

In February 1953 Bonatti and Carlo Mauri made the first winter ascent of the North Face of the Cima Ovest di Lavaredo, cementing his reputation in the front line of the sport and making him a natural pick for the K2 venture.

In its traumatic aftermath, Bonatti was so disenchanted that he vowed not to join a major expedition again, although he and Mauri made the first ascent of Gasherbrum IV in 1958. In 1955 Bonatti had made a sensational climb in the Alps, a five-day solo ascent of the Southwest Pillar of the Dru that is still considered one of the masterpieces of modern Alpinism. He made further important ascents in the Alps and other ranges before retiring from major climbing in 1965, when he was 35. He pursued a distinguished career as a photo-journalist for the next 20 years and died, aged 81, in 2011.

'It was a very simple scene,' ran the official account credited to Compagnoni and Lacedelli. 'Yet as we surveyed it we were assailed by an indescribable tumult of emotions.' The two men embraced, then flung themselves onto the snow in order to remove their oxygen masks. They tied the flags of Italy, Pakistan and the Italian Alpine Club to an ice-axe for the summit photographs. Compagnoni lost a glove, snatched by the wind, and Lacedelli gave him one of his own. After half an hour they set off on their descent, having taken one more look at the summit: '... that windswept solitude where it would probably be true to say that we had both just experienced the greatest moment of our lives.' Even that seemingly straightforward account of reaching the summit was later to add fuel to the controversy.

Compagnoni and Lacedelli endured an epic descent to Camp 8, surviving several falls before stumbling into their colleagues' arms at 11.00 p.m. Both had suffered frostbite, and as their hands began to thaw they endured 'another night of suffering, anxiety and bitter cold'. Meanwhile, technical difficulties with the expedition radios had prevented Desio from making contact with the summit teams, and it was not until the evening of 1 August that two climbers arrived with the news of success. 'The tears streamed from our eyes as we embraced the two men,' Desio recorded. The next day Compagnoni and Lacedelli reached base camp 'utterly exhausted and in desperate need of sleep'.

Desio wasted no time in dispatching telegrams to Italy to broadcast news of the expedition's success. He penned an address to the expedition members: 'By your efforts you have won great glory for your native land, whose name is on the lips of men throughout the world...Today all Italians are rising to acclaim you as worthy champions of your race.' Compagnoni and Lacedelli were acclaimed as national heroes and the whole team was granted an audience with Pope Pius XII.

If the two summit climbers endured a bitter night at Camp 8, bitter is also the most suitable term to describe the aftermath. When Desio's official account appeared, Bonatti felt he had been given short shrift. Mahdi, whose efforts had been equally vital in ensuring the expedition's success, and whose loss had been far greater, was all but written out of the expedition history. As he pondered events, Bonatti's fundamental suspicion was that Compagnoni and Lacedelli had pitched Camp 9 higher than they had agreed precisely so that he would not be able to find it and rule out any possibility that he could join the summit party. It was a remarkable suggestion, implying that Compagnoni and Lacedelli had placed him and Mahdi in mortal danger through their unscrupulous behaviour. Yet it was eventually proved that Bonatti was right.

After the expedition, there were no fewer than four lawsuits arising from the disputes over what had happened on the mountain. In the most sensational, Bonatti sued over extraordinary allegations emanating from Compagnoni that Bonatti had tried to race him and Lacedelli to the summit, had purloined some of the oxygen for himself, and had deserted Mahdi. In 1966 Bonatti won the case and was vindicated on all counts.

The rows rumbled on until 2004 when Lacedelli broke ranks with Compagnoni and gave his own account. Lacedelli revealed that it was Compagnoni who wrote the official summit account, even though it had been credited to both men. Lacedelli made damning remarks about Desio, saying that he was incompetent and authoritarian, and loathed by most of the climbers. As for Compagnoni, Lacedelli described him as a sycophant whose account of events high on the mountain had been false in key respects. Most important of all, Lacedelli confirmed Bonatti's worst suspicions. Compagnoni had indeed been determined that Bonatti should not take part in the summit attempt and for that reason had sited Camp 9 far higher than he had promised – and against the wishes of Lacedelli, who considered it 'a most dangerous and stupid position'.

There were other crucial falsehoods in Compagnoni's account, ranging from the time they left Camp 9 to where and when they ran out of oxygen – all designed, as Lacedelli saw it, to buttress the case against Bonatti and blacken his reputation. Lacedelli went so far as to assert that Compagnoni and Desio had formulated a plot to dishonour Bonatti, who had been served up as a 'sacrificial goat'.

For Bonatti and his supporters, Lacedelli's revelations rang entirely true. Compagnoni did his best to respond in a blustering interview of his own. But the emergence of other crucial details concerning the oxygen equipment further undermined Compagnoni's account. There was a poignant aftermath that showed the wounds were still festering. In 2004 Bonatti was awarded the Grand Cross of the Knights of Italy, the country's highest civilian honour. But after discovering that Compagnoni was to receive the decoration, Bonatti sent his back.

Bonatti was finally entirely vindicated in 2008, when the Italian Alpine Club declared that it fully accepted his version of events (an earlier declaration by the Italian Alpine Club in 2004 had been more equivocal). 'This historic truth', the club stated, 'restores full dignity and respect to the memory of a great mountaineering achievement.' The Italian Alpine Club may have been optimistic in contending that the scars of the controversy would be healed so easily. But Bonatti himself declared: 'Complete historic truth and all dignity have been restored to this Italian achievement and, after 53 years, have now awakened once more in our country a sense of national pride and joy.'

Everest sequel – the British on Kangchenjunga

In June 1953, three weeks after the expedition he led had climbed Mount Everest, John Hunt was asked at a press conference in India to name mountaineering's next goal. 'Kangchenjunga,' he replied.

Hunt amplified his answer in unequivocal terms. 'Those who first climb Kangchenjunga will achieve the greatest feat in mountaineering,' he said. 'It is a mountain which combines not only the severe handicaps of wind, weather and very high altitude, but technical climbing problems and objective dangers of an order even higher than those we encountered on Everest.'

It might seem surprising that Hunt should emphasize the dangers of Kangchenjunga in comparison with his team's achievements on Everest. But Hunt knew more about Kangchenjunga than he was letting on. In 1937 he and his wife had failed in an attempt to reach the crest of its North Ridge from the Sikkim side. British climbers had returned to the mountain after the war and if the Swiss had succeeded in climbing Everest in 1952 the British had planned to attempt Kangchenjunga as a consolation prize. Now that Everest had been climbed, Kangchenjunga remained a highly desirable and challenging objective – all the more so since the Italian ascent of K2 meant that it was now the highest unclimbed peak in the world.

In 1954 a British reconnaissance team returned to Kangchenjunga. It delivered enough encouragement (see box, page 144) for Hunt to propose that the Alpine Club should send a full-size expedition in 1955. Hunt chaired the organizing committee, which included representatives of the Royal Geographical Society. The cost was £18,000 – modest by today's standards – and it was met from the proceeds of the 1953 Everest expedition, which was already providing a steady income from the expedition book and film, lectures and photographic rights.

The obvious choice for leader was Charles Evans, Hunt's deputy on Everest. Hunt had valued his calm, reasoned support and Evans had demonstrated that, like Hunt, he was prepared to go into the front line. In 1953 Evans had made the first summit attempt in partnership with Tom Bourdillon (see pages 115–119), leaving the South Col at 6.00 a.m. on 25 May, and becoming the first climbers to reach the South Summit. But because of the problems Evans was having with his oxygen set, he and Bourdillon reluctantly decided that they should return to the South Col.

Evans, a softly spoken Welshman, was to win unstinting praise from his 1955 colleagues, who considered him intelligent, of sound judgment and with a non-autocratic manner. George Band felt that Evans, a surgeon, was keen to form a group whose members would fit well together. As a leader, 'he wasn't one to shout things from the rooftops. He just got on with the job in a quiet sort of way'. Tony Streather commented: 'He would make a suggestion, and we would all get on and do it.'

Evans and expedition secretary Alf Bridge began their detailed planning in August 1954. With departure due in six months, the most urgent task was to recruit the team. Eight climbers were selected, with a wide range of experience between them. Band had taken part in the 1953 Everest expedition, albeit as its youngest member. Streather was a British Army officer who had been on K2 with an American team in 1953 and took part in the dramatic retreat from the Abruzzi Ridge, or Spur, which culminated in the death of Art Gilkey. Three other members had climbed previously in the Himalayas.

JOE BROWN – THE MANCHESTER MOUNTAINEER

Joe Brown, chosen to make the first summit attempt on Kangchenjunga with George Band, was a talismanic figure of British climbing. Born in 1930, into a working-class family in Manchester, he first climbed as a boy using a discarded washing line for a rope. Together with a group of friends, who included fellow Mancunian Don Whillans (like Brown, he worked in the building trade), he developed his skills on the gritstone edges of the Peak District, rapidly pushing standards to new levels. They moved on to Snowdonia, where Brown led a memorable series of new routes, including Cenotaph Corner and Cemetery Gates on Dinas Cromlech in the Llanberis Pass. In 1954 Brown and Whillans made their first trip to the Alps where they made the first ascent of the West Face of the Aiguille du Blaitière and the

third – and fastest at that time – of the West Face of the Dru, Brown's selection for Kangchenjunga (above, he climbs the final wall) not only confirmed his technical reputation but also marked the altered social face of climbing. The year after Kangchenjunga, Brown and three colleagues made the first ascent of the Mustagh Tower in the Karakoram.

Brown continued to climb at the highest standards in Britain, particularly on Clogwyn D'ur Arddu in Snowdonia and Craig Gogarth, Anglesey. He achieved high public recognition through a series of spectacular climbs televised by the BBC. In 2012, at the age of 82, he delighted an audience at the Royal Geographical Society in London by relating his experiences on Kangchenjunga during a celebration of its first ascent.

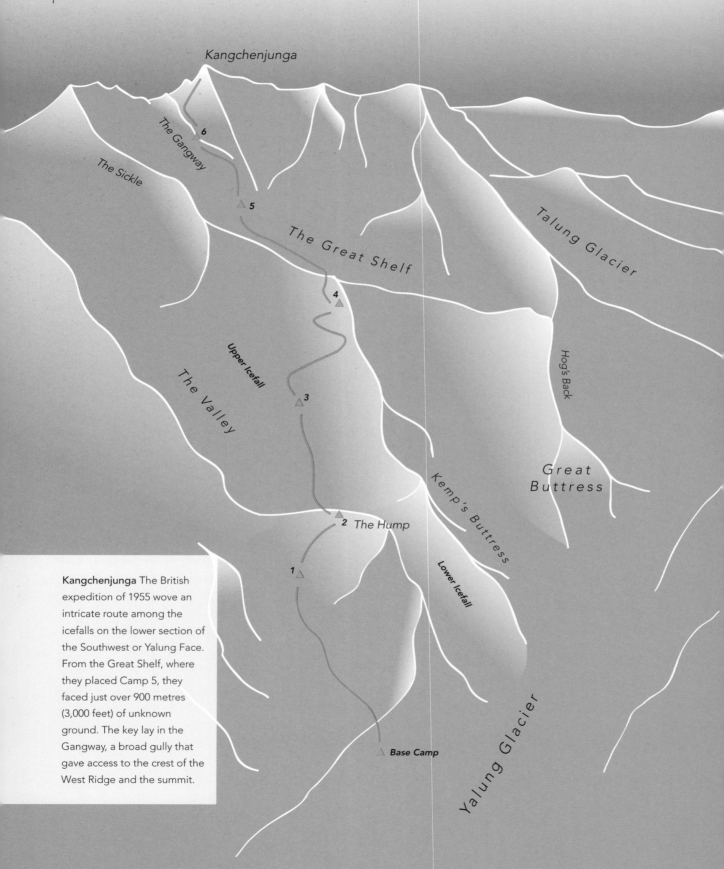

Kangchenjunga

The Gangway

The Sickle

6

5

The Great Shelf

Talung Glacier

4

Upper Icefall

Hog's Back

3

The Valley

Great
Buttress

2 The Hump

Kemp's Buttress

1

Lower Icefall

Kangchenjunga The British
expedition of 1955 wove an
intricate route among the
icefalls on the lower section of
the Southwest or Yalung Face.
From the Great Shelf, where
they placed Camp 5, they
faced just over 900 metres
(3,000 feet) of unknown
ground. The key lay in the
Gangway, a broad gully that
gave access to the crest of the
West Ridge and the summit.

Base Camp

Yalung Glacier

The most intriguing choice was Joe Brown. One of the three expedition members who were new to the Himalaya, he more than compensated with his astonishing record as a rock climber. His selection also brought recognition of climbing's spreading social base. The 1953 Everest expedition members had been drawn from the middle- and upper-class nexus that comprised the English climbing establishment. Brown, from a working-class family in Manchester, was employed in the building trade. Brown had not expected to be invited to join the expedition. On receiving a telegram from Evans, he wrote, 'I was completely surprised – and very pleased'. There was still a gulf of culture and expectation between Brown and the other members. Evans told Brown that his costs would be met from expedition funds, but he should bring £20 pocket money. Brown noted wryly: 'I couldn't tell him that I hadn't got £20.'

Kangchenjunga had been the subject of exploration since at least 1848, when the British explorer and botanist Joseph Hooker came within a few miles of it while journeying in Sikkim and made a series of pencil sketches of the mountain. The eminent Alpinist Douglas Freshfield trekked around the massif in 1899 in the company of the celebrated Italian photographer Vittorio Sella. Freshfield published a book that listed potential routes to the summit in which he declared, referring to the glacier descending 24 kilometres (15 miles) through Nepal on the southwest side of the main peak: 'The rockwall at the head of the Yalung glacier might be overcome by the help of a shelf conspicuous to the right of a horseshoe cliff. The western ridge would be gained close to the foot of the final peak.' It was Freshfield who adapted

The abyss A member of the 1955 British Kangchenjunga expedition contemplates a fragile-looking snow-bridge across a crevasse. The expedition encountered difficult and dangerous conditions on the Yalung Glacier – 'my idea of hell,' one climber said. The expedition then spent a week trying to negotiate the Lower Icefall before finally finding a safer route.

RECONNAISSANCE OF KANGCHENJUNGA

There were three reconnaissance expeditions to Kangchenjunga ahead of the 1955 expedition. In 1951 the Welsh climber Gilmour Lewis and Swiss climber George Frey made a preliminary foray along the Yalung Glacier. In 1953 Lewis returned with John Kempe, a former RAF Spitfire pilot who became headmaster of a school in India (and was later headmaster at Gordonstoun.) After further scrutiny from the Yalung Glacier, they judged that an ascent via the Southwest, or Yalung, Face was feasible.

Kempe was back in 1954, this time with a six-man party intent on examining possible ascent routes from closer at hand. They concluded that the key lay in the Great Shelf, a massive hanging glacier between 7,163 metres (23,500 feet) and 7,772 metres (25,500 feet) on the Yalung Face. Reaching it, they admitted, presented 'an immense problem' as it lay above a steep, unstable icefall – and the team was daunted by the 'predominant steepness' of the mountain's upper face. Kempe and his team presented their findings to a meeting at the Alpine Club in late 1954, warning above all that any future expedition would need to avoid the avalanches that swept the face. Despite the manifest problems, John Hunt and his colleagues took enough encouragement from the findings to mount their expedition the following year.

the name from the Tibetan and settled on its European spelling, Kangchenjunga, which is taken to mean the 'five treasures of the (high) snow'.

Six years later the notorious Aleister Crowley made an attempt from the Yalung Glacier. The team reached higher than 6,100 metres (20,000 feet) but lost four men in an avalanche. The next major expeditions approached from the east, via Sikkim. German teams made attempts in 1929 and 1931, reaching around 6,100 metres (20,000 feet) each time. They had to contend with storms and avalanches and lost a total of five men through falls and illness. Six years later Hunt, his wife Joy and a third climber, Reggie Cooke, failed in their bid to reach the main col on the ridge connecting the summit and the neighbouring Twins peak.

Following the Second World War, expeditions were compelled to approach the mountain via Nepal, as Sikkim had closed its borders in a bid to preserve its independence from China to the north and India to the south (it was eventually annexed by India in 1975). Three freelance reconnaissances, culminating in the 1954 venture, were the prelude to the British expedition of 1955.

The expedition reached Darjeeling in early March and trekked into the massif. It reached the Yalung Valley on 23 March and then had to find a route up the Yalung Glacier. With the glacier's jagged, unstable footing, scoured by an unrelenting wind, team member

John Clegg considered it 'my idea of hell'. The climbers set up base camp at the head of the glacier on 12 April and over the next 24 hours, by Band's count, heard 48 avalanches crashing down the Southwest Face. The climbers were further daunted when they studied photographs taken by the Indian Air Force (IAF). The final ridge looked even worse than they had feared, Band wrote: 'A jagged knife-edge with a clump of pinnacles half-way and with tremendous cliffs on either side... It was all rather depressing.'

Their next task was to find a way to the Great Shelf. They spent a week trying to establish a route through the Lower Icefall, which rose above the glacier, before concluding it was far too dangerous. They switched to the Western Rock Buttress on the far side of the icefall, moving base camp to a knoll known as Pache's Grave, the burial place of one of the climbers killed in 1905. The new line proved safer and easier than the Lower Icefall. Even so, the lead climbers had to negotiate a funnel that felt like an ambush site and then climb a slope that carried a clear avalanche risk.

On 27 May Band and New Zealander Norman Hardie reached a feature on the buttress that they had named the Hump, then descended a 152-metre (500-foot) gully that took them near the top of the notorious Lower Icefall. They sited Camp 2 at 6,218 metres (20,400 feet) and judged the terrain above 'more stable and less terrifying' than expected. After fixing Camp 3 on an ice-platform at 6,645 metres (21,800 feet), the expedition consolidated its position by ferrying 1.5 tons of supplies, much of it oxygen equipment, to the camp, now designated Advance Base.

On 12 May the expedition moved up once more, siting Camp 4 at 7,163 metres (23,500 feet). The next day came the breakthrough, when Evans and Hardie

The Great Shelf Members of the 1955 team ascend a steep ice-field on Kangchenjunga's Yalung Face. After climbing the Upper Icefall, the expedition established Camp 4 at the foot of the Great Shelf, a huge ice-terrace that offered access to the upper reaches of the mountain.

Band's prospect George Band, photographed by Joe Brown, shortly after the two climbers reached the crest of Kangchenjunga's West Ridge. The summit is some 60 metres (nearly 200 feet) further on. Behind them the ridge runs to the summit of Yalung Kang, Kangchenjunga's west peak.

Summit view Expedition members descend from Camp 5 on Kangchenjunga. The camp, at 7,711 metres (25,300 feet) was sited near the top of the Great Shelf. From there the summit climbers followed the rightward ascending gully (centre of photo) known as the Gangway, then struck up the rocks to the right to the summit.

climbed to the foot of the Great Shelf. They pushed on to establish Camp 5 beside a steep ice-cliff where, at 7,711 metres (25,300 feet), they were higher than any previous climbers. As they had foreseen, this was the equivalent in both logistical and psychological terms of the South Col on Everest – launch pad for the summit. The achievement was significant in another way. This was supposedly a reconnaissance expedition, preceding a full attempt the following year. The climbers descended to base camp for a meeting on 14 May. In his account, Evans diplomatically referred to the tasks that remained, including 'exploration of the final ridge'. Band described that climactic meeting without any inhibition, describing the 'air of expectancy' among the climbers in the tent as they waited for Evans to arrive. 'Since we were all fit, every one must secretly have longed to be chosen for a summit bid.'

Evans entered with a mug of tea in his hand. Then, without ceremony, he announced his dispositions. Following consolidation of the higher camps, Band and Brown would make the first attempt; a second by Streather and Hardie would follow. The team celebrated with a supper of tomato soup, stewed steak, roast potatoes and peas, pineapple and custard dessert, and Ovaltine, followed by the expedition's second and last bottle of rum.

After Camp 5 had been stocked, Band and Brown moved up to Camp 4, but were pinned in their tents by a storm that raged for 60 hours. 'We had to sit and wait while our chances seemed like sand running away through our fingers,' Band recorded. The weather cleared on 22 May and Band and Brown, plus a support team, moved up to Camp 5, only to discover that it had been wrecked by an avalanche. They disinterred the tents but there was no food that night, only mugs of tea brewed by the indomitable Sherpas.

On 24 May Band and Brown, with other climbers in support, pushed on to the Gangway, a steep snowfield that offered a route onto the West Ridge and the summit beyond that the summit. At 2.00 p.m., having reached 8,199 metres (26,900 feet), they carved out a narrow ledge for their tent. It hung over the ledge in an alarming manner, so the two men drew matchsticks to see who took the outside berth. Band lost, and passed an anxious night.

A fine day dawned on 25 May and Brown and Band set off at 8.15 a.m. Having studied the IAF images, they planned to move out of the Gangway and traverse the mountain's Southwest Face, rather than continue directly to the summit ridge, which had looked so daunting. They lost a precious 90 minutes by exiting onto the face too early. After locating the correct line, they ascended steep mixed ground before moving on to the crest of the ridge. They had been climbing for five hours and stopped to remove their oxygen masks and snack on lemonade, toffee and mint cake.

It was 2.00 p.m. – with 122 metres (400 feet) still to climb, Band calculated they would have to reach the summit by 3.00 p.m. if they were to make it back to Camp 6 by nightfall. They made fast progress but then found the ridge blocked by a sheer rock wall. As Band recorded, the wall was broken by several vertical 6-metre (20-foot) cracks. It proved an irresistible temptation for Brown. 'I knew that at sea level I could climb it quite easily,' Brown said, 'but at that height you don't know just how long your strength's going to last.' Brown – who later rated the pitch as 'v diff' by sea-level standards – turned his oxygen to maximum flow and soon pulled over the top of the wall. He called down: 'George, we're there!'

When Band joined Brown at the top of the wall, he found that they were close to the final snow cone, which rose for another 1.5 metres (5 feet). Evans had promised the Sikkimese authorities that they would not step onto the summit out of respect for Kangchenjunga's status as a holy mountain. Even though the expedition had climbed from Nepal, Brown and Band kept the promise. But for all intents and purposes, Kangchenjunga had been climbed. The two climbers' principal response, wrote Brown, was of relief at not having to take any more upward steps – coupled with 'a great feeling of peace and tranquillity'.

It was 2.45 p.m. Band and Brown photographed each other and the view from the summit, with the neighbouring mountaintops emerging from a sea of cloud; nearly 130 kilometres (80 miles) away rose the great triumvirate of Lhotse, Makalu and Everest. After half an hour Band and Brown began their descent. Their oxygen ran out after an hour but they continued without mishap, reaching Camp 6 by dusk, where they were congratulated by Hardie and Streather. Brown, who had briefly removed his goggles during the ascent, was in agony that night from snow-blindness. The next day Hardie and Streather went to the summit, discovering that they could avoid the rock wall where Brown had performed his heroics by following a snow ridge a short distance beyond.

The team cleared the mountain by 28 May. 'The one cloud on our happiness,' Band recorded, was the death from a stroke two days earlier of a high-altitude Sherpa, Pemi Dorje. He was buried near Pache's Grave on the Yalung Glacier. Otherwise the expedition was notable for the mature way it had handled the risks of forging a route on a largely unknown peak. It was free of the disputes that disfigured other major expeditions of the period and in fact made little impact on the British consciousness, perhaps sated by the Everest triumph two years before. In this case the satisfaction was more personal, as Evans recorded when the team looked back at the peak during its trek to Darjeeling: 'The mountain seemed to embody the spell of all far places, of all the high snows and hidden valleys that are waiting.'

The dual Swiss expedition of 1956: Everest and Lhotse

The Swiss team that set up its Advance Base camp in Everest's Western Cwm on 18 April 1956 had high expectations and an impressive provenance. Four years before, Swiss climbers had overcome a succession of barriers on the approach to Everest, opening up the routes to the summits of both Everest and Lhotse. Their efforts had proved crucial in preparing the ground for the triumphant British Everest expedition the following year. The Swiss dual attempt on both Lhotse and Everest in 1956 was thus undertaken with the sense that theirs was a mission waiting to be fulfilled – and one where the Swiss were owed their due.

The Swiss expedition of 1952 was the first to reach the dangerous Khumbu Icefall and the first to stand in the Western Cwm, the giant valley of ice that had been glimpsed – and named – by George Mallory in 1921. Above them soared the West Face of Lhotse, rising some 1,524 metres (5,000 feet) from the head of the Western Cwm to Lhotse's summit at 8,516 metres (27,940 feet). To the north, one of Lhotse's three summit ridges dipped to the South Col, the midpoint between Lhotse and Everest.

The British had honourably shared the fruits of their 1951 reconnaissance with the Swiss, with Eric Shipton recommending that they approach the South Col by way of Lhotse's West Face. But the Swiss concluded that the icefall occupying its lower slopes presented too many risks. They concluded that it would be safest to climb a giant rock rib to its north, which they dubbed L'Eperon des Genevois (the Geneva Spur). Climbing the spur proved far harder than the Swiss had anticipated but in May 1952 they eventually overcame it and then descended 61 metres (200 feet) to reach the South Col, thus notching another historical first. A few days later Raymond Lambert and Tenzing Norgay had to turn back from around 305 metres (1,000 feet) below the summit.

The Swiss returned with a mostly new team after the 1952 monsoon. At first they persevered with the Geneva Spur, but after a Sherpa was killed by falling ice they switched to the West Face and established a zigzag route through the icefall, which proved less intimidating than expected. They established camps at around 7,148 metres (23,450 feet) and 7,498 metres (24,600 feet), then made an ascending leftward traverse to the South Col, pioneering the approximate route used by all Everest expeditions climbing via the South Col to this day. That was almost the limit of their endeavours. On 20 November Lambert led a small group of climbers a short distance above the col before the cold and wind forced them to abandon their summit attempt.

For all the rivalry with the British, the Swiss were gallant enough to share their knowledge and experience of Everest, which included pointing out the advantages and salient features of the route up the West Face of Lhotse. The British followed the same line in spring 1953, finding the face so arduous that at first it appeared their attempt had stalled. After that triumphal first ascent, the British interrupted their journey home at Zurich Airport where the Swiss 1952 climbers toasted them with champagne. The British returned the courtesy, telling the Swiss that they deserved 'half the glory'.

It was with the awareness that the summit of Lhotse was an attractive and feasible target that an international team returned to the Western Cwm in the post-monsoon season of 1955. It included climbers from Switzerland and Austria and was led by the Swiss-American Norman Dyhrenfurth, who went on to head the first American ascent of Everest in 1963. Largely following the 1952 Swiss post-monsoon route, it established its highest camp at 7,589 metres (24,900 feet). On 16 October a four-man team, including two Sherpas, set off on its summit attempt. Three turned back after

three hours, leaving the Austrian Ernst Senn to press on alone. He climbed to a point at 8,108 metres (26,600 feet), reaching the foot of a couloir that slices a route most of the way up the final summit pyramid. Senn's oxygen supply ran out and he was compelled to turn back. He was pinned in Camp 5 by a five-day storm before he was able to descend to safety.

So when the Swiss returned again in 1956, it was in the reassuring knowledge that most of the problems of the ascent had been solved, save for the tantalizing final couloir, also known as the Lhotse Groove. The team of 11 climbers was headed by Albert Eggler, a lawyer, soldier and Alpinist from Bern, selected by the Swiss Foundation for Alpine Research to bring a degree of professionalism and organization it felt had been lacking in 1952. Eggler recruited a team of German-speaking climbers from the Oberland and the valleys of the upper Rhone. They included one survivor from the 1952 expeditions, Ernst Reiss, who had taken part in the post-monsoon attempt. With characteristic thoroughness, Eggler obtained permits from the Nepalese to attempt both Everest and Lhotse – fourth-highest peak in the world and the highest still unclimbed. Eggler cannily declined to specify which peak was the expedition's principal objective, preferring to keep his options open.

Opting for the route used by the 1952 post-monsoon and 1955 expeditions, the 1956 Swiss team took its first steps on the Lhotse icefall on 2 May. It made 198 metres (650 feet) on the first day. The next day, in perfect weather and ideal snow and ice conditions, it climbed a further 457 metres (1,500 feet), placing the team far ahead of the rate achieved by the British in 1953. 'We felt convinced that our venture

Danger ahead The Swiss Everest/Lhotse expedition of 1956 camped in the Khumbu Icefall, the tumbling river of ice that forms a formidable barrier below the Western Cwm. 'All were impressed by its savagery and instability,' declared expedition leader Albert Eggler.

Yellow Band A Swiss climber at the Yellow Band, a layer of limestone running across Lhotse's West Face. The Swiss fixed ropes across the band to assist the Sherpa porters in carrying loads between Camps 5 and 6.

was going to succeed,' Eggler wrote. On 5 May the lead climbers reached the site of the 1955 expedition's Camp 5 where they found a priceless cache of eight oxygen bottles, which they gratefully added to their own supplies. Meanwhile, they were consolidating the route and securing fixed ropes to assist the Sherpas in their load-carrying.

On 6 May seven of the climbers, including Eggler, met in Camp 3 to consider their options. Should they attempt Lhotse or Everest? Or both? And if the latter, which should they attempt first? They decided, in short, to go for broke and attempt both. They would establish a camp on the South Col as a preliminary to an attempt on Everest. At the same time the first party in a position to do so was to launch what Eggler called 'a single, determined assault on Lhotse'.

The next day the climbers moved back up the face. There was a momentary crisis when the sirdar fell ill and had to be evacuated from the mountain. But by 9 May two climbers, Ernst Schmied and Fritz Luchsinger, had placed Camp 6 at 8,001 metres (26,250 feet), excavating a snow-platform large enough to hold their two-man tent. The camp was sited just below the top of the Geneva Spur and it enabled the team to install a winch that would save them 305 vertical metres (1,000 vertical feet) of load-carrying. The team was ideally positioned to prepare an attempt on Lhotse, but was abruptly hit by a spell of bad weather that shelved all plans for a week.

When the storms eased, the team moved back up to the highest camp, which was occupied on 17 May by Luchsinger and Reiss, the 1952 veteran. Luchsinger had already proved himself a survivor, having recovered from a near-lethal attack of appendicitis during the approach march. Dawn on 18 May was cold and windy, driving plumes of snow from the ridges above them. Following a restless and anxious night, the two men left the camp at 9.00 a.m., heading for the Lhotse Groove. They were using open-circuit oxygen equipment and had an immediate setback when Luchsinger found that his supply hose was blocked with ice. He had brought a back-up set but the time spent effecting a switch cost a precious hour. By then they had lost all feeling in their hands and feet, and felt grateful that they could at last move on.

Snow conditions were good and after another hour they reached the foot of the notorious couloir where – to their 'delight and surprise' – they found good firm snow. They climbed nearly 140 metres (450 feet) in the next hour as the angle gradually steepened to 50 degrees. Around noon they reached a 30-metre (100-foot) rock step that had been identified in photographs as the crux of their ascent. They overcame it via a steep and narrow snow groove that called for the most demanding climbing of the ascent. The groove widened as they approached the top of the couloir, assailed now by an intensifying wind. They emerged onto steep snow and stood on a saddle between Lhotse's twin summits.

The lower summit, to their right, was 30 metres (100 feet) above them; the higher and true summit rose to the left for another 46 metres (150 feet). They climbed a band of green rock and cut steps with their ice-axes to a stance below the final snow-crest. Luchsinger joined Reiss on the stance as they crouched and waited for a lull in the

Western Cwm Six Swiss climbers (opposite, bottom) in the great ice basin, the Western Cwm, which was the key to reaching both Everest and Lhotse. Beyond them rises Lhotse's West Face, with its icefall prominent in the lower section.

Summit shot Fritz Luchsinger (below), photographed by Ernst Reiss, on Lhotse's summit. Behind him is Lhotse's lower South Summit and beyond that the connecting ridge with Nuptse

wind. Then they hauled themselves over the crest – 'almost as sharp as a knife-blade' – and looked down on the cloud smothering the East and South faces of the mountain. 'We were on the summit of Lhotse.'

The ascent from Camp 6 had taken six hours. The two men exchanged few words: Reiss noted that they were 'overwhelmed by the incomparable magnificence and savagery of the view'. They removed their oxygen masks, drove their ice-axes into the snow and hung their rucksacks from them. They attached the flags of Switzerland and Nepal to the axes, together with a woollen monkey they had been carrying as a mascot. They posed for the statutory summit photographs in some difficulty, exhausted from their efforts, battered by the wind and all too aware of the tiny platform they were occupying, falling away on all sides. Far below they glimpsed the expedition camps where their colleagues were waiting for news and, beyond the head of the Western Cwm, the Southwest Face of Everest. They headed down after three-quarters of an hour.

The descent, cautious and painstaking, took three hours. The couloir acted as a wind tunnel, driving snow and ice into their faces. They fixed a rope to down-climb the rock step in the couloir and reached Camp 6 at 6.15 p.m. They had to excavate their tent from the snow before they could brew soup and tea. During the night the tent collapsed under the weight of fresh snow and they had to put on their boots to go out to clear it. In the morning they continued their descent to Camp 5, to be greeted by Eggler and other team members. Eggler noted that they were immensely tired – 'but happy beyond words'. Their hands and feet were numbed, but recovered

Lhotse The Swiss expedition of 1956 followed the route through the treacherous Khumbu Icefall pioneered by the British reconnaissance expedition of 1951 and used again by the Swiss in 1952 and the British in 1953. On the Lhotse Face the climbers avoided the Geneva Spur and sited Camp 6 below the South Col. From there it was a six-hour climb to the summit, unlocked by ascending the Lhotse Groove.

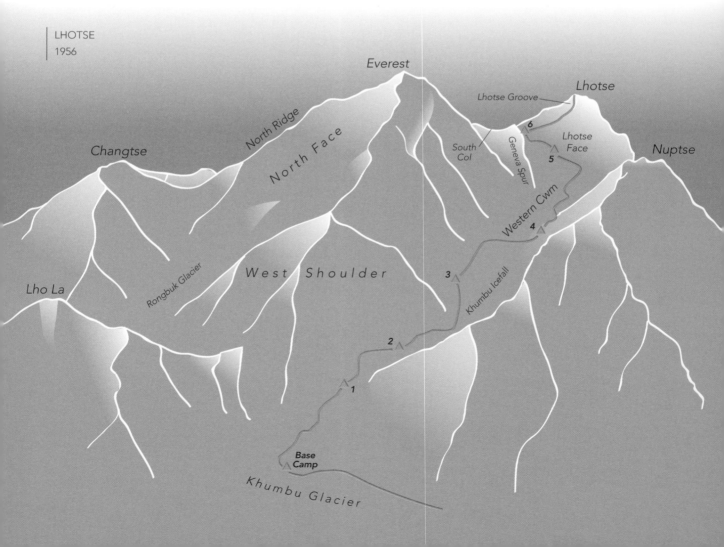

LHOTSE
1956

after massage, and they were rewarded with a hot brew of gruel and a tot of cognac.

The Swiss had thus achieved the first ascent of what was then the highest of the unclimbed peaks — and the first ascent by Swiss climbers of an 8,000-metre (26,246-foot) peak. 'We were thrilled to the core,' wrote Eggler.

The Swiss were now determined to make the second ascent of Everest itself. The Swiss established a camp on South Col on 21 May and on 22 May Ernst Schmied and Jürg Marmet set off on their summit bid. They camped that night at 8,397 metres (27,550 feet) and reached the summit around 1.00 p.m. on 23 May. They were followed the next day by Adolf Reist and Hansrudolf von Gunten, crowning a multiple triumph for a well-organized and harmonious expedition, and bringing deserved success for climbers from a nation that had played such a crucial role in the first ascent of Everest.

On 29 May the entire team was back in base camp and was gratified to hear the BBC relay congratulations from John Hunt, leader of the 1953 British team, and the summit pair, Ed Hillary and Tenzing Sherpa. It was a proud moment for the Swiss, recalled Eggler, particularly as they had benefited from the experiences of the British team three years earlier. He also recorded that the team had survived the three ascents unscathed: 'We were all deeply thankful, and to our recognition of our good fortune was slowly added the knowledge that the finest and rarest days of our life lay behind us.'

From Everest This view of Lhotse was taken by Swiss climbers on Everest's Southeast Ridge. The final couloir, named the Lhotse Groove, is the black gash that rises leftwards to the notch between the two summits.

9

Opening New Frontiers: 1961–the Present

Doug Scott

During the ten years after the ascent of Annapurna in 1950, 12 more summits over 8,000 metres (26,246 feet) were reached. It was an incredibly productive decade – and all the more remarkable since so little had been achieved in the preceding 55 years of climbing in the Himalaya, commencing with Mummery's attempt at Nanga Parbat in 1895.

The Second World War had been a significant catalyst for change. Equipment improved, particularly with the invention of nylon, which provided a more durable, lighter and more wind-resistant fabric for clothing and tents. Down clothing became standard, boots warmer and stoves were improved to match the scientists' demand that climbers took their rehydration seriously. There were other more profound changes, in particular that to the political landscape of Central Asia. The Chinese overran Tibet and closed it to foreigners. As a consequence Nepal, which had been completely shut off for climbing, now welcomed foreigners to reconnoitre and climb some of its huge number of unexplored mountains.

A shifting landscape

The political climate was as changeable as the weather. After China invaded India in 1962 not only India but also Nepal and Pakistan restricted access to border areas and therefore to the majority of the Himalaya's challenging peaks. Bhutan was to open and shut to climbers as did Tibet, which opened up to Iranian climbers in 1978 and then to all climbers the following year. Vast areas of Tibet had always been off limits, and in 2008 restrictions were imposed due to riots in the lead up to the Beijing Olympic Games. However, it can be said that overall there are more mountains in Central Asia available than ever before.

Wars not only alter the political map but also bring about social and economic change. After about 1960 climbing became more socially inclusive, and by the 1970s it was also more affordable as the cost of air travel tumbled relative to salaries. And as mountaineers, trekkers and cultural tourists poured into the Himalayan countries it generated funds to improve the infrastructure. Roads were built into the high Himalaya where only barefoot porters and mule trains had gone before. In Pakistan and India it was a border dispute that gave impetus to this construction programme. As tourism reached the highest settlements – and climbers reached higher still – the local economies benefitted, but at a cost to the environment and cultural heritage as the old traditional ways of life were eroded in the face of Western materialism.

After the war, climbing in Britain was no longer the preserve of the Alpine

God's rays The sun's rays pour down on the Southwest Face of Everest, bathing it in an almost ethereal light.

Club and climbers with an Oxbridge background. Joe Brown, a jobbing builder from Manchester, was invited onto the 1955 Kangchenjunga Expedition and by the 1960s anyone with initiative could take advantage of the increased affluence and the ease of relatively cheap travel. In most other countries climbing had already moved towards the inclusion of climbers from all social groups, particularly in Austria and Germany.

Routes and styles

On the climbing front, mountaineering progressed – as it always has, with rare exception – from the obvious, most straightforward, risk-free route to the more difficult. The harder route was only attempted first, as happened on Everest in the 1920s and 1930s, when local or regional politics precluded access to the easier one. Eventually, the first ascent was achieved when Hillary and Tenzing climbed the Southeast Ridge in 1953, the easiest route up the mountain. The second ascent of the mountain was made in 1960 via the next most convenient route, the North Ridge, by the Chinese. In 1963 came the Americans to climb the steeper West Flank and then to traverse over and down the Southeast Ridge. After the Nepalese lifted the ban on climbing that had been imposed from 1964 to 1969 the Japanese came to the Southwest Face. After six more reconnaissances and attempts it was finally climbed in 1975 by the British. That was not the end of the story of the southwest side of Everest, for the Poles climbed the South Pillar route in 1980 and two years later the Russians climbed a much steeper route still, to the left of the British route. Other major routes followed on the north side, including the Northeast Ridge and on the Kangshung, or East, Face. Many other new routes and variations have generally filled in the gaps between these more obvious features.

Although the explorations of the mountain are always going to be of the most interest, there is also the evolution of style. Generally this has resulted in fewer people using less equipment to the point when, in 1978, Reinhold Messner and Peter Habeler climbed Everest without using oxygen. Climbers gradually moved from large-scale 'siege' tactics towards an ascent of Everest in Alpine-style small teams until in 1980 Messner again climbed Everest, but this time solo without anyone else on the mountain to help him. In the same year the masters of cold climbing arrived from Poland led by Andrzej Zawada, who made the first winter ascent of Everest. On 16 February 1980 Leszek Cichy and Krzysztof Wielicki reached the summit after a supreme effort of will in battling the winter cold all the way from the South Col.

This illustration of climbing development has been replicated on all the world's major peaks, from Africa to the Arctic, the Andes to Alaska, and from Europe to Central Asia and beyond. That is not to say there was a mad rush to establish new routes. In fact the majority of climbers in the Himalaya were content to repeat the original routes with very little new route activity until the 1970s when Himalayan climbing really came into its own. Only on Everest and Nanga Parbat were new routes put up before 1970.

Airless duo Reinhold Messner (above, left) and Peter Habeler (above, right) are shown just before their 1978 ascent of Everest – the first climbers to reach the summit without the assistance of oxygen. The climb was beset with problems, including an attack of food poisoning that struck Habeler, but in the end the pair managed to climb from the South Col to the summit in just eight hours.

Everest: the 'West Side story'

When the North Ridge, which had defeated so many British attempts during the interwar period, was climbed in 1960 by three Chinese in the dead of night, having climbed the second step of the summit barefoot and without definitive summit photographs, doubt was cast upon the validity of the ascent. However, over the years – after more scrutiny of the photographs and knowing that the Chinese definitely climbed Everest in 1975 – the claim has been accepted by climbing pundits.

Three years after the Chinese, the Americans climbed Everest, first by the original route and then, three weeks later on 22 May 1963, by a new route up the West Flank, over the summit and down the original route, thus completing every climber's classic ideal by climbing up one side and descending the other. This was an amazing achievement and has continued to inspire climbers to this day. How does the 'West Side story' fit into the history of climbing on Everest? It is in a class all of its own, for it was here more than on any other climb that a point of no return was reached and therefore a total commitment made. The summiteers were Tom Hornbein and Willi Unsoeld, who had to contend not only with the difficulties of the climb and the vagaries of the weather but also in maintaining the interest of the rest of the expedition, including the leader Norman Dyhrenfurth, in the West Ridge attempt.

The expedition had left the USA with high expectations: the main aim being to put the first American on the summit via the South Col, as well as to climb Lhotse and Nuptse. The idea of putting up a new route on the western side of Everest was only mentioned during a training climb on Mount Rainier. Thanks to the persistence

Night climb Messner and Habeler leave Advance Base camp during their ultimately successful oxygen-free summiting of Everest. Although they climbed as a separate two-man team they joined a larger Austrian expedition and were able to make use of their facilities, including a tent where the duo brewed a much-needed cup of tea just short of the Hillary Step.

'West side climbers' Both Tom Hornbein (above, right) and Willi Unsoeld (above, left) were strong champions of the proposal to tackle the West Ridge during the 1963 American Mount Everest Expedition, and, even when resources were shifted to the Southeast Ridge route, declined to abandon the attempt on the new route. As they reconnoitred the West Shoulder, the snowy outcrop that led onto the West Ridge, they were rewarded with a remarkable view (opposite, right) up the West Ridge. As Hornbein later wrote: 'Our eyes climbed a mile of sloping sedimentary shingles, black rock, yellow rock, grey rock to the summit.'

of those most interested – Hornbein and Unsoeld – a decision was finally made, during the walk into Everest, to include the West Ridge in the expedition's itinerary. Nuptse was left out of the planning, although Lhotse would be attempted if there were sufficient oxygen. This large expedition, of 19 members, gravitated into 'West Ridgers' and 'South Colers' based on old friendships, those whose primary goal was the summit, and others who were more interested in a new way to the top. Naturally, there was some friction between these groups. As described in the official book of the expedition, *Americans on Everest* by James Ramsay Ullman: 'There were long, sometimes heated discussions as Tom persistently pushed the West Ridge cause. Those who agreed with him thought he was an idealist, the champion of pioneering and adventure as against the easy road of cheap success. Those who disagreed were not above calling him a fanatic who put his personal preferences above the common goal.' Disagreements were only resolved after Jim Whittaker, with Sherpa Gombu, became the first American to stand on the summit.

A workable plan then unfolded that would complete the expedition to the satisfaction of all concerned – both those wanting to repeat the Southeast Ridge route and the 'West Side climbers', since a team would be dispatched to the South Col with the option to summit in support of the 'West Side climbers' coming over the summit and down to the South Col.

On the West Ridge, Al Auten, Barry Corbet and Dick Emerson together with various Sherpas put in many days of load-carrying up to a site for Camp 4. During this period they had to contend with illness, blizzards and hurricane-force westerly winds. On 15 May the camp was fully established with a final carry by Unsoeld and Hornbein, who then occupied it. The following day they checked out the 'Diagonal Ditch', which provided a relatively easy way to the snowfields below the couloir

that they hoped to ascend and thereby avoid the steep rocks of the actual West Ridge. Because it was Tom Hornbein's idea the couloir has forever been known as the Hornbein Couloir, although at the time it was not known whether it could be climbed since the upper part narrowed, going through a yellow band of rock, and then twisted out of sight.

The build-up of supplies continued until there were three tents at Camp 4. During a storm in the middle of the night of 18 May, Corbet and Auten were alarmed to find that their tent was suddenly sliding down the mountain completely out of their control until miraculously, after about 45 metres (150 feet) they stopped in a trough in the slope. A retreat was enforced upon the group down to Camp 3. With the attrition of men and materials it was decided to reduce the West Ridge attempt to just one team. Emerson was not well, Auten had always decided upon a support role, leaving Corbet gallantly to give up his chance, acknowledging the special relationship that existed between Hornbein and Unsoeld.

On 20 May, in perfect weather, everyone available moved back up to the battered Camp 4 from where they hoped to establish a Camp 5 in the couloir. The next morning Auten and Corbet set off across the Diagonal Ditch and into the couloir, cutting bucket steps for the heavily laden Sherpas following behind. At 2.00 p.m. they located a ledge at the foot of the yellow band of rock at about 8,300 metres (27,230 feet) that would just accommodate a two-man tent. After this magnificent effort at route-finding and step-cutting, Auten, Corbet and the Sherpas retreated back down the fixed rope to Emerson, who was there in support. For Hornbein and Unsoeld, and all the team, the parting was made with considerable emotion. They

A network of routes
Since the first summiting of Everest in 1953 via the Southeast Ridge, more than a dozen other routes up the mountain have been successfully climbed, particularly via the Northeast Ridge, pioneered by the Chinese in 1960 and the route from the West Ridge across the North Face opened up by the Americans in 1963.

OTHER ROUTES TO
THE TOP OF EVEREST

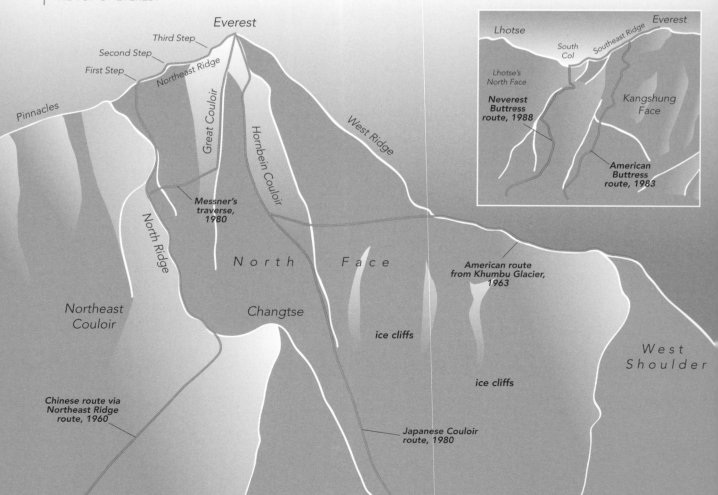

were a close-knit group who had shared many climbs together over the years and all envisaged going where no one had been before. With about 542 metres (1,778 feet) left to go, Hornbein and Unsoeld put up their tent and moved in, fully aware of their precarious position since it was anchored to a peg driven only half an inch into the shattered rock of the yellow band and then tethered to their ice-axes, which were pushed up to the hilt into soft snow, pinning down the outside corners. Unsoeld planted a Tibetan prayer flag that had been left by one of the Sherpas, commenting, 'I think we'd better count on this'.

The tent and the occupants survived the night and they did not awake until 4.00 a.m., whereupon they began to melt snow over their butane stove. Even with the advantage of gas over the old paraffin primus stove it took them three hours of preparation before they could begin climbing. By 11.00 a.m. they had only managed to climb 122 metres (400 feet) through the yellow band of rock, snow and hard ice. After a rest, Hornbein went ahead to tackle an 18-metre (60-foot) cliff of rotten rock where he found 'an unlimited selection of hand-holds, mostly portable'. Unsoeld went back into the lead, but after two more hours of climbing they were only at 8,504 metres (27,900 feet). They called base camp on the walkie-talkie and spoke to Jim Whittaker who suggested rappelling. Unsoeld replied: 'There are no rappel points, Jim, absolutely no rappel points. There's nothing to secure the rope to so it's up and over for us today....' Hornbein wrote of that moment, 'to go down now, even if we could have, would be descending to a future marked by one huge question: what might have been? It would not be a matter of living with our fellow man but simply living with ourselves, with the knowledge that we had had more to give.'

They continued more easily for after 30 metres (100 feet) the yellow band was all beneath them and the tongue of hard snow gave them the opportunity to climb together until they stopped for a lunch of lemonade, turning to slush ice, and frozen kippers. The pair then moved together diagonally up and across slabs of rotten shale and snow leading over to the rocks on the crest of the West Ridge. Suddenly they could look down 2,438 metres (8,000 feet) to the tents of Advance Base camp nestling in the Western Cwm. They now climbed without crampons on firm rock and 'experienced the joy of delicate moves on tiny holes,' wrote Hornbein, considering it 'a wonderful pleasure almost like a day in the Rockies'. Back on snow and crampons they moved together until finally they came to the tattered American flag that Jim Whittaker and Sherpa Gombu had planted on the summit three weeks before. It was now 6.15 p.m. with the last of the sun's rays coming in horizontally across the summit. After 20 minutes they left all summit thoughts and impressions to concentrate on the descent.

Footprints in the snow were an indication that not long before members of the support party, Lute Jerstad and Barry Bishop, had been on the summit. Since Unsoeld had led most of the way up, Hornbein came down as anchorman, moving rapidly down the ridge, with the two taking the Hillary Step in their stride and reaching the South Summit by 7.15 p.m., thankful for the guiding footprints. By 7.30 p.m. it was dark; their flashlights faded and the tracks became hard to follow. They stumbled on down, shouting into the gusting wind and hoping a returning voice would indicate Camp 6. Finally they heard voices and at 9.30 p.m., still 305 metres (1,000 feet) above Camp 6, they came across Jerstad and Bishop absolutely exhausted, shivering and shaking, curled up together in the snow. At Hornbein's insistence they all moved off, with him in the lead, stopping and starting as Bishop collapsed frequently with fatigue. After three hours they had only gone down another 122 metres (400 feet), where they stopped, unable to find a safe passage through an area of rocks. Hornbein and Unsoeld wrapped themselves around each other while Jerstad and Bishop lay

HIMALAYAN CLIMBING AND THE USE OF STIMULANTS

On 19 May 2009 Jesse Easterling, an American client on a commercial trekking expedition to the South Col route on Everest, had to be evacuated from base camp suffering from an overdose of the steroid dexamethasone, known as Dex. He was brought back from the brink in the intensive care unit of a Kathmandu hospital. Easterling had been taking Dex several times a day for a month since his arrival at Lukla (Everest) airstrip. He had suffered paranoia verging on a psychotic breakdown, and only after a blood transfusion was he fit enough to fly home.

Drugs have been carried and occasionally used to help climbers in extremis for many years. Hermann Buhl took Pervitin (amphetamine) after he fell down an Alpine crevasse. He was very impressed with the way it seemed to revitalize his body so quickly. Having felt 'its marvellous effects', on his final push climbing solo on Nanga Parbat in 1957, he took two Pervitin tablets at the Bazhin Gap. After summiting he had to bivouac out in the open, with very little warm clothing. He took three more tablets that helped him down to his companions waiting at the top camp, 41 hours after leaving it.

On the traverse of Everest in 1963 Dr Tom Hornbein gave Dexedrine (Dexamphetamine) tablets to help the exhausted support party, Lute Jerstad and Barry Bishop. On the South Col of Everest in 1996 one man, who had been given up for dead when eight other clients and guides perished in a storm on the mountain, revived on his own. Beck Withers collapsed in the snow and spent a night in the open. Although his face and limbs were severely frostbitten, and his eyesight considerably impaired, he rose up and staggered towards a tent where he attracted the attention of others. No one expected him to survive the night, never mind descending the Lhotse Face and the Khumbu Icefall. Pete Athens, who had climbed Everest many times, had abandoned his plans in order to help rescue others. He had himself taken Dex several times before and injected 4 milligrammes into Withers's thigh. It may have been a life-saver, since he continued his miraculous recovery and was able to descend the mountain with the help of Athens and Todd Burleson, and later go home to his wife and family.

No one is critical of such drugs being carried on a mountain that might 'bring life back to a dead person', as an article 'Climbers' Little Helper' in *Outside* magazine acknowledged in April 2013. Since the Easterling case, however, the mountaineering world has begun to question the use of drugs such as Dex, Sildenafil, EPO, and so on, that enhance performance.

Now that the majority of Everest climbers use commercial trekking agencies, those agencies have a responsibility to warn clients of the dangers of taking drugs at altitude. British doctor David Hillebrandt, President of the UIAA Medical Commission (the UIAA is the International Mountaineering and Climbing Federation), is concerned that climbers are easily obtaining such drugs online and are using them by following advice found on the internet. He says climbers should seek unbiased advice and be honest: 'The vital principle must be honesty with oneself and honesty with ones' peers just as one would be expected to declare points of aid (bolt or peg) on a rock climb, so one should declare the use of pharmacological aid.' Hillebrandt and his colleagues on the commission are intending to issue guidelines relating to the problems involved in taking drugs at altitude. The use of performance-enhancing drugs in recreational mountaineering is separate to their use during ice climbing and indoor climbing competitions – events policed by the World Anti-Doping Agency (WADA), which maintains the integrity of these contests by enforcing doping regulations and testing.

strung out apart and alone. Hornbein warmed his frozen toes on his friend's stomach. Unsoeld unfortunately declined Hornbein's offer to reciprocate.

With the dawn all four moved on down, helped into Camp 6 by Dave Dingman and Girmi Sherpa who plied them with mugs of tea, following which they moved on down the Lhotse Face and the Western Cwm before staggering into Advance Base camp at 10.00 p.m. Over the next few days the exhausted and injured men went to Namche Bazaar, from where a helicopter evacuated Unsoeld and Bishop to Kathmandu and then home. Weeks of painful rest culminated in amputations of fingers and toes. Hornbein was left to contemplate that 'half of me seemed to have gone with him; the other half was isolated from my companions by an experience I couldn't share and by the feeling that something was ending that had come to mean too much'.

Everest: the Japanese attempt on the Southwest Face

By 1969 and the lifting of the Nepali ban on climbing from their territory the Japanese had gained experience in the Himalaya that was second to none. They had made the first ascents of the eighth-highest summit, Manaslu (8,156 metres/26,759 feet), in 1956; Chogolisa (7,654 metres/25,111 feet) in 1958; Himal Chuli (7,864 metres/25,800 feet), Api (7,132 metres/23,399 feet) and Noshaq (7,492 metres/24,580 feet) in 1960; Chamlang (7,319 metres/24,012 feet) and Saltoro Kangri (7,742 metres/25,400 feet) in 1962; Baltoro Kangri (7,312 metres/23,989 feet), Saipal (7,034 metres/23,077 feet) and Sharpu (7,100 metres/23,294 feet) in 1963; Gyachung Kang (7,922 metres/25,990 feet) and Annapurna South (7,256 metres/23,805 feet) in 1964; and Ngojunmba Ri (7,800 metres/25,590 feet) in 1965, one of the last peaks climbed before Nepal closed its doors to mountaineering.

In Japan, because of a popular devotion to Shintoism and Buddhism, people had always taken to the mountains as pilgrims, worshipping at the shrines of temples built far from the dwelling places of men. However, before the Second World War brought about profound changes in Japanese society, the chance to indulge in modern mountaineering was confined to an élite group of students from the privileged class, particularly when it came to climbing abroad. One notable climb was made in the Himalaya before the war: in 1931 an expedition from Rikkyo University in Tokyo climbed Nanda Kot (6,861 metres/22,510 feet) in the Garhwal Himalaya by the Northeast Ridge. None of the party had climbed anywhere else other than Japan and all their equipment was made in Japan. The future of Japanese climbing was looking bright until the war in the Pacific intervened.

By the end of the American occupation in 1952, Japan had embraced democracy in all spheres of life and activities that were once only for the select few were now open to everyone. This included modern mountaineering, which attracted masses of people who went out onto the crags and mountains for their recreation, providing an outlet for their supressed energies and the frustrations of wartime privation.

Sixty-four Japanese expeditions had gone to the Himalaya by 1965, accounting for 22 virgin summits. Japanese mountaineers were therefore well placed to take advantage of the lifting of the Nepalese ban and make the next logical step on the flanks of Everest – up the 2,286-metre (7,500-foot) Southwest Face.

In the pre-monsoon season of 1969 the Japanese Alpine Club sent out a small reconnaissance party prior to sending a larger group in the autumn. When the Japanese returned the weather was perfect and, unusually, there was very little wind and good firm snow conditions on the lower slopes of the face. All through October they pushed on up the central couloir, establishing three camps, with Camp 5 at 7,785 metres (25,600 feet). From this top camp they pushed the route to just below the base of the rock band on 31 October. The lead climbers were Naomi Uemura, Masatsugu Konishi, Hiroshi Nakajima and Shigeru Satoh. They had gained valuable information as to the route and also that they needed to overcome the difficulty of erecting tents at the top of the couloir, where the snow cover was sparse, by bringing out specially designed tent platforms. They returned to Japan to report on their findings and make plans for a full attempt in the spring of 1970.

The 1970 expedition decided that one group would attempt the Southwest Face of Everest while the other simultaneously attempted the original Southeast Ridge route. The Japanese brought out 39 climbers and employed 77 Sherpas, all of whom would work together until Advance Base camp had been established in the Western Cwm, from where the expedition would split. The organizers had decided unilaterally which climbers would go on which route – a decision that caused a degree of unrest.

Hiromi Otsuka changed his mind several times, under pressure from those anxious to climb their new route rather than the ordinary one, but he still concentrated most of the expedition's resources and personnel on the original route. Naomi Uemura and Teruo Matsuura reached the summit on 11 May followed by Katsutoshi Hirabayshi and Sherpa Chotare the next day. Hirabayshi had checked out the upper part of the Southwest Face by climbing down a short distance from the South Summit. He thought it looked very difficult – and so it proved to be, because the winter winds had stripped the face almost bare of snow.

The Southwest Face team, although fewer and without Uemura who had been on the previous two reconnaissances, made good progress establishing Camp 4 on 6 May, pitching the tents on duraluminium platforms. On 8 May Masatsugu Konishi and Akira Yoshikawa reached around 7,800 metres (25,590 feet). Two days later Katsuhiko Kano and Hiroshi Sagano, supported by two Sherpas, climbed higher to a point devoid of snow, where they removed their crampons and for 122 metres (400 feet) climbed on rock in good weather to the base of the rock band on the left side and at a height of 8,050 metres (26,410 feet). From the high point they could see an obvious ramp leading up left to the West Ridge. Above the start of the ramp a narrow cleft forked right, cleaving through the rock band and leading up to the broad strip of snow above it. They knew that climbing the gully would not be easy but thought it was possible. Full of optimism, they dropped back for a rest at Advance Base. Unfortunately, on the way down Kano was struck by a falling rock, as was Nakajima the same afternoon. Otsuka suddenly called off the attempt because of the danger of falling rocks and also his calculation that the rock band could not be climbed before the arrival of the monsoon. He therefore put the mission effort back to the original route, but bad weather came in and the expedition was terminated on 20 May. It naturally begs the question, had the Japanese put all their resources and manpower towards climbing on the Southwest Face, would they have succeeded in establishing a significant new route on Everest? The odds are that they would have done so.

The Southwest Face expedition of 1971

In the spring of 1971 Norman Dyhrenfurth returned to Everest as leader, with Jimmy Roberts as co-leader, of an international expedition to tackle not only the Southwest Face but also the West Ridge direct. There were nine climbers earmarked for the Southwest Face and ten for the West Ridge. Roberts coordinated the Sherpas at base camp and Dyhrenfurth took control of events between base camp and Advance Base. The two groups had self-selected since Dyhrenfurth, unlike Otsuka the year before, firmly believed in a democratic style of leadership.

All went reasonably well until the death of Harsh Bahuguna, a member of the West Ridge party from India, in the most awful circumstance. He was caught on a fixed rope while retreating down from the ridge in a storm that rapidly worsened. He reached a point where he could move no further and by the time other members of the team reached him he was beyond help, despite a final, valiant rescue attempt by Don Whillans. For ten days Harsh Bahuguna remained hanging there, not far from

Advance Base. After the storm ended, many of the team contracted a debilitating virus, the food supplies proved inadequate and it was realized that there were not enough Sherpas to cover both the climbing objectives. The West Ridge was abandoned in favour of the South Col and the Southeast Ridge, something several of the West Ridge team preferred to ensure a better chance for the summit.

After everyone had returned from the funeral and cremation of Harsh, at Gorak Shep, it was realized that there were not even enough porters to keep both teams supplied. Jimmy Roberts proposed abandoning the original route to concentrate resources on getting up the Southwest Face. Dyhrenfurth had put this to a vote, including the Sherpas. Michel and Yvette Vauchers were absent, away at the icefall, and only Carlo Mauri and Pierre Mazeaud voted for the South Col. The Sherpas naturally preferred the shorter, more straightforward snow slopes of the face rather than the long flog up to the South Col.

The Vauchers, Mauri and Mazeaud regarded this as an Anglo-Saxon plot to get the British up to the summit at all costs. After much debate, all four decided to go home. Yvette in particular was angry that the vote had denied her the opportunity to make the first female ascent of Everest and maybe the first husband and wife ascent.

Sickness took a heavy toll on those remaining. Dyhrenfurth, immobilized by a virus, ceded the leadership of the expedition to Jimmy Roberts and Don Whillans became climbing leader. Dougal Haston, Reizo Ito, Naomi Uemura and the two Austrians Wolfgang Axt and Leo Schlommer were the only other climbers still fit.

They all returned to the face at the end of April, occupying the campsites and duraluminium platforms established by the Japanese the year before with box tents designed by Whillans. On 5 May Camp 5 at 7,925 metres (26,000 feet) was occupied, from where Whillans and Haston first inspected the left-hand break through the rock band. Conditions had evidently changed since the Japanese were there; the pair found it lacked a campsite and was too steep, so they tried to find a break on the right and were able to establish a Camp 6 at 8,291 metres (27,200 feet). With the weather intermittently bad, most of the team descended to rest and to conserve supplies but Whillans and Haston remained. Resultant tensions led to Schlommer and Axt both departing the expedition, adding weight to the conspiracy theory that it was a British plot. The two Japanese, Ito and Uemura, gave continuous and loyal support, seemingly without concern as to who pioneered the route.

Whillans and Haston climbed above Camp 6 and looked round to the right, to the very edge of the Southwest Face, to a point where they saw a relatively easy route across broken ground to the Southeast Ridge. Taking that way out would not have gone down well, so they continued to check out a snow-filled corner or gully directly below the South Summit. After about 90 metres (300 feet) Whillans came back down from his high point and they both agreed to abandon the attempt. Supplies were coming up intermittently but not enough to support the hard climb ahead to the top of the rocks – about 245 metres (just over 800 feet) at that point and still with a long way to the summit. The main reason for the retreat was primarily the problem of climbing steep rock at more than 8,230 metres (27,000 feet) in high-altitude boots and clothing and cumbersome oxygen equipment.

Success on the Southwest Face in 1975

Further expeditions were mounted in the spring and autumn of the following year, the first one German and the second British, but neither succeeded. The German expedition was dogged by problems. Felix Kuen and Adi Huber reached 8,300 metres

First up Japan's Junko Tabei plants the flag of her native country and Nepal on the summit of Everest on 16 May 1975. Tabei, who had survived an avalanche on the way up, became the first woman to reach the top of Everest, and in 1992 she became the first female climber to complete the ascent of the Seven Summits (the highest peak on each of the seven continents).

(27,231 feet) before they had to give up in the face of high winds and insufficient supplies with which to sit it out. Nothing had been gained on the mountain except to reconfirm the need for good leadership of a homogenous group of strong climbers. This was in evidence from October through to November in the British team led by Chris Bonington – its problem lay in having arrived too late in the season. In the face of shrieking westerly winds Haston and Doug Scott did not reach Whillan's high point. If there was to be a next time then it would have to take place earlier in the season and be directed at the left-hand gully.

A year later, in autumn 1973, the Japanese returned. Again they divided their resources, between the Southwest Face and the original South Col route. Although they reached Camp 6 on the face, no further progress was made from there and bad weather towards the end of October made them give up. However, from the South Col two Japanese climbers went all the way to the summit on 26 October – the first ever expedition to climb Everest in the post-monsoon season.

By the autumn of 1975, when Bonington had again managed to 'book' Everest, six of his team had been to the Southwest Face before and three of them twice. There had never been an expedition to the mountain that was so experienced. Drawing on that, they came in earlier, walking in through the monsoon to take advantage of the window of opportunity that is provided as the monsoon draws back and before the onset of the westerly jet stream. They arrived to establish base camp on 22 August.

One group after another pushed a safe route through the Khumbu Icefall then along the magnificent Western Cwm. By the time they were installed in Camp 2 they were several days ahead of the leader's most optimistic forecast. Bonington had climbed Annapurna II (7,937 metres/26,040 feet) in 1960 and Nuptse (7,861 metres/25,790 feet), by the South Face, in 1961. In 1970 he led the successful climb up Annapurna's South Face. His planning and enthusiasm, coupled with sterling work by Dave Clarke, Mike Thompson (food), Adrian Gordon (Camp 1 organization) and Mike Cheyne's Sherpas, gave the team the means to push on rapidly up the face itself to Camp 5. They had countered the potential avalanche danger by siting Camp 4 much lower than previously, under a protective rock buttress, and Camp 5 was now situated to the right of the central couloir. Old Everest hands remembered only too well losing 16 tents in 1972 because of avalanche, rock fall and the power of winter winds. A large team of Sherpas and all the climbers had contributed to the build-up: Alan Fiffe, Ronnie Richards, Mick Burke and Scott to Camp 3; Nick Estcourt and Paul Braithwaite to Camp 4; and Haston, Peter Boardman, Martin Boysen and Hamish MacInnes to Camp 5.

From there Bonington, Richards and Scott set off across the central couloir, fixing rope to within about 45 metres (150 feet) of the left-hand gully. They went down the ropes still unsure if the tongue of snow leading into the gully continued all the way up and linked with the upper snowfields. The following day Braithwaite and Estcourt went up to find out. From the previous high point Braithwaite led a long pitch across steep, friable ribs of rock that were sheathed in a layer of powdered snow. After very difficult and insecure climbing, he reached the base of the gully. They then led up over chock stones and on to hard, avalanche-pressed snow until the pair reached an amphitheatre at the top. Estcourt led up mixed rock and snow on the right to gain a ramp, with his crampons scraping ineffectually through two inches of powder covering loose and brittle rock angled at 65 degrees. They eventually reached a point where they were certain there was a way through to the upper snowfield and a site for Camp 6 above the rock band. It had been a great effort since they had run out of oxygen negotiating the hardest climbing on the face.

On 22 September Haston and Scott moved up the fixed ropes, into the great cleft and out up the ramp to the high point. Ang Phurba carried the tent as Scott led up another 90 metres or so (300 feet) of difficult ground to a site for Camp 6 on the crest of a snow arête. Thompson, Bonington, Burke and Pertemba all came up with vital loads – an impressive carry, especially for Bonington who had now been at or above Camp 5 for nine days. They all descended, leaving Haston and Scott to erect the tent. Bonington had requested that whoever went first should fix more rope across the upper snowfield so that something tangible would be there to help the next attempt if that one failed. They led out more than 450 metres (nearly 1,500 feet) of rope and returned to Camp 6 to prepare for their summit attempt.

The next morning, after mugs of tea and a fry-up of corned beef, Haston and Scott set off with light sacks containing a stove and a billycan for hot water, four 'dead men' belay plates, four pitons and one hammer. They swung leads from the end of the rope up to the foot of the South Summit couloir, where Haston's oxygen set became blocked with ice. An hour passed as they used a Swiss penknife to release a blockage. More time was spent on the 9-metre (30-foot), 65-degree amorphous yellow rock step in which Scott put three pegs. From a fourth he belayed Haston up, who then led all the way up the couloir to the South Summit. The unconsolidated powder snow made the going slow and they did not arrive at the South Summit until 3.30 p.m. On finding the snow of the Summit Ridge more consolidated they continued along the ridge, with Haston climbing the Hillary Step all banked up with monsoon snow. Scott led on towards the summit.

At 6.00 p.m. they walked up onto the summit to rest, eat and photograph the wonderful display of colour as the sun set. Their headlamps failed when descending the Hillary Step and their oxygen had run out, so they thought it prudent to bivouac at the South Summit, where they already had a small hollow, left over from their afternoon brew stop, to enlarge into a cave. There they sat on rucksacks for nine hours in temperatures of around minus 40 degrees C. That they survived the highest bivouac ever, just 100 metres (328 feet) below Everest's summit, with no sleeping bag or oxygen and – as it turned out – without suffering frostbite, was to give them and others more confidence about what and how they might climb in the future.

The climbing of the Southwest Face had shown that if enough men and materials are used by an experienced, cohesive group of climbers, employing numerous Sherpas, and that if they are well led, using oxygen and fixing ropes to the top camp, then given reasonable weather and snow conditions, success is more or less guaranteed even on the highest Himalayan face. This had already been demonstrated in 1970 on Chris Bonington's Annapurna South Face expedition and on the Rupal Face of Nanga Parbat. All members of the expedition who continued to climb did so with far less assistance from Sherpas, oxygen and fixed ropes. Elsewhere the trend back to basics was already underway, even on the highest peaks.

Towards Alpine style in the Himalaya

The big national expeditions to K2 (Italians), Everest (British), Kangchenjunga and Nanga Parbat (Germans/Austrians) tended to obscure the fact that the approach to the Himalaya had begun as lightweight efforts and the majority of climbs continued to be made lightweight – and in some cases were made in pure Alpine style, without any fixed ropes and yo-yoing up and down, building up supplies at fixed camps. Tom Longstaff climbed Trisul (7,120 metres/23,359 feet) with Karbir Burathoki and the Brocherel brothers of Courmayeur. They went from the Trisul Glacier (around 5,290 metres/17,355 feet) in one long day on 12 June 1907 to record the highest peak ever climbed at the time, and in pure Alpine style from the glacier. In the same year the Norwegians Ingvald Monrad Aas and Carl Wilhelm Rubenson attempted Kabru (7,394 metres/24,258 feet), 11 kilometres (7 miles) south of Kangchenjunga. On 20 October they set off from their high camp (6,706 metres/22,000 feet) and gained the connecting ridge between the twin summits of the mountain only to be stopped 30 metres (100 feet) below the main summit by violent winds that threatened to blow them off the mountain. Alexander Kellas, the Aberdonian chemist, also climbed lightweight style (with Sherpa support) on numerous peaks in the Himalaya, mainly in Sikkim. In 1910 he had a field day climbing Pauhunri (7,125 metres/23,375 feet) and Chomo Yummo (6,829 metres/22,404 feet) among others peaks in Sikkim.

The Swiss climbed Jongsong Peak (7,462 metres/24,481 feet) in 1930, Frank Smythe's British Expedition made the first ascent of Kamet (7,756 metres/25,446 feet) in 1931 and the ascent of Nanda Devi (7,816 metres/25,643 feet) was achieved by Bill Tilman and Noel Odell in 1936. All these expeditions were modest in their approach and in the manpower employed when compared with the attempts on Everest.

The first ascent of Cho Oyu (8,201 metres/26,906 feet) was made by an Austrian expedition in a style well ahead of the times – not pure Alpine style, but with less men and materials than on any previous ascent of an 'eight-thousander'. Sepp Jochler, who had already climbed the North Face of the Eiger; the geologist, explorer and amateur climber Herbert Tichy; and Pasang Dawa Lama reached the summit on 19 October 1954. This was the first ascent of an 8,000-metre (26,246-foot) peak to be made post-monsoon and in lightweight style. Pasang was a strong and experienced climber who had been with the Americans on K2 in 1939 and had almost summited with leader Fritz Wiessner, and he performed the most amazing feat on the Cho Oyu expedition. On 16 October Pasang was down in Namche Bazaar collecting supplies when on the way back to base camp he heard that a strong Swiss expedition had abandoned Gaurisankar and was now intent on climbing Cho Oyu. Pasang hurried back to join the Austrians, leaving Thami (3,800 metres/12,467 feet) that

morning and racing over the Nangpa La (5,716 metres/18,753 feet) to the Austrian base camp – all on 17 October. On the 18th he climbed up to Camp 4 at 7,010 metres (23,000 feet) and on the 19th was on the summit at 26,750 feet. His first words when he met the Austrians were: 'Have the Swiss reached the summit?' When they answered 'no', he said, 'Thank God for that, I would have cut my throat'. There were few Sherpas who were so motivated – and even to this day it is unlikely that anyone has performed such a feat of endurance as to climb 4,401 metres (14,439 feet) in four days over rough country up to 8,201 metres on an unclimbed peak.

In 1957 it was again the Austrians who took another step forward towards Alpine-style climbing at altitude with their first ascent of Broad Peak without oxygen and for being the first group to tackle an 8,000-metre (26,246-foot) peak without porters. Marcus Schmuck, Fritz Wintersteller, Kurt Diemberger and Hermann Buhl reached the summit on 9 June, although this inspiring climb was marred throughout the planning and execution of the climb by controversy that continues to this day. Sadly, a few days after summiting Broad Peak, Hermann, one of the greatest Alpinists of all time who had made the first ascent of Nanga Parbat solo, fell through a cornice while attempting to climb Chogolisa with Diemberger. His body was never recovered. In the light of the success on Broad Peak and the attention given to the death of Buhl, the climbing of Skilbrum (7,360 metres/24,147 feet) has largely been overlooked. Schmuck and Wintersteller left Broad Peak base camp on 18 June to camp, at 6,000 metres (19,685 feet), below Skilbrum. The next day they reached the summit at 4.00 p.m. and the following day they were back at base camp by 8.30 a.m. after a round trip of 52 hours completely self-contained and therefore in Alpine style.

On Everest the large, siege-style expeditions continued to operate but every once in while a smaller group of more adventurous spirits would arrive to attempt a new route in lightweight style. In 1982 Chris Bonington organized a small team to tackle

Teeth of rock The jagged terrain around Cho Oyu, the world's sixth-highest peak at 8,201 metres (26,906 feet). The mountain was first seriously attempted by the 1952 British Everest reconnaissance expedition, which was thwarted by an ice-cliff. When the Austrians Tichy and Jöchler and the Nepalese Pasang Dawa Lama summited it in May 1954, it became the fifth 8,000-metre (26,246-foot) mountain to be climbed.

the unclimbed Northeast Ridge. Bonington, Dick Renshaw, Peter Broadman and Joe Tasker eventually established three snow caves along the ridge, the highest of them at 7,850 metres (25,754 feet). On 4 May they climbed and fixed rope most of the way up the first pinnacle of the ridge and then descended down to base camp. Renshaw had experienced a mild stroke high up on the pinnacle and Bonington decided that he was just too exhausted to continue, so only Boardman and Tasker went back up the mountain, intending to go Alpine style from the end of their fixed rope to the summit. On 15 May they were seen that evening, through a telescope, at the base of the second pinnacle but after that neither man was seen again for ten years, until 1992 when Kazakh climbers found Peter's body sat in the snow. Possibly Joe had fallen and Pete succumbed to exhaustion retreating alone.

On 5 August 1988 Russell Brice and Harry Taylor managed to climb the Pinnacle Ridge in its entirety to where it joined the North Ridge. However, too exhausted to continue upwards, they retreated down the North Ridge and North Col to base camp.

In 1995 a large Japanese expedition of 13 climbers from Nihon University and 31 Sherpas fixed a huge amount of rope up the Northeast Ridge and around and over the Pinnacles to enable them to reach the North Ridge and the summit of Everest on 11 May. The assistance that fixed ropes provide is obvious from the fact that the Japanese climbers descended from the summit of Everest to their Advance

New approaches The 1976 American Nanda Devi expedition was marked by disagreements between a traditional siege-style approach (favoured by John Roskelley) and lighter Alpine-style tactics championed by Willi Unsoeld. In contrast to the 1936 expedition, the Americans pushed up the West Face of the mountain and then overcame the formidable North Buttress to reach the summit on 1 September. The expedition, though, cost the life of Unsoeld's daughter Nanda Devi, who was named after the mountain.

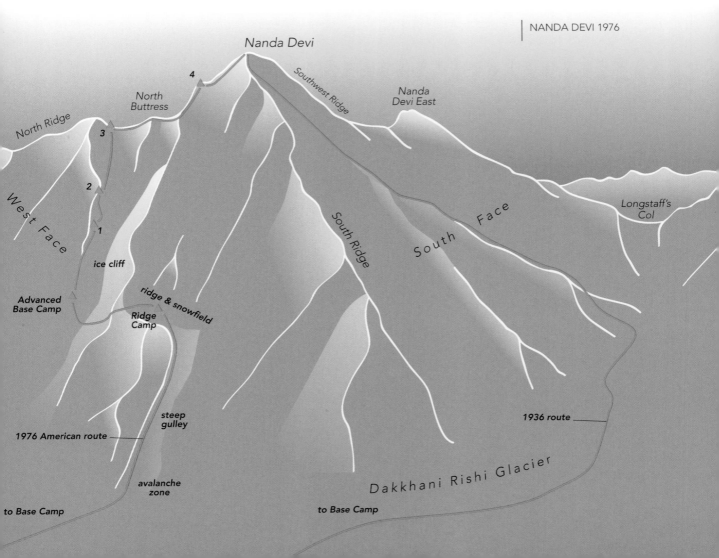

NANDA DEVI 1976

Base in a day, having left at 8.15 a.m., they slid down the ropes, racing along the
ropes between the Pinnacles, and reached the camp at 6.16 p.m., just as the sun
was setting. These fixed ropes and fixed camps backed up with Sherpa support have
made it possible for all kinds of records to be broken on Everest that are not a lot to
do with the progress and development of pure climbing. Disabled people have now
climbed Everest, with one leg and even with no legs, and so has a blind person. Now
there is an ever-widening gap between the youngest and oldest ascentionists, and in
May 2013, 80-year-old Yuichiro Miura, with his son Gota, became the current oldest
person to climb the mountain.

In total contrast, Switzerland's Erhard Loretan and Jean Troillet, who had made
a rapid ascent of Dhaulagiri together, decided to climb the north side of Everest in
total Alpine style. They skied to the foot of the face on 28 August 1986 and started
climbing at 11.00 p.m. by the light of their head torches. The men reached the foot of
the Hornbein Couloir and after a long rest they set off again the following evening,
reaching the summit at 2.00 p.m. on 30 August after 31 hours of climbing. Their
descent was even more spectacular, since they were down in three and a half hours
after glissading most of the way on their backsides! It has to be said that to set off to
climb Everest without sleeping bags, tent or rope, even on an established route, takes
some courage – but then they were two of the world's finest mountaineers, who knew
how to keep the margins of safety satisfyingly narrow.

Alpine style on Nanga Parbat

Nanga Parbat continues to provide an arena for ground-breaking climbing, following
on from Reinhold Messner's remarkable solo climb up the Diamir Face in 1978, when
he became the first to make an absolutely solo ascent of an 'eight-thousander' by
a new route. In 2005 the Americans Vince Anderson and Steve House climbed up
the central pillar of the Rupal Face, between the Messner route of 1970 and the
Kukuczka–Carsolio route of 1985, both of which employed fixed rope. Anderson and
House took on the steepest section of this, the highest face in the entire Himalaya,
completely Alpine style. On the first day they climbed about 1,600 metres (nearly
5,250 feet) from their base camp, and during the next five days they continuously
moved up over steep rock, mixed rock and ice, often with poor belays and frequent
rock falls. On 6 September they arrived on the summit as the sun was setting, having
made one of the most difficult routes on any 8,000-metre (26,246-foot) summit.

K2 – THE NEW ROUTES

The pace of progress climbing on other peaks was slower than that of Everest but the climbs made were no less adventurous or dramatic. It was not until 1978 that an alternative route on K2 was found. It was pioneered by the Americans with Lou Reichardt and Jim Wickwire reaching the summit first via the Northeast Ridge, and a long traverse across to the Shoulder of the original route. Reichardt made the ascent without using bottled oxygen. In 1981 K2's West Ridge was climbed by a Japanese expedition that included the exceptionally strong and gifted local climber Nazir Sabir. It was Sabir who at a critical time motivated the team to continue and led most of the route to the summit, which he reached with Eiho Otani on 7 August.

When China opened up its side of K2 the Japanese quickly organized an expedition to the North Ridge, which they climbed in 1982 (above, Naoe Sakashita waves the flags of Japan and China on 14 August 1982). The Poles climbed the central rib of the South Face in 1986, and in the same year the so-called Magic Line, the South Sou'west Pillar, was climbed by Polish and Slovak climbers.

Two of France's strongest Alpinists, Pierre Beghin and Christophe Profit, climbed the Northwest Ridge and North Ridge with just two friends in support at their base camp. Although the French climbing was not exploratory it was nevertheless a very bold undertaking that connected the previous routes to the summit and back down in two days. The summit photographs they took as the sun was setting on 15 August were witnessed by a French trekking group down at Concordia, astonished to notice flashlights going off on the summit several miles above them. Beghin and Profit descended through the night all the way down to their tents, having made a magnificent, Alpine-style ascent of the world's second-highest peak.

In 1994 a Basque expedition climbed the South–Southeast Ridge of K2, pioneered by an Anglo-French team as far as the Shoulder in 1983. The Basques were the first to connect the ridge to the summit and open an alternative, and probably easier, way than the Abruzzi Spur.

A large Russian team arrived to fix rope to the West Face direct in 2007. Its ranks included veterans of the Jannu North Face, which had taken several weeks to siege using thousands of feet of fixed rope, bolts and porter ledges. Several teams had previously prospected the possibility of climbing the West Face in Alpine style but had given up because conditions were not favourable. The Russians had no intention of doing other than fixing rope, which they did up to about 7,850 metres (25,754 feet). After two and a half months of such work, during which they established seven camps, they reached the summit of K2 on 21 October and again on the 22nd: a real team effort, with 11 of the 16-man expedition reaching the summit. The climb came in for some criticism in the *American Alpine Journal* whose editors felt that, whatever the rights and wrongs of sieging these last great problems, 'it was unethical to abandon thousands of feet of fixed rope and hundreds of pounds of equipment and provisions on K2's slopes'.

The other magnificent achievement was accomplished in 2012 when the whole of the Mazeno Ridge was climbed to the summit and a descent made down the Kinshofer Route after a journey of about 13 kilometres (8 miles). The Mazeno Ridge had been attempted Alpine style in 1992 by Serge Effimov, Doug Scott, Ang Phurba and Nga Temba. With each climber carrying 25 kilogrammes (55 pounds) they gained the ridge after two bivouacs. They continued along the ridge climbing over points at 6,825 metres (22,441 feet), 6,880 metres (22,572 feet) and

Abruzzi again Until 1978, K2 had been climbed by just a single route (and only summited twice). In that year two expeditions tackled the mountain: a British attempt up the West Ridge led by Chris Bonnington failed, after Nick Estcourt died in an avalanche; the American expedition under John Whittaker which aimed at the North-East Ridge was successful. An attempt at a direct approach up the ridge proved too difficult, and in the end the summit team traversed across the East Face to the Abruzzi Ridge and completed the ascent along the route of the 1954 Italian expedition.

6,970 metres (22,867 feet), the first of several summits, but gave up after five days through exhaustion.

The Americans Steve Swenson and Doug Chabot finally climbed all eight summits of the Mazeno Ridge to the Mazeno Gap. Unfortunately illness and deteriorating weather forced them to descend by the Schell Route. This attempt in 2004 had been a magnificent effort and in great style with just a single rope and minimum gear.

In 2012 British climbers Rick Allen and Sandy Allan, as part of a larger group, achieved one of the finest climbs ever made in the Himalaya. During late June Rick and Sandy, with Cathy O'Dowd and three Sherpas, reached 6,200 metres (20,341 feet) and returned to base camp having left food, equipment and short sections of fixed rope for their return. On 2 July, now fully acclimatized, they set off climbing all eight of the Mazeno peaks to the Mazeno Gap. It had been hard going, since nearly all the route was around 7,000 metres (nearly 23,000 feet) with Grade IV ice, complicated rocky sections and a lot of soft, unstable snow. Consequently they did not reach the Mazeno Gap until 10 July. Only Rick and Sandy continued towards the summit of Nanga Parbat with the remainder of the team descending the Schell Route on 13 July.

Rick and Sandy attempted to keep on the crest of the ridge but were forced by a rock step to drop down the north side and skirt around ribs of rock in thick cloud. They eventually reached the summit on 15 July, then headed off down the Kinshofer Route. Both men knew this route for they had climbed up it in 2009, along with many other people, but now there was no sign in the deep snow of anyone else on this side of the mountain until they were nearly in base camp. On 19 July they

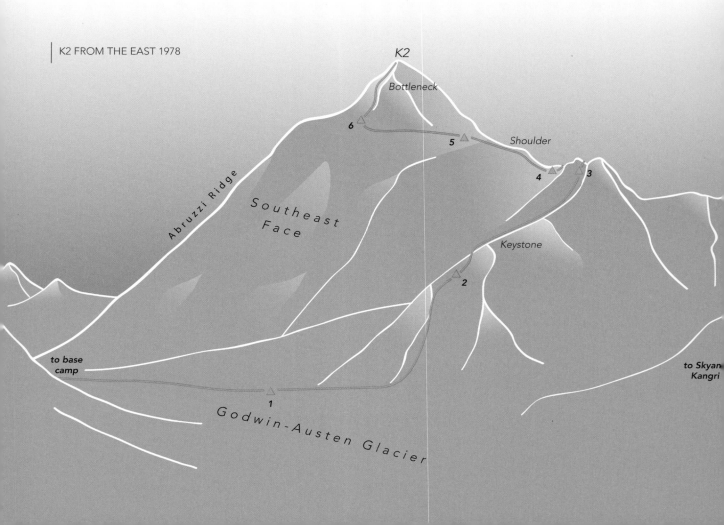

K2 FROM THE EAST 1978

K2

Bottleneck

6

5

Shoulder

Abruzzi Ridge

Southeast Face

4

3

Keystone

2

to base camp

to Skyang Kangri

1

Godwin-Austen Glacier

NOVEL WAYS ON KANGCHENJUNGA

On Kangchenjunga it was 22 years before Indian Army climbers found another way to the summit with the help of a detachment of Ladakh Scouts, 16 climbers and continuous fixed rope. Prem Chand and Nima Dorje reached the summit on 31 May 1977 via the Northeast Ridge after a very impressive final push.

In total contrast the next new route was established in lightweight style by a four-man team with just two Sherpas.

Frenchman Georges Bettembourg supported up to the last bivouac, then Boardman, Scott and Tasker climbed, without oxygen, via the steep West Face (left, pictured under the Pinnacles on the West Ridge) and North Ridge to reach the summit on 16 May 1979. This was the first time a major peak had been climbed lightweight and without oxygen being available on the mountain. Many new and difficult variations followed on the main peak and on the subsidiary peaks. All the 'five treasures' were traversed by the Russian–Kazakh–Ukrainian climbing team in 1989.

Of all the many great routes pioneered in the Kangchenjunga area, the Slovenian ascent of the south peak (8,476 metres/27,808 feet) was exemplary. Marko Prezelj and Andre Stremfelj climbed the South Ridge to the summit after five bivouacs on 30 April 1991. They had climbed completely Alpine style and often solo, up pitches of Grade VI rock and sometimes vertical, even overhanging, ice. At 8,100 metres (26,574 feet) they joined part of the Russian route and followed and used the Russian fixed ropes to the summit. For this climb they received the first Piolet d'Or award for mountaineering.

arrived to be well looked after by members of a Czech expedition with whom they rested, fed and rehydrated. They had gone for two days without liquid because the flint had dropped out of their lighter.

This was a remarkable climb by anyone's standards – climbing high for 18 days, mostly on a ridge, thereby exposed to the vagaries of the weather – but what made this climb exceptional was the fact that Sandy was 56 years old and Rick 58. Their peers acknowledged this achievement in April 2013 when, in Chamonix, they were presented, along with five other expeditions, with the Piolet d'Or – an award established in 1992 that now recognizes all such inspiring climbs.

Hard technical climbing

There has been such an explosion of interest in Himalayan climbing, particularly after 1970, that space permits only a brief outline of the new climbs made in recent times. Although many courageous and innovative climbers cannot therefore be mentioned, the following technical climbs, mostly achieved on peaks around 6,000 to 7,000 metres (nearly 20,000–23,000 feet), reveal how the world's finest Alpinists and rock climbers have added the extra challenge of altitude to technical difficulty.

Joe Tasker and Dick Renshaw went to the Garhwal in 1975. They left their lonely, unattended base camp to climb 1,524 metres (5,000 feet) up the South Face

LAST OF THE 'EIGHT THOUSANDERS'

The last of the 8,000-metre (26,246-foot) summits to be climbed was Shisha Pangma (8,013 metres/26,289 feet). It was a team effort achieved after a long siege by Chinese and Tibetan climbers via the northern snow slopes up to the North Ridge, with ten members following the ridge to the summit on 2 May 1964.

It was not until 1982 that another significant route was established on the mountain. Roger Baxter Jones, Alex MacIntyre and Doug Scott first climbed nearby Pungpa Ri (7,445 metres/24,425 feet) in a three-day Alpine push. They then set off, now fully acclimatized, for the hitherto unvisited South Face, where they had a completely virgin, 3,000-metre (9,840-foot) face to climb. They reached the summit on 28 May and descended by a couloir on the right of the face. The round trip was made with three bivouacs over four days of rare good weather.

In autumn 1990 three faster men arrived to climb another new route on the South Face. Voytek Kurtyka, Erhard Loretan and Jean Troillet climbed up the left-hand couloir to the central summit, reaching the main summit by 10.00 a.m. The trio was back at base camp less than 24 hours after leaving it.

of Dunagiri (7,066 metres/23,182 feet) in six days of continuous climbing. With all the usual storms and snowfall to contend with it took a further five days to descend, during which time Renshaw's fingers were badly frostbitten. This was a hallmark ascent and an indication of things to come. In the same year a less technical but equally impressive climb was made in the Karakoram when Messner and Peter Habeler climbed Hidden Peak (Gasherbrum I) by a new route on the Northwest Face from their supply dump at 6,700 metres (21,981 feet). For Habeler, Tasker and Renshaw these were tremendous achievements because all three were on their first visit to the Himalaya.

Spurred on by his success on Dunagiri, Tasker joined up with Peter Boardman in 1976 to climb the West Face of Changabang. This was one of the most technically difficult climbs made at the time by two men. Over a period of 40 days they fixed 610 metres (2,000 feet) of rope on this 1,539-metre (5,050-foot) face during which time they survived hanging bivouacs, hard rock climbing and intense autumn cold.

In 1977, in the central Hindu Kush, the 2,438-metre (8,000-foot) East Face of Koh-i-Bandaka (6,840 metres/22,441 feet) was climbed by a group containing Alex MacIntyre, John Porter, Jan Wolf and Voytek Kurtyka (who thought it was harder and more dangerous than the North Face of the Eiger). They negotiated the steep ice and unstable rock bands of this formidable face in six days, Alpine style. Andrzej Zawada, the leader of this expedition, and Terry King, made an Alpine ascent of the 1,981-metre (6,500-foot) North Face of Koh-e-Mandras in five days of dangerous, mixed climbing. This was the start of a fruitful period of Anglo-Polish climbing.

A far more technical climb took place that year when Americans Kim Schmitz, Dennis Hennek, John Roskelley, Galen Rowell and Jim Morrissey climbed Trango Tower (6,257 metres/20,528 feet). This team of expert, big wall climbers took four days to follow a line up ice-ramps and steep granite walls at 5.8 A1.

At the same time in the summer of 1977, Bonington and Scott climbed the Ogre (7,285 metres/23,901 feet) in lightweight style from the ice plateau, negotiating pitches of 5.9 A1. They had a lot of trouble descending after Scott broke both legs on the first abseil and four days later Bonington smashed his ribs. Thanks to the help afforded by Mo Anthoine and Clive Rowland they managed to get down to the glacier in eight days. The second ascensionists of the Ogre – 24 years later – thought the final tower must have been the hardest rock climbed at the time at that altitude.

In 1978 the Americans George and Jeff Lowe, Jim Donini and Michael Kennedy climbed 2,134 metres (7,000 feet) up the very steep granite and ice-choked gullies of the north ridge of Latok I (7,145 metres/23,441 feet). The final 150 metres (almost 500 feet) of this beautiful line could not be taken because of Jeff Lowe's illness. It has been attempted many times since without success. Over in the Garhwal that same year, MacIntyre, Porter, Zureck and Kurtyka established a very hard rock climb on the South Buttress of Changabang after an eight-day push from base camp.

In 1979 Roskelley and Schmitz with Ron Kauk and Bill Forest climbed up a 762-metre (2,500-foot) narrow gully to the foot of the 1,067-metre (3,500-foot) East Face of Uli Biaho Tower (6,109 metres/20,042 feet). They spent 12 days climbing this continuously steep wall with ten nights spent in hammocks. They graded it VII (A4). It was the hardest big wall climb ever made in the Himalaya. Roskelley had earlier that year made the first ascent of Gaurisankar (7,115 metres/23,343 feet), by the horrendous West Face using siege tactics.

In 1981 Doug Scott and Georges Bettembourg, with Greg Child and Rick White from Australia, climbed up the East Pillar and head wall of Shivling in a continuous 13-day push, negotiating 60 pitches of steep rock (Grade 5.9 A3) and mixed ground (French grade TD-ED ['*tres difficile*' and '*exceptionale difficile*'], as used in the Alps). It was found that big wall climbing did not mix so well on contrasting snow arêtes and gully ice. The weight of gear for one detracts from the other, making it altogether a very strenuous and time-consuming business. They had snowfall every day to contend with.

Roskelley and Rowell returned to Nepal in 1982 with fellow American Vern Clevenger and Englishman Bill O'Connor to make the first ascent of Cholatse (6,440 metres/21,128 feet) by the Southwest Ridge, which included some 30 pitches of hard green ice. Roskelley thought it one of the hardest climbs of its type in the Himalaya. In the Gangotri Mountains of India, Scottish climbers Allen Fyffe and Bob Barton climbed the huge, granite Southwest Buttress of Bhagirathi III (6,454 metres/21,174 feet) just across the Gangotri Glacier from Shivling. After fixing seven ropes at the start they climbed continuously for 11 days. Unfortunately, the firm granite gave way

Cold camp American John Roskelley peeks out of his bivouac high on the summit plateau of Cholatse. The 6,440-metre (21,128-foot) mountain was the last major unclimbed peak around the Khumbu Valley, until Roskelley and his climbing companions Vern Clevenger, Galen Rowell and Bill O'Connor scaled its Southwest Ridge in April 1982.

to shattered rock and shale near the summit. They descended down the North Ridge in a day. The following year Chris Bonington and Jim Fotheringham pioneered a new mixed route on Shivling's unclimbed West Summit involving mixed rock and ice. They topped out after a bold, continuous five-day push.

Elsewhere in India, Renshaw and Stephen Venables made the first ascent of Kishtwar Shivling (6,040 metres/19,816 feet) via the North Face in a five-day push. This 1,500-metre (4,921-foot) route involved vertical ice and the climbing of superb granite cracks, slabs and open corners at Grade V and Grade VI.

By 1984 climbers were pushing out up ever-steeper walls high in the Himalaya and Karakoram with the confidence and courage to move continuously up, day after day, without fixed ropes. The Norwegians Hans Christian Doseth and Finn Doehli climbed the huge Southeast Face of Trango Tower. This ascent is possibly the most demanding big wall climb in the Himalaya. Tragically, as the two were abseiling down, they met with an accident. Their battered bodies were discovered after a helicopter reconnaissance.

In autumn 1984 Ganesh II (7,111 metres/23,330 feet) was climbed via the huge South Face in nine days by British climbers Nick Kekus and Rick Allen. They met with Grade V difficulties on the rock and long sections of steep ice. It took them three days to descend. This was a just reward for the setbacks and tragedy that had dogged Kekus's previous bold expeditions to Kalanka, Shivling and Annapurna III.

On 3 October two Catalans, Nils Bohigas and Enric Lucas, reached the middle summit (8,051 metres/26,414 feet) of Annapurna by way of the huge 3,000-metre (9,842-foot) South Face. They acclimatized thoroughly first by spending five weeks

THE TYRANNY OF NUMBERS

In 1986 the Nepalese decided no longer to restrict the mountains of Nepal to just one expedition a season. From then on, anyone that could pay could go. By 1987 there were over 250 people at Everest base camp; today there are often more than 1,000 people milling about the south base camp in May. The same has happened on the Tibetan side, especially since a blacktop road has been built right up to the north base camp. At these honeypot locations on Everest, and to a lesser extent on the ordinary routes up other 'eight thousanders' and attractive peaks such as Ama Dablam, there is no longer the opportunity for peace and serenity. In fact in spring 2013 a fight erupted between three regular climbers on a private expedition and Sherpas fixing ropes on the Lhotse Face for commercial expeditions.

Some of the problems arising from the tyranny of numbers, such as waste disposal and deforestation for firewood, are being managed. The problems that have not been are on the mountain: the mass of people joining commercial expeditions to climb 8,000-metre (26,246-foot) peaks. On Everest clients have died of hypothermia and oedema through having to wait several hours at the Hillary Step (above, the traffic on 19 May 2012 when 234 summited), where a bottleneck forms as up to 300 guides and clients make their way up and down with no alternative.

Everest must appear much diminished in the eyes of the public, who have been led to believe it is just an overcrowded rubbish tip, where climbers leave other climbers to die alone in the snow. In 2006 40 clients and guides passed Englishman David Sharp in a state of collapse just below the first step on the Northeast Ridge. He was sat next to the body of an Indian climber who had been there ten years. The Indian, with two companions, had got into difficulties; unable to move, he asked for help from passing Japanese climbers, who refused on the way up and again on the way down. Although not all those who ignored David Sharp had actually seen him, because of obstructed views caused by oxygen masks and goggles, others were blinkered by their ambitions. The tabloid press declared that the 'Good Samaritan principle' no longer existed among climbers.

Yet more often, as with the ocean racing fraternity, climbers have given up their ambition to help others. Don Whillans was on Masherbrum (7,821 metres/25,660 feet) in 1957 and only about 45 metres (150 feet) away from making the first ascent. His partner, Joe Walmsley, was exhausted and hypothermic, so Whillans turned his back on the summit and took his friend down. In 2008 international climbers formed a rescue group to help the stricken Spanish mountaineer Inaki Ochoa high on Annapurna. The attempt failed, despite a supreme effort by the speed climber Uli Steck from Switzerland. But, as Stephen Venables wrote, 'Although they could not save Inaki ... he did not die alone'.

HELICOPTER RESCUES

Tomaz Humar, who had previously climbed the South Face of Dhaulagiri, set off up the Rupal Face of Nanga Parbat in 2005. He pushed off in bad weather to head off a rival, American, expedition but he then got into serious difficulty and called for a rescue. The crew of the Pakistan Army helicopter (pictured left, heading off to try to locate him) that responded, bravely winched him off from about 6,000 metres (19,685 feet) and in so doing nearly ditched. Humar was so cold he was unable to detach himself from his belay, but luckily the belay snapped under the strain and he was propelled into the air – only missing the helicopter thanks to the skill of the pilot who tilted his machine to one side.

In 2009 Humar again went climbing solo, this time up the huge South Face of Langtang Lirung in Nepal. He fell during the descent and, with a broken back, called for a helicopter on his mobile phone. Sadly, the pilot only located his body the day after he had perished up at around 6,300 metres (20,669 feet) on 8 November. (In 2010 three climbers were lifted off Annapurna from almost 7,000 metres/22,966 feet, and before that, in 2005, a helicopter had actually hovered over Everest, touching the summit with its skis.)

In 2011 two other experienced climbers were trying a new route on Ama Dablam where they got into difficulties on dangerous snow and dialled for a rescue. A new French helicopter came in and rescued David Gottler from Germany, before quickly returning to pick up Hiraide Kazuya from Japan. It was hovering just a few centimetres above his head when the rotor blade struck a snow cornice and hurtled down the Northeast Face, killing the pilot, Sabin Basnyat, and the rescue operator, Purna Awale. With incredible courage, another pilot and rescue operator flew in a helicopter the next day and brought Kazuya to safety.

This tragedy was a timely reminder that a helicopter rescue at 6,000 metres (19,685 feet) or more in the Himalaya is not as easy as at 4,000 metres (13,123 feet) in the Alps. The outstanding Italian climber and helicopter pilot Simone Moro requests climbers not to expect too much: 'Very few pilots have the skills and mental preparation to achieve such flights ..... It's necessary to manage the power, which is often not enough in rescues above 6,300 metres.'

Commitment to the Himalayan climb reduces as communication devices and helicopters become more efficient and powerful. Pre-war expedition climbers took the long boat journey out to the region, spending many days, if not weeks, at sea then long periods of retrieving expedition stores from customs before walking on to base camp for several more weeks along exposed footpaths and across rickety suspension bridges. They never expected news from home until back in Rawalpindi, Kathmandu or Delhi. Back then the climber left home and city to be in the mountains as a self-contained party, like a commando unit operating behind enemy lines. On the mountain the climbers had to look after themselves, since there was no rescue service.

Most private, tight-knit groups of friends heading for the Himalaya today expect, having taken out suitable insurance, that if there is an accident a helicopter will fly in to save their lives. With the introduction of more powerful helicopters, such as the French Ecureuil AS 350B3, climbers are increasingly aware that if they do get it wrong then, as in the Alps, such a rescue is indeed a strong possibility.

The pros and cons of this situation have been debated ever more strongly since the outstanding Slovenian climber in the Annapurna Sanctuary climbing Fluted and Tent Peaks before starting to climb the South Face, which they did in a continuous six-day push. They encountered difficulties of Grade V+/A2 and near-vertical sections of ice. They descended the Polish Spur to the left of their new line in one long, 18-hour day using up all their rack of gear. The last abseil was from their one remaining peg. This is now seen as an epoch-making climb on account of the scale; the objective dangers, requiring the climbing to be efficient and fast; and the sheer difficulty of the walls and gullies, needing great skill, determination and endurance.

By October 1986 Reinhold Messner had not only climbed Everest without oxygen, climbed Nanga Parbat by a new route solo and climbed Everest solo, he had also became the first climber to ascend all 14 8,000-metre (26,246-foot) summits. He then moved on in other directions: into Green Politics, making epic journeys across hot deserts and polar wastes, and creating mountain museums in the north of Italy. Meanwhile, in 1987 the renowned Polish climber Jerzy Kukuczka became the second climber to ascend all the 'eight thousanders', but climbed four in winter and ten by new routes, including variations.

In 1985 Voytek Kurtyka from Poland, a former climbing partner of Kukuczka, joined Robert Schauer from Austria to achieve the distinction of climbing, in Alpine style, one of the most difficult mountain routes in the world when they ascended the west rib of the 'Shining Mountain', Gasherbrum IV (7,924 metres – over 26,000 feet, but under 8,000 metres). This achievement took 13 days of hard climbing over steep compact marble upon which, since they had no drilling equipment, it was difficult to find belays pitch after pitch. Being completely self-contained they had heavy sacks but used up all their supplies of food and fuel as the ascent went on for longer than planned due to heavy snowfall. The deep snow prevented them from going up to the summit.

In 1988, from 24 June to 14 July, Kurtyka, with Erhard Loretan, made the first ascent of the East Face of Nameless Tower. They had to make three attempts due to storms and because of the technical difficulty of this 29-pitch big wall climb. Two years later, in 1990, they made one-day ascents of Cho Oyu and also the South Face of Shisha Pangma, both with Jean Troillet. Loretan went on to become the third person to climb all the 'eight thousanders'.

The last 25 years

Despite the changed circumstances of Everest (see box, page 179), on the east side of the mountain climbers may find solitude and the opportunity to pioneer new routes in small teams of friends – as the Anglo-Americans did in 1988 when they climbed the Kangshung Face to the South Col. Stephen Venables went on alone up the Southeast Ridge to the summit without oxygen.

This inspiring climb was just one of so many put up in the last 25 years. There was Mick Fowler and Victor Saunders over in the Karakoram, climbing the 2,100-metre (6,890-foot) Golden Pillar of Spantik (7,028 metres/23,057 feet) in 1987. In 1992 the Slovenians Marko Prezelj and Andrej Stremfelj climbed the horrendous 2,000-metre (6,562-foot) Southeast Face of Melungtse in two and a half days, up and down after making the first ascent of the mountain. During the summer of 1997 Fowler was back in the Himalaya, now with Stephen Sustad, to follow Andy Cave and Brendan Murphy up the North Face of Changabang. They climbed every pitch without the divorcing experience of the second jumaring up the rope. The Australian Andrew Lindblade and New Zealander Athol Whimp climbed directly up the North Face

OXYGEN

The debate over the use of canned oxygen began on the early Everest expeditions in the 1920s and has continued ever since. George Finch, an early proponent of oxygen, saw its use in line with the development of better clothing, snow goggles, thermos bottles and the use of caffeine as a stimulant. He hypothesized that if an oxygen pill could be manufactured then 'not a soul would oppose its use'.

Many today would disagree and be opposed to taking any such pill, along with other performance-enhancing drugs. Such a pill is unlikely in the near future and most Everest climbers will continue to carry oxygen in bottles. However, it is interesting to note that until the Russian lightweight oxygen cylinders came on the market recently, borrowed from the space industry, the weight of the bottles actually outweighed the physiological benefits of imbibing their contents.

In general there is no substitute for acclimatization. It will be far more satisfying – and a less dangerous experience – if instant gratification is avoided and climbers acclimatize one day at a time. Dr David Hillebrandt's observations seem eminently sensible (see box, page 162). It is up to the individual to decide what he imbibes, but since climbing is a game, albeit with unwritten rules, there is a requirement that in the reporting of a climb to others the report is honest. No one could quibble if someone used oxygen and fixed ropes and they were able to report that the bottles, the rope and the fixed camps were all removed from the mountain and the maxim 'leave no trace' was respected.

of Thalay Sagar in fine style. Jules Cartwright and Richard Cross climbed a route attempted ten times previously on Ama Dablam, and they made it to the summit after moving continuously for ten days in 2001. The same year the renowned Russian climber Valery Babanov climbed the central peak of Meru, solo, and in 2003 he opened up a new way up the South Face of Nuptse with Yuri Koshelenko. In 2002 Mick Fowler and Paul Ramsden climbed an amazing ice runnel up the North Face of Siguniang (6,250 metres/20,505 feet) in China. The French climbers Yannick Graziani and Christian Trommsdorff made the first ascent of Pumari Chhish South (7,350 metres/24,114 feet), taking a beautiful line up the South Face, climbing in Alpine style for five days. In 2008 Kazuya Hiraide and Kei Tangiguchi climbed the East Face of Kamet (7,756 metres/25,446 feet) by a superb 1,800-metre (5,905-foot) logical line never previously attempted, now called Samurai Direct. In August 2011 Saser Kangri II East (7,518 metres/24,665 feet), the second-highest unclimbed peak in the world, was climbed in Alpine style on the first attempt by the American climbers Mark Richey, Steve Swenson and Freddie Wilkinson.

In 2013 the jury of the Piolets d'Or awarded all six nominees, from the climbs achieved in 2012, a Golden Ice-Axe to emphasize the non-competitive nature of mountaineering and that it is not about winners and losers but climbing for its own sake, as it was in the beginning and still is for the majority of climbers.

It would seem that it is in the makeup of many of us to take an interest in those who make epic journeys and hard climbs, going where no man had gone before. From mountaineering's earliest days the exploits of climbers have been followed avidly by the public, especially those activities on the flanks of Everest. It was Cicero in the first century BC who observed: 'What has always fascinated man most is the unknown.' It is this facet of human nature that will keep Himalayan exploration on course for another 100 years or more.

(Following pages)
Karakoram winter Kazakh climber Denis Urubko and Italian Simone Moro make steady progress as the sun rises on Gasherbrum II in February 2011. The climb was the first successful winter ascent of the mountain. Moro had previously been forced to turn back just 200 metres (almost 660 feet) from the summit of Broad Peak, and was determined to prove that the 'eight thousanders' of the Karakoram could be climbed in winter. The picture was taken by American Cory Richards, the team's third member, who was to win an award for his film of the expedition, 'Cold'.

Further Reading

CHAPTER 1 *Madeleine Lewis*

Burrard, Sidney Gerald. *A Sketch of the Geography and Geology of the Himalaya Mountains and Tibet.* Superintendent Government Printing: Calcutta, 1907–1908.

Isserman, Maurice and Weaver, Stewart. *Fallen Giants: A History of Himalayan Mountaineering from the Age of Empire to the Age of Extremes.* Yale University Press: New Haven and London, 2010.

Mason, Kenneth. *Abode of Snow: A History of Himalayan Exploration and Mountaineering from Earliest Times to the Ascent of Everest.* Diadem Books: London, 1987.

Molnar, Paul and Tapponnier, Paul. 'The Collision between India and Eurasia' in *Scientific American.* Volume 236, No. 4, April 1977, pages 30–41.

Zeitler, Peter K. and Meltzer, Anne S., et al. 'Erosion, Himalayan Geodynamics, and the Geomorphology of Metamorphism' in *GSA Today.* Volume 11, January 2001, pages 4–9.

Zurick, David and Pacheco, Julsun. *Illustrated Atlas of the Himalaya.* University Press of Kentucky: Lexington, 2006.

CHAPTER 2 *Georgios T. Halkios*

Aris, Michael. *Bhutan: The Early History of a Himalayan Kingdom.* Aris & Phillips Ltd: Warminster, 1979.

McKay, Alex and Balikci-Denjongpa, Anna. (Eds.) *Buddhist Himalaya: Studies in Religion, History and Culture.* Namgyal Institute of Tibetology: Gangtok, 2008.

Petech, Luciano. *Mediaeval History of Nepal (c. 750–1480).* Istituto Italiano per il Medio ed Estremo Oriente: Rome, 1958.

Rizvi, Janet. *Trans-Himalayan Caravans: Merchant Princes and Peasant Traders in Ladakh.* Oxford University Press: New Delhi, 1979.

Singh, Madanjeet. *Himalayan Art: Wall-Painting and Sculpture in Ladakh, Lahaul and Spiti, the Siwalik Ranges, Nepal, Sikkim and Bhutan.* Macmillan: London, 1968.

Snellgrove, David L. and Skorupski, Tadeusz. *The Cultural Heritage of Ladakh.* Prajna Press, Boulder, 1977.

Tobdan. *History and Religions of Lahaul: From the Earliest to Circa A.D. 1950.* Books Today: Delhi, 1984.

CHAPTER 3 *Stewart Weaver*

Cameron, Ian. *Mountains Of The Gods: The Himalaya and the Mountains of Central Asia.* Facts on File Publications: New York, 1984.

Fleming, Peter. *Bayonets to Lhasa: The First Full Account of the British Invasion of Tibet in 1904.* Harper: New York, 1961.

Hopkirk, Peter. *The Great Game: On Secret Service in High Asia.* John Murray: London, 1990.

Hopkirk, Peter. *Trespassers on the Roof of the World: The Secret Exploration of Tibet.* John Murray: London, 1990.

Keay, John. *Explorers of the Western Himalayas, 1820–1895.* John Murray: London, 1996.

CHAPTER 4 *Stewart Weaver*

Keay, John. *The Great Arc: The Dramatic Tale of How India Was Mapped and Everest Was Named.* Harper Collins: New York, 2000.

Mason, Kenneth. *Abode of Snow: A History of Himalayan Exploration and Mountaineering from Earliest Times to the Ascent of Everest.* E.P. Dutton & Co.: New York, 1955.

Meyer, Karl and Brysac, Shareen. *Tournament of Shadows: The Great Game and the Race for Empire in Central Asia.* Counterpoint: Washington, D.C., 1999.

Waller, Derek. *The Pundits: British Exploration of Tibet and Central Asia.* University Press of Kentucky: Lexington, 1988.

Wessels, C.J. *Early Jesuit Travellers in Central Asia, 1603–1721.* Nijhoff: The Hague, 1924.

Chapter 5 *Amanda Faber*

Curran, Jim. *K2: The Story of the Savage Mountain.* Hodder & Stoughton: London, 1995.

French, Patrick. *Younghusband: The Last Great Imperial Adventurer.* HarperCollins: London, 1994.

Isserman, Maurice and Weaver, Stewart. *Fallen Giants: A History of Himalayan Mountaineering from the Age of Empire to the Age of Extremes.* Yale University Press: New Haven and London, 2010.

Mason, Kenneth. *Abode of Snow: A History of Himalayan Exploration and Mountaineering from Earliest Times to the Ascent of Everest.* Diadem Books: London, 1987.

Mitchell Ian R. and Rodway, George W. *Prelude to Everest.* Luath Press Ltd.: Edinburgh, 2011.

Tenderini, Mirella and Shandrick, Michael. *The Duke of the Abruzzi: An Explorer's Life.* Bâton Wicks Publications: London, 1997.

Chapter 6 *Stephen Venables*

Howard-Bury, C.K. *The Reconnaissance of Mount Everest, 1921.* Edward Arnold & Co.: London, 1922.

Mason, Kenneth. *Abode of Snow: A History of Himalayan Exploration and Mountaineering from Earliest Times to the Ascent of Everest.* Diadem Books: London, 1987.

Pallis, Marco. *Peaks and Lamas: A Classic Book on Mountaineering, Buddhism and Tibet.* Shoemaker & Hoard: New York, 2004.

Sale, Richard and Cleare, John. *On Top of the World: Climbing the World's 14 Highest Peaks.* CollinsWillow: London, 2000.

Shipton, Eric. *Eric Shipton: The Six Mountain-Travel Books.* Bâton Wicks Publications: London, 2011.

Smythe, Frank. *The Six Alpine/Himalayan Climbing Books.* Bâton Wicks Publications: London, 2000.

Tilman, W.H. *The Seven Mountain Travel Books.* Diadem Books: London, 1991.

Unsworth, Walt. *Everest: The Mountaineering History.* The Mountaineers: Seattle, 2000.

Venables, Stephen and Fanshawe, Andy. *Himalaya Alpine-Style: The Most Challenging Routes on the Highest Peaks.* Diadem Books: London, 1995.

Chapter 7 *Mick Conefrey*

Douglas, Ed. *Tenzing: Hero of Everest*. National Geographic Books: Washington, D.C., 2003.

Herzog, Maurice. *Annapurna: The First 8,000 metre Peak*. Cape: London, 1952.

Hillary, Edmund. *High Adventure*. Hodder & Stoughton: London, 1955.

Hunt, John. *The Ascent of Everest*. Hodder & Stoughton: London, 1953.

Izzard, Ralph. *The Innocent on Everest*. Hodder & Stoughton: London, 1955.

Morris, James. *Coronation Everest*. Faber & Faber: London, 1958.

Norgay, Tenzing. *Tiger of the Snows: The Autobiography of Tenzing of Everest with James Ramsay Ullman*. Putnam: New York, 1955.

Noyce, Wilfrid. *South Col: One Man's Adventure on the Ascent of Everest, 1953*. William Heinemann: London, 1956.

Shipton, Eric. *That Untravelled World: An Autobiography*. Hodder & Stoughton: London, 1969.

Unsworth, Walt. *Everest: The Mountaineering History*. (3rd edition.) Bâton Wicks Publications: London, 2000.

Chapter 8 *Peter Gillman*

Band, George C. 'The Conquest of Kanchenjunga' in *Sports Illustrated*. Volume 3, No. 14, 3 October 1955, pages 46–55.

George Band, Tony Streather, Michael Westmacott, Doug Scott, with Dr Peter Catterall. 'A Kangchenjunga Seminar' in *The Alpine Journal*. Volume 101, No. 345, London, 1996, pages 17–30. Brown, Joe. *The Hard Years: his autobiography*. Gollancz: London, 1967.

Braham, T.H. 'Kangchenjunga Reconnaissance; 1954' in *The Himalayan Journal*. Volume 19, 1955–1956.

Braham, Trevor. 'Kangchenunga: The 1954 Reconnaissance' in *The Alpine Journal*. Volume 101, No. 345, London, 1996, pages 33–35.

Buhl, Hermann. *Nanga Parbat Pilgrimage: The Lonely Challenge*. Hodder & Stoughton, London, 1956.

Curran, Jim. *K2: The Story of the Savage Mountain*. Hodder & Stoughton: London, 1995.

Desio, Ardito. *Ascent of K2*. Elek Books: London, 1955.

Dittert, René, Chevalley, Gabriel and Lambert, Raymond. *Forerunners to Everest: An Account of the Two Swiss Expeditions to Everest in 1952*. George Allen & Unwin: London, 1954.

Douglas, Ed. 'A Quiet Triumph' (interview with George Band) in BMC, Manchester (posted at www.thebmc.co.uk.), 22 May, 2005.

Eggler, Albert. *The Everest-Lhotse Adventure*. George Allen & Unwin: London, 1957.

Eggler, Albert. 'The Swiss Expedition to Everest and Lhotse, 1956' in *The Himalayan Journal*. Volume 20, 1957.

Evans, Charles. *Kangchenjunga: The Untrodden Peak*. Hodder & Stoughton: London, 1956.

Herligkoffer, Karl. *Nanga Parbat*. Elek Books: London, 1954.

Hunt, John. *The Ascent of Everest*. Hodder & Stoughton: London, 1953.

Isserman, Maurice and Weaver, Stewart. *Fallen Giants: A History of Himalayan Mountaineering from the Age of Empire to the Age of Extremes*. Yale University Press: New Haven and London, 2008.

Kurz, Marcel (Edited by). *Mountain World 1952*. George Allen & Unwin, London, 1953.

Marshall, Robert. 'Re-writing the History of K2 ~ a story all'italiana' in *The Alpine Journal*. Volume 110, No. 354, London, 2005, pages 193–200.

Marshall, Robert. *K2: Lies and Treachery*. Carreg: Ross-on-Wye, 2009.

Messner, Reinhold. *The Naked Mountain*. The Crowood Press: Marlborough, 2003.

Murray, W.H. *The Story of Everest*. Dent: London, 1953.

Sale, Richard and Cleare, John. *On Top of the World: Climbing the World's 14 Highest Peaks*. CollinsWillow: London, 2000.

Viesturs, Ed with Roberts, David. *K2: Life and Death on the World's Most Dangerous Mountain*. Broadway Books: New York, 2009.

Chapter 9 *Doug Scott*

Bonington, Chris. *Everest the Hard Way: The First Ascent of the South West Face*. Hodder and Stoughton: London, 1976.

Bonington, Chris; Boysen, Martin; Hankinson, Alan; Haston, Dougal; Sandhu, Balwant; and Scott, Doug. *Changabang*. Heinemann: London, 1975.

Brown, Joe. *The Hard Years: His Autobiography*. Gollancz: London, 1967.

Venables, Stephen and Fanshawe, Andy. *Himalaya Alpine-Style: The Most Challenging Routes on the Highest Peaks*. Diadem Books: London, 1995.

Habeler, Peter. *The Lonely Victory: Mount Everest '78*. Simon & Schuster: New York, 1979.

Harvard, Andrew and Thompson, Todd. *Mountain of Storms: The American Expeditions to Dhaulagiri*. New York University Press: New York, 1974.

Hornbein, Thomas F. *Everest: The West Ridge*. The Sierra Club: San Francisco, 1965.

Krakauer, John. *Into Thin Air: A Personal Account of the Mt. Everest Disaster*. Villard: New York, 1997.

Messner, Reinhold. *The Crystal Horizon: Everest – The First Solo Ascent*. Mountaineers Books: Seattle, 1989.

Ridgeway, Rick. *The Last Step: The American Ascent of K2*. Mountaineers Books: Seattle, 1980.

Roper, Robert. *Fatal Mountaineer: The High-Altitude Life and Death of Willi Unsoeld, American Himalayan Legend*. St. Martin's Griffin: New York, 2003.

Roskelley, John. *Nanda Devi: The Tragic Expedition*. Stackpole Books: New York, 1987.

Stevens, Stanley F. *Claiming the High Ground: Sherpas, Subsistence, and Environmental Change in the Highest Himalaya*. University of California Press: Berkeley, 1993.

Tasker, Joe. *Everest the Cruel Way*. Eyre Methuen: London, 1981.

Venables, Stephen. *Everest: Kangshung Face*. Odyssey Books: London, 1989.

A full and detailed guide to the international climbing grades employed in this chapter can be found at: http://www.spadout.com/wiki/index.php/Climbing_Grades

General bibliography

Isserman, Maurice and Weaver, Stewart. *Fallen Giants: A History of Himalayan Mountaineering from the Age of Empire to the Age of Extremes*. Yale University Press: New Haven 2008

Baume, Louis C. *Sivalaya: Explorations of the 8000 Metre Peaks of the Himalaya*. Mountaineers Books: Seattle, 1979.

Mason, Kenneth. *Abode of Snow: A History of Himalayan Exploration and Mountaineering from Earliest Times to the Ascent of Everest*. E.P. Dutton & Co.: New York 1955.

Picture Credits

Alamy/David Gee 30; Urban Golob 84-85; MARKA 130 bottom; Mary Evans Picture Library 46; Galen Rowell/Mountain Light 177; The Photolibrary Wales 58; Mikhail Turnovskiy 100 bottom. **Archiv des Deutschen Alpenvereins, München** 78, 79, 124, 127, 130 top. **Archives Reinhold Messner** 157. **Corbis**/Bettmann 173; Franck Charton/Hemis 33; Fridmar Damm 39; Paul Harris/JAI 29 top; Hulton-Deutsch Collection 72; Image Plan 48; Christian Kober/JAI 170; Colin Monteath/Hedgehog House/Minden Pictures 16, 94-95, 134; National Geographic Society 36; Galen Rowell 80, 87; Jochen Schlenker/Robert Harding World Imagery 22; Nichole Sobecki 25. **Courtesy of Club Alpino Italiano - National Library, Torino** 64. © 2013 - **Fondazione Sella, Biella, Italy** 54, 66-67, 70. **Getty Images**/Alinari via Getty Images 10; Anindo Dey Photography 52; Apic 60; Barry C. Bishop/National Geographic 158 left and right, 159; British Library/Robana via Getty Images 53; English School 34; fotoVoyager 21; Lee Frost 31; Ace Kvale 178 left; Mondadori via Getty Images 137, 138; Amir Mukhtar 128-129; Ignacio Palacios 43; Planet Observer 12; Popperfoto 14, 122; Cory Richards 184-185; SSPL via Getty Images 44, 47; Alex Treadway 15; W. & D. Downey 56; Werner Forman Archive 40. **Georgios T. Halkias** 27, 29 bottom. **Robert Harding**/Gavin Hellier 98-99. **Hedgehoghouse New Zealand**/Colin Monteath 90, 93. **Peter Hillary** 6. **John Lee** 4-5. **Nature Picture Library**/Leo & Mandy Dickinson 156. **NASA Images** 9. **Christina Partsalaki** 24, 26, 28, 32. **Press Association Images**/AP 166, 181. **Rex Features**/Galen Rowell/Mountain Light 2-3. **Royal Geographical Society** 38, 51, 61, 81, 100 top, 105, 108, 115, 116 left; George Band 119, 141, 146; Joe Brown 144; L.V. Bryant 83; Charles Evans 143, 145; Alfred Gregory 96, 109, 111 centre, 111 bottom, 113, 117, 123; Edmund Hillary 116 right, 118; John Hunt 110; A.M. Kellas 68; George Lowe 111 top, 112, 120; Maull & Polyblank 49; J.B. Noel 77; Hermann de Schlagintweit 50; A.F.R. Wollaston 74. **Doug Scott** 168-169, 172, 175. **Swiss Institute for Alpine Research** 149, 150 top, 150 bottom, 151, 153. **Subin Thakuri (Utmost Adventure Trekking/www.utmostadventure. com)** 179. **The Bridgeman Art Library**/Private Collection 37. **TopFoto** 101; The Granger Collection 69; Ullsteinbild 89. **Stephen Venables** 178 right. **Ed Webster** 75, 88, 91, 107, 136, 154, 180. Feature box background images: John Lee. Feature box background textures: Shutterstock.

Index